Family Day Care

of related interest

Child Welfare Policy and Practice
Issues and Lessons Emerging from Current Research
Edited by Dorota Iwaniec and Malcolm Hill
ISBN 1 85302 812 6

The Early Years
Assessing and Promoting Resilience in Vulnerable Children 1
Brigid Daniel and Sally Wassell
ISBN 1 84310 013 4

Parenting in Poor Environments
Stress, Support and Coping
Deborah Ghate and Neal Hazel
ISBN 1 84310 069 X

Small Steps Forward
Using Games and Activities to Help Your Pre-School Child with Special Needs
Sarah Newman
ISBN 1 85302 643 3

Approaches to Needs Assessment in Children's Services
Edited by Harriet Ward and Wendy Rose
ISBN 1 85302 780 4

Lone Mothers in European Welfare Regimes
Shifting Policy Logics
Edited by Jane Lewis
ISBN 1 85302 461 9

Family Day Care

International Perspectives on Policy, Practice and Quality

Edited by Ann Mooney and June Statham

Jessica Kingsley Publishers
London and Philadelphia

First published in the United Kingdom in 2003
by Jessica Kingsley Publishers Ltd
116 Pentonville Road
London N1 9JB, England
and
325 Chestnut Street
Philadelphia, PA 19106, USA

www.jkp.com

Copyright ©2003 Jessica Kingsley Publishers

Library of Congress Cataloging in Publication Data
Mooney, Ann, 1950-
    Family day care: international perspectives on policy, practice and quality/Ann Mooney and June Statham.
        p.cm
    Includes bibliographical references and index.
    ISBN 1-84310-062-2 (pbk : alk. paper)
    1. Family day care. 2.Child care services. 3. Child care--Government policy. I. Statham, June. II. Title.

HQ778.5 .M66 2003
362.71'2--dc21
                                                              2002034069
British Library Cataloguing in Publication Data
A CIP catalogue record for this book is available from the British Library

ISBN 1 84310 062 2

Printed and Bound in Great Britain by
Athenaeum Press, Gateshead, Tyne and Wear

Contents

Part II: Understandings of Family Day Care

Part III: Carers' and Parents' Perspectives

List of Figures

List of Tables

For Nell, who was born as this book reached completion,
and for Nellie, who has lived a long and productive life.

Preface

This book had its origins in an international conference organized by the European Early Childhood Education Research Association, which was held at the Institute of Education, University of London in August 2000. At the conference, a group of researchers in the field of family day care met to discuss their work, and realized that there was much to be learnt from comparing the way family day care is organized and understood in different countries. Although much has been written about day care centres, the care of children by non-relatives in a home-based setting has received very little attention. This is despite the fact that such care is often the main type of formal provision used by working parents for children under the age of three.

We therefore decided to bring together a collection of chapters by key family day care researchers, describing how family day care operates in their countries and presenting findings from recent or ongoing research. Additional contributions were invited from a number of countries not represented in our original group, to ensure the inclusion of a range of welfare systems, different ways of organizing child care services, and different stages of family day care development (expanding, declining or newly emerging). Countries such as Greece, Italy and Spain, where family day care is a relatively uncommon type of formal child care service, have not been included.

We would like to acknowledge the support of colleagues within the Thomas Coram Research Unit, in particular Peter Moss, whose encouragement and support played a key role in the genesis of this book. We would also like to thank the family day care researchers for their patience in coping with the many demands we have made of them during the editing process. Their chapters raise a number of common issues and concerns that all countries currently have to address. We hope that this book will encourage reflection and contribute to the debate about how family day care may develop in the future.

Ann Mooney and June Statham

CHAPTER ONE

Across the Spectrum

An Introduction to Family Day Care Internationally

June Statham and Ann Mooney

Family day care has received very little attention from researchers and policy makers, despite being an important form of childcare in many countries. This introductory chapter suggests why this might be so, and provides an overview of the key issues that are raised by the contributors to this book. Much can be learnt from cross-national comparisons, and the chapter discusses some common themes and significant differences that emerge from this compilation of research into family day care in ten different countries, from Western and Central Europe to the United States, New Zealand and Australia.

Introduction

This book explores the subject of family day care, known as childminding in the UK, from an international perspective. As more women enter the labour market and the demand for childcare increases, the provision of childcare has a high profile in many countries, and family day care plays a significant role. It has been estimated that well over a million children in Western Europe are in this form of day care at any one time (Karlsson 1995). In some countries, such as the UK and the United States, family day care is the major source of formal childcare for children whose parents work. As well as a service for working parents, family day care can also provide education and learning opportunities for young children and their families, and a potential source of employment.

Despite its important role in many countries, there has been remarkably little research into this childcare service. Even when family day care is the most significant form of care for children under three, it is often disregarded or overlooked in official policy making. European countries such as France, Denmark, Finland and Sweden are well known for their day care centres, but also have a high proportion of children under three attending home-based care. However, one researcher has described how, when discussing day care with local and national policy makers in such countries, 'no one says anything about family day care until I ask about it specifically, and then the descriptions and explanations are always offered with a hint of embarrassment' (Cochran 1995, p.66). When the UK government was introducing a scheme in the mid 1990s to provide free part-time nursery education for four-year-old children in a variety of public and private settings, childminding was at first conspicuously absent from the types of service that could be approved to provide nursery education (see Chapter Five).

To some extent, this reflects a view of family day care as being little more than substitute mothering, something that requires little in the way of professional training or qualifications. Peters and Pence (1992) have described how family day care is 'seen by many as not much different from out-of-home care by close relatives or friends', and Cochran suggests that this service is viewed somewhat sceptically by the early childhood education community 'because it is not "professional" – that is, designed and run by university-trained early childhood educators'. There are other interpretations of the term 'professional' which are explored in many of the chapters of this book, such as having a particular body of theory and practice, or having a career structure and respected status. However, Cochran concludes that 'family day care continues to exist because it is popular with parents, not because it is popular with the profession' (Cochran 1995, p.67).

Another explanation for the lack of attention paid to family day care is put forward by Karlsson in her report for the European Commission Childcare Network. In many countries, there has been a conflict between those who think mothers should care full-time for children and those who favour centre-based care for all, with neither side valuing or supporting the idea of a properly resourced family day care service (Karlsson 1995, p.58). It has also been suggested that the lack of research on family day care is attributable in part to the 'invisibility' of family day care, in part to the difficulties of conducting research in this 'private-yet-public' setting, and in part to the lack of a synthesis of knowledge that can generate and drive programmatic research efforts (Peters and Pence 1992).

In this book, we begin to redress the balance by bringing together research-based information on the situation of family day care in ten different countries in the industrialized world. The scope of the book is international, including not only western and central Europe but also Israel, the United States, Australia and New Zealand. Each chapter draws on the author's recent or current research into family day care. The studies adopt a variety of methodologies. Many are guided implicitly or explicitly by Bronfenbrenner's ecological model, and consider factors affecting family day care services at different levels – the individual child, their immediate environment, and the wider social and political context in which childcare services operate (Bronfenbrenner 1979). The methods used range from socio-anthropological research involving 'urban strollings', where family day carers are accompanied on their excursions in the neighbourhood; to observation in the carers' homes; analysis of their daily diaries of activities; large-scale surveys; and individual interviews with family day care providers, parents using the service, public officers and policy makers.

Many studies start from the perspective of the family day care providers themselves, arguing that their views and experience are essential to reach an understanding of their work and have too often been ignored (see for example Chapters Eight, Nine and Thirteen). One notable omission, however, is the perspectives of children themselves. Although a number of studies report on the daily lives of children in family day care, this is described through the eyes of their carers or the researcher/observer. There is an increasing body of research seeking the views of children themselves on their experiences in different kinds of environments, often using innovative techniques such as mapping, tours and photography (Clark and Moss 2001) to help young children make their views known. It would be interesting to extend such work to family day care settings.

Each chapter includes an overview of the way that family day care is organized, financed and regulated in that country. We all tend to take for granted our own way of doing things, yet the differences between countries in how family day care operates can provide useful insights into how the service is conceived and how it might develop. In editing this book, we found that many of our queries to authors on early drafts related to information that they had not included because it was considered too obvious to mention. The book offers readers a unique opportunity to understand the way in which family day care is conceptualized and organized in ten countries, and to use this understanding to reflect on practice in their own country.

Across the spectrum

The provision of home-based non-parental care for young children has a long history. Early examples of parents paying other people to provide childcare, in the carers' rather than the child's home, can be seen in practices such as wet-nursing (see Chapter Ten) and 'baby-farming', where large numbers of infants were cared for while their mothers (usually single or widowed) were in paid employment (Cameron 2002). Informal care arrangements between parents and non-relative childcare providers have existed for many years. But family day care as a formal service has developed in very different ways and at different points in time in the countries described in this book.

In some places, such as Hungary and the former East Germany, family day care has only emerged as a formally recognized childcare service in the last decade, reflecting changing social and economic circumstances that have weakened traditional policies of widespread state-funded childcare centres (see Chapters One and Two). Israel, too, has developed a formal family day care service relatively recently, partly in response to concerns about the quality of care provided in some childcare centres (see Chapter Six). Other countries have a longer history of family day care, in some cases developed from the foster care service (Karlsson 1995). However, while family day care is just emerging in some countries or expanding in others, such as New Zealand and Australia, elsewhere this form of provision is declining. In Sweden, for instance, nearly half of all children in public childcare in 1977 were in family day care, but this had fallen to only 10 per cent by 1999 (see Chapter Nine). In England, the number of childminders has fallen over recent years (Chapter Seven), and the government has commissioned research to explore why there has been this drop and what could be done to reverse it (Mooney, Moss and Owen 2001).

Women may enter family day care through different routes.[1] For many it is something they do to enable them to earn an income while remaining at home with their own young children. For these women, family day care may be a stopgap until they are able to take up other employment, or it may turn into a longer term commitment (see for example Chapter Seven). In countries such as Sweden, with high levels of childcare and maternal employment and with most family day care providers employed by the local authority, women are more likely to enter this work as a chosen occupation rather than as a way of staying at home with their own children. The pattern is different again in countries such as Hungary and the former East Germany, where many women have taken up family day care when made redundant from their jobs in state-funded day care centres due to the economic upheavals in both countries. Family day care offered an alternative source of employment with children, although as Chapters Two and Three both show, such providers have sometimes attempted to overcome the disadvantages of isolation and poor economic viability by coming together to provide care in what are effectively 'mini-nurseries'.

These differences between countries can help to clarify the kind of questions we need to be asking about this form of childcare service. Should family day care be viewed as a career or a profession? Is it a business? What would this mean in terms of training and qualifications and working conditions? Many of the chapters in this book explore such issues, and raise important and thought-provoking questions. What does quality mean in this form of provision? How can standards be improved and assured? Can family day care be 'professionalized' – for example, through higher standards, better working conditions, training, qualifications and support – without losing its essential nature? How far is it possible for family day care to develop a distinctive pedagogical approach, which is neither substitute mother nor group pedagogy? How can the tensions, for example between centre-based and home-based services and between providing care and running a small business, be resolved? And, more fundamentally, can family day care survive in a changing world if it is not able to adapt? The traditional recruits for family day care work have generally been women with low levels of qualifications who have had extended periods out of the labour market. This group is shrinking fast as women have gained better access to jobs, education and training.

Many of the chapters discuss the concept of family day care providers as 'substitute mothers'. This traditional perception is underpinned by theories of attachment that suggest young children need to be cared for by one maternal figure (Bowlby 1971). In many countries, the words used to describe providers of home-based care reinforce this perceived affinity with mothering. The term in common use often translates as something to do with 'mother', such as *tagesmutter* in Germany, *onthaalmoeder* in Flemish

Belgium, and *dagmamma* in Norway and Sweden (further examples are given in Karlsson 1995, p.6). In official language, however, there has been a move away from such terminology towards more gender-neutral words, such as *dagbarnvårdare* ('day child carer') in Sweden, and the term 'family day care' now used in many English-language countries. In the hope that language will shape ways of thinking, recent official documents in New Zealand have replaced the term caregiver with educator, to reflect the changed view of family day care work as providing education as well as care (see Chapter Four).

When family day care is viewed through the lens of maternal care, it can create a conflict between the affective, caring aspects of the work and being paid to care. This love/money dilemma is especially acute where day care providers are self-employed and subject to market forces, since they are in effect running small businesses. They have to find customers, charge enough to make a living without pricing themselves out of the market, and engage in financial and contractual negotiations with parents. These circumstances can create tensions in the relationship between providers and parents, which usually do not occur in other forms of childcare provision.

One way of alleviating such tensions could be to break the contractual link between parent and family day care provider. In some countries, a third party – the local authority, or a private or voluntary agency – takes responsibility for placing children, collecting fees and paying providers. In England, this intervention is usually limited to children who are judged to be 'in need' and who are offered family day care by welfare officers as a way of supporting their families at a time of crisis (see Chapter Eleven). But other chapters in this book describe different scenarios. In Sweden, almost all family day care providers are employed by their local government, with working hours and pay negotiated with local trade unions (Chapter Nine). In New Zealand, Australia and Israel providers working within the formal family day care service remain self-employed but their work is organized by an agency. These types of working arrangements may create more opportunities to improve family day care providers' working conditions and pay than when they are operating within the private market. However, improvements to working conditions, such as introducing pensions, leave and sickness benefits, raising salaries and imposing higher training standards, will remain a challenge unless there is adequate public funding of the service.

The conditions under which family day care providers carry out their work are likely to affect the quality of care which they are able to offer children. We use the term 'care' in its broadest sense, to include education, family support and all the other functions that early childhood services perform. There is increasing recognition that these different functions cannot be separated (Mooney and Munton 1997), and that early childhood services need to be provided within an integrated, strategic framework (Organisation for Economic Co-operation and Development 2001). However, administrative responsibility for childcare and pre-school services remains split in many countries, with education services for children over three located within education, while childcare services are located within welfare. Three of the countries featured in this book (New Zealand in 1986, Sweden in 1996 and England in 1998) have integrated responsibility for early years, compulsory schooling and childcare within the education system although, as described in Chapter Eleven, services for 'children in need' in England are still organized within a welfare framework.

The theme of quality, and how to improve standards in home-based care services, runs through many of these chapters. Most countries have some system for regulating family day care services, although the extent of regulation varies a great deal. Often there are basic standards of health and safety which all family day care providers must meet (although in the United States some providers are exempt, and most countries also have unknown numbers of family day care providers who operate illegally). A growing trend is for higher standards to be encouraged through various mechanisms, for instance by linking to public funding (examples are given in New Zealand, the UK, Israel and Australia in Chapters Four, Five, Six and Twelve) or through voluntary accreditation systems (Chapter Thirteen).

Although quality is an issue of common concern in many countries, as a concept it often lacks clarity (Dahlberg, Moss and Pence 1999; Moss and Pence 1994). Implicit or explicit in a number of the chapters in this book is an exploration of what is meant by quality in family day care. The need for a culturally sensitive definition of quality is emphasized by Kathy Modigliani (Chapter Thirteen). Sarah Wise and Ann Sanson (Chapter Twelve) examine what parents from different ethnic groups look for in childcare services. Irene Kyle suggests the need to extend the concept of quality to include the notion of personal agency and an 'ethics of care', and to pay more attention to the conditions that are needed to foster such qualities in family day care providers (Chapter Eight).

The different authors agree on some of the factors that hinder the development of a high quality family day care service. One is the low level of qualifications and training generally expected of family day care providers. Ways of improving this are suggested in various chapters, such as distance-learning training approaches (Chapter Four), video-aided supervision (Chapter Six), childminding networks (Chapter Five) and accreditation schemes (Chapter Thirteen). Another barrier to development is the poor pay and employment conditions of many family day care providers. Looked at from one perspective, this may be a convenient way to supply society with an important service for a very low cost. But this raises issues about equal opportunities in the labour market, which are addressed by Liane Mozère in her chapter on the employment situation of a group of family day care providers living in an underprivileged area of France (Chapter Ten).

A higher level of public funding for family day care would help to address some of these problems. The chapters on France, the new Germany and Hungary (Ten, Three and Two) illustrate the difficulty of sustaining the family day care service without significant government funding. However, a lack of financial support is not the only barrier facing family day care. The low status of this work is highlighted by many of the contributors to this book. Even in Sweden, where the employment conditions of family day care providers are relatively good, local government policies frequently favour day care centres over home-based care, and the number of children using this form of provision has consequently fallen. We come back to the need to define what it is about family day care that makes it special and justifies developing it as a particular service for young children and their families. In Chapter Nine, Malene Karlsson suggests the importance of self-reflective practice, and describes how some Swedish family day care providers meet together on a regular basis to reflect on their work and develop an understanding of the ideas and knowledge that underpin their childcare practice. A similar point about reflective practice has been made elsewhere (e.g. Dahlberg *et al.* 1999; Malaguzzi 1993). We hope that the material in this book will encourage readers to reflect on their own practice, challenging assumptions and stimulating critical thinking.

Structure of the book

The book is broadly organized around three main themes, although there is considerable overlap between the chapters in the issues they address. The first part covers policy and organization. It addresses the ways in which governments in different countries intervene to set standards and provide training and support for family day care providers, and the extent to which they have adopted strategies to develop quality services. It also considers policy and organization in two countries – the former East Germany and Hungary – where family day care is just emerging as a recognized service, after many decades when childcare policy was limited to state-funded group day care.

The chapters in the second part of the book focus on understandings of family day care, and investigate how day care providers conceptualize their work, what they think makes for 'good care,' and their attitudes towards training and towards family day care as a career.

The final part considers how family day care meets the diverse needs of children and their parents, particularly 'children in need' and families with varying cultural backgrounds. It addresses issues such as cultural values and how they influence decisions about childcare and quality. This section also considers the extent to which family day care providers can support vulnerable families whose children are placed in the service by welfare agencies.

The themes of quality, training and the role and status of family day care permeate all the chapters. These are important issues, which are of increasing concern in many countries. The final chapter draws out the some of the key implications for policy and practice from the material presented in the book, and considers how family day care might develop in the future.

References

Bowlby, J. (1971) *Attachment and Loss, Vol. 1: Attachment.* Aylesbury: Pelican.

Bronfenbrenner, U. (1979) *The Ecology of Human Development.* Cambridge MA: Harvard University Press.

Cameron, C. (2002) 'An historical perspective on changing child care policy.' In J. Brannen and P. Moss (eds) *Re-thinking Children's Care.* Buckingham: Open University Press.

Clark A. and Moss P. (2001) *Listening to Children: The Mosaic Approach.* London: National Children's Bureau.

Cochran, M. (1995) 'European child care in global perspective.' *European Early Childhood Education Research Journal 3*, 1, 61–72.

Dahlberg, G., Moss, P. and Pence, A. (1999) *Beyond Quality in Early Childhood Education and Care: Postmodern Perspectives.* London: Falmer Press.

Gunnarsson, L., Korpi, B.M. and Nordenstam, U. (1999) *Early Childhood Education and Care Policy in Sweden: Background Report Prepared for the OECD Thematic Review.* Stockholm: Ministry of Education and Science.

Karlsson, M. (1995) *Family Day Care in Europe: A Report for the EC Childcare Network.* Brussels: European Commission (Equal Opportunities Unit).

Malaguzzi, L. (1993) 'Fundamentals of the Reggio Emilia approach to early childhood education,' *Young Children,* November, 9–12.

Mooney, A., Moss, P. and Owen, C. (2001) *A Survey of Former Childminders. Research Report 300.* London: Department for Education and Science.

Mooney, A. and Munton, A.G. (1997) *Research and Policy in Early Childhood Services: Time for a New Agenda.* London: Institute of Education, University of London.

Moss, P. And Pence, A. (Eds) (1994) *Valuing Quality in Early Childhood Services: New Approaches to Defining Quality.* London: Paul Chapman Publishing.

Organisation for Economic Co-operation and Development (OECD) (2001) *Starting Strong: Early Childhood Education and Care. Paris: Organisation for Economic Co-operation and Development.*

Peters, D. and Pence, A. (1992) 'Family Day Care: Issues and information needs.' In D. Peters and A. Pence *Family Day Care: Current Research for Informed Public Policy, 1–6.* New York: Teachers College Press.

Notes

1   It is almost always women who provide family day care. Less than 1 per cent of childminders in England are men, and even in Sweden, where there is a policy of encouraging men to enter childcare work, the proportion of men rises to less than 5 per cent (Gunnarsson, Korpi and Nordenstam 1999). We return to this issue of gender imbalance in the concluding chapter.

Part I

Policy and Organization

CHAPTER TWO

Some Unique Features of the Emerging Family Day Care Provision in Hungary

Home-like?

Marta Korintus

The emergence of a home-based childcare service is a recent phenomenon in Hungary, with its tradition of state-funded day care centres, and there are still only a handful of family day care providers. Most have previously worked in centres that were closed down, and have turned to family day care as a way of continuing to work with young children. Marta Korintus, who was a member of the working group that developed the model and the criteria for family day care in Hungary, describes the reasons for the development of the service, the process involved, and the difficulties faced in establishing a family day care service in the absence of significant financial support from the government.

Introduction

This chapter charts the development of family day care in Hungary, discussing the context in which the process occurred, the issues that arose in the development of this new kind of provision, and the attempts made to address them. The chapter is unique in that it is the first attempt to describe the emergence of family day care as a service in Hungary and to analyze why it evolved as it has over the past ten years. This provision was rare during the years of state socialism, since the state financed only centre-based childcare. Furthermore, self-employment or running a small business would not have been possible during this period. The idea of childcare in domestic settings arose in response to the changing economic circumstances that accompanied the political changes that occurred in 1989 and 1990.

In recent years, demographic and political changes have had a dramatic impact on family life and employment in Hungary. There has been a steady decline in the population, which now stands at approximately ten million. This decline is due to a number of reasons including a lower birth rate (from 150,000 births in 1980 to under 100,000 in 2000), poor health and reduced life expectancy among men. There are fewer marriages, more children born out of wedlock and a higher divorce rate. Consequently more children live in lone parent households, which have risen from 19 per cent in 1990 to 29 per cent in 1999. Finally, the number of families where several generations live together has declined with a corresponding increase in the number of single households. The average size of households decreased from 2.8 to 2.6 between 1980 and 2001.

In the 1990s, following the transition to a multi-party state, the country moved from a planned to a market economy. The process resulted in the dismantling of state-owned property and the restructuring of the economy accompanied by a great upsurge of private enterprises. These changes had a dramatic effect on employment. Different employment opportunities and working patterns emerged. Unemployment rose and the living standards of a great proportion of the population fell. More people now work in the private sector, in retail and in small industries and more now work longer and/or irregular hours. Women have a lower rate of participation in the labour market than was previously the case. Although women outnumber men by 4 per cent, more men (63.3%) than women (49.7%) are in work. Several factors contribute to women's low level of employment, including earlier retirement, child rearing, and a lack of part-time jobs. Despite attempts to increase opportunities for part-time work through different employment strategies, part-time employment is still rare in Hungary. Only 4 per cent of the workforce had part-time jobs in 2000. Women with low levels of education in particular have difficulty re-entering the labour market after childbirth.

Before 1989, parents with dependent children received state support, resulting in fewer inequalities within Hungarian society. A wide range of social benefits had been established by the end of the 1980s, despite the fact that funds were increasingly being diverted from health, social services, education and culture to support a failing economy.

However, the political changes led to debates about whose responsibility it is to care for children, pay for childcare and meet the changing needs of families. There was (and still is) a consensus on these issues. Although it is the responsibility of parents to bring up and care for children, it is recognized that parents need help with this task. The Hungarian government signed the UN Convention on the Rights of the Child very soon after it was issued. Furthermore, the introduction of the notion of motherhood as a profession (that is, as pension-earning years), and the acknowledgement of non-parental childcare as a basic service (Protection of Children Act No. XXXI, 1997) all reflect the recognition that society shares the responsibility of child rearing with parents.

Family benefits and non-parental childcare services are seen as a complementary system for helping parents with young children. The social (family) benefit system includes family allowance, which is paid monthly to families with children; maternity benefit; and a childcare leave and assistance arrangement (including paid leave to care for sick children). Maternity benefit and childcare leave are available until the child's third birthday. Parental leave and financial support as a means of supporting mothers to stay at home when their children are young was first introduced at the end of the 1970s. Since then, the system has undergone many modifications and today fulfils two functions. In areas where childcare services are available, mothers can choose whether to take full parental leave (36 months) or return to work sooner. However, in areas that lack childcare facilities, mothers can use parental leave to avoid the need for childcare services. This system, whether chosen freely or out of necessity, makes it possible for families to solve their childcare needs.

However, the financial support for parental leave is low compared to wages. Most families need two incomes to live on and many women need to work to support their families. Thus, many mothers prefer to return to work when childcare is available rather than take parental leave. Yet, despite this need for childcare, the number of childcare places has declined and the decline has outstripped the declining birth rate. This means that there is a growing demand for affordable and accessible childcare services. Furthermore, childcare services increasingly need to accommodate the changing employment patterns of parents.

Childcare in Hungary

In Hungary, there is a long tradition of organized childcare and kindergarten education. The first full-time kindergarten for 3 to 6-year-old children (*óvoda*) opened in Hungary in 1828, the first such institution in Central Europe. The first childcare centre for children under three (*bölcsöde*) was established in 1852, only eight years after the world's first (in Paris in 1844). There has been more or less systematic development of early childcare and education services ever since. However family day care, as formal care, did not exist until 1993, when legislation for providing such a service was first introduced. Unofficially, family day care existed only to a small extent during the state socialist years. Officially, during this time, there was full female employment. A nationwide publicly funded network of childcare centres and kindergartens provided care for those children whose mothers worked and there was no need for family-based services.

Whereas all provision was financed from the state's budget before 1990, the tendency since has been for the state to withdraw from direct involvement, to decentralize and to pass many of its previous responsibilities to local government. Its regulatory function is retained but the intention has been to give local government and agencies providing services more independence and flexibility within the legislative framework. Currently the major task of national government is to provide the legal framework; to secure earmarked (normative) funding for care services; to ensure the necessary education for staff working with children, youth and adults, and to introduce the framework for supervision and quality assurance.

It is important to briefly describe childcare funding, since it has had an effect on the development of family day care, as we shall see later. There are three major sources of funding: national government, local government and parental fees. The government annually sets the normative support (earmarked funding) for each type of service. Some services do not receive normative support. The type of service and the decision of the council determine the contribution made by local authorities. Parental fees are regulated for services receiving central government funding and/or contracted by local authorities. The small proportion of services not in these categories can set their own fees, which have to cover the full cost of the care provided.

The Protection of Children Act (1997) defines the basic services that local authorities are required to provide. Basic services include childcare for children under three and kindergarten. Service provision can be undertaken directly by the local authority, in partnership with other agencies or by means of contracting out the service. The Act also stipulates that parents should have access to a childcare place for their child(ren) should they want one. In reality, most local authorities do not provide childcare for children under the age of three, although it is their statutory duty. Lack of funding, the availability of childcare leave and assistance, and there being no precedent for public advocacy or challenging the local authorities' inability to fulfil their legal duty account for this situation. The majority of children under the age of three are cared for at home by the mother or by relatives (mainly the grandmother). Non-parental childcare is provided almost entirely in public childcare centres.

Childcare centres (Bölcsőde)

Childcare centres offer full-time care for children between the ages of 24 weeks and 3 years, who live with their parents. Children with developmental delay can come to the centre until they are four years old. Children with special needs can remain until they are six if the parents wish and/or if no other suitable place is available. About 8–10 per cent of the age group attend childcare centres, which come under the responsibility of the Ministry of Health, Social and Family Affairs.

There has been a decline of almost 60 per cent in the number of places since 1985. The main reason for the closures was the financial difficulty many local authorities experienced. Employers, who until 1989 had supported about a quarter of the places, have largely withdrawn from childcare provision and the non-governmental sector has not become involved. Childcare centres in small towns and villages were hit hardest since maintaining a centre proved to be too expensive for the limited budgets of small local authorities. Of the 3200 local authorities in Hungary, only 216 maintain one or more childcare centres. The distribution of childcare places among these local authorities indicates that about 60 per cent of the places are in Budapest or in other bigger towns, about 28 per cent in smaller towns and only 10 per cent in villages.

Kindergartens (Óvoda)

Kindergartens offer centre-based full-time care and education for children from the age of three until starting school at six, although in some circumstances children may not start school until the age of seven.

Attendance at kindergarten is compulsory for five-year-olds, as preparation for school. About 91 per cent of children aged between three and six attend kindergartens, which are under the auspices of the Ministry of Education.

Because childcare leave and assistance is available to parents until their child is three, the demand for kindergartens, and coverage, has always been greater than for childcare centres. For a child over the age of three, kindergarten is practically the only option available for working parents. Nevertheless, there has been a small decrease in the number of places in this type of provision too. This has resulted in a growing number of children who are not admitted because of the shortage of places.

Family day care (Családi napközi)

Family day care provides care for children up to the age of fourteen, in the home of the provider or in another home-like environment. The maximum number of children one can look after at any time is five if the provider is working alone, and seven if there is a helper. However, it is quite normal to find family day care sites where two licensed providers work together and thus the number of children goes up to ten to fourteen. The children in family day care homes do not attend childcare centres, kindergartens or after-school care. Like childcare centres, family day care is under the responsibility of the Ministry of Health, Social and Family Affairs.

After-school care (Iskolai napközi)

This is mainly for children at elementary school, which caters for children between six and fourteen. These schools provide care and activities in the afternoon after classes have finished.

Home childcare service (Házi gyermekfelügyelet)

This service provides care for children up to the age of fourteen, in their own homes, for a period of time when the parents need help in looking after the child and the care of the child cannot be ensured in any other way. Local authorities provide this service when families experience particular problems.

Table 2.1 Details of childcare provision in Hungary

Type of service	Number of institutions	Number of places available	Number of children enrolled	Number of workers	Number of qualified workers
Childcare centre (Bölcsőde)	532	24,960	29,520	9630	5548
Family day care (Családi napközi)	31	272	852[1]	n.a.	n.a.
Home childcare service (Házi gyermekfelügyelet)	12	n.a.	312	26	n.a.
Kindergarten (Óvoda)	4,643	366,245	365,704	55,673	31,409
After-school care (Iskolai napközi)	3151[2]	-	340,677	12,407	n.a.

1   Many children do not attend family day care full-time, so places are shared.
2   Number of schools providing after-school care.

Sources: Ministry of Social and Family Affairs, 2000 (data on childcare and child protection services), Central Statistical Office, 2000

As can be seen from Table 2.1, kindergartens and after-school care are the two most commonly used services, followed by childcare centres. There are as yet very few family day care and home childcare services because these are relatively new forms of provision.

The need for family day care

Several factors led to the emergence of family day care as a childcare service in Hungary. These included the closure of centres, particularly in rural areas, the growing need for women to return to the labour market before their childcare leave ended and the changing patterns of employment resulting in a need for more diverse services. In an attempt to meet parents' changing needs, some childcare centres began to offer part-time care, 24-hour care and mother-toddler groups.

In 1996, the National Institute of Day Care Centres (BOMI) undertook a survey of over six hundred parents using childcare centres (Papp 1997).[1] Four hundred and seventy-three questionnaires were returned, forty-one of them completed by fathers. Although the main aim was to find out who used day care for their child and why, and what parents thought about the provision, it did shed light on the need for services to diversify. This has been the only study to look at parental needs, views and expectations. Findings relevant to the issue under discussion include:

- The main motivation for using childcare was economic. Some women were asked by employers to return to work as soon as possible after giving birth. The wish to work or to pursue a career was ranked only third among the answers.

- The majority of the mothers and almost all of the fathers worked full-time. Most of the mothers had regular work hours, whereas 36 per cent of the fathers had rotating schedules.

- Ninety-six per cent of parents were satisfied with the childcare provision, but over half (53%) would have liked additional services (such as part-time care, foreign language classes and swimming lessons).

- Seventy-two per cent of the families needed help from someone else for childcare occasionally, and 93 per cent received regular help from grandparents.

The survey showed that even those families who used childcare would have welcomed diversification of the existing centre-based provision. They would have liked centres to offer more flexible hours, additional services and sometimes, more educational provision. They also needed occasional help in looking after their children, even though centres were open for 12 hours a day. The Institute considered that developing home-based services such as family day care was one of the ways in which childcare could be diversified. This provision was thought to be suitable for families preferring family-type care for their children, and especially suitable for rural areas where local governments are too small to maintain childcare centres. Family day care also offered a potential employment opportunity for women, many of whom had lost their jobs in childcare centres during the economic transition.

The process of developing family day care in Hungary

The Family Day Care Working Group, a small group of people with expertise in childcare, was set up in 1992. The purpose of the group was to study examples of family day care abroad and to develop a model for Hungary. In developing a model, the Working Group identified a number of issues including:

- What level of quality can be ensured in domestic settings?

- What kinds of support do family day care providers need and what can they expect?

- How can a good balance between centre-based care and family day care be achieved when the latter is less expensive for local authorities?

Clearly, there were advantages to developing a new system, such as regulating it from the beginning, but there were also many difficulties to be solved. This necessitated some tough decisions and some compromises.

Quality and setting standards

The long history of organized childcare in Hungary had contributed to a high level of quality in the childcare centres. It was important to establish and ensure an equally high level of quality in the new form of childcare. It was clear from the beginning that regulation was a means to ensure good quality. A decision was made that family day care providers had to be licensed, and standards for licensing were developed. However, the Working Group were faced with a dilemma: if standards were too high, it might be impossible for many prospective providers to care for children, especially in poorer areas. Would high quality in terms of the care environment have to be compromised to enable local care for children who were growing up in less affluent areas, where it might not be possible to meet certain requirements (e.g. homes where there is no tap water or sewage provision)? The Working Group developed standards for premises that those living in the 'average home' could meet, but which ensured the safety and healthy development of children. To be licensed a provider must meet the following list of criteria. They must:

- hold the necessary approvals and documents (e.g. from the police, the fire department and the health and hygiene agency) for the provider and/or her premises

- be a fit person to provide care

- conform to health and safety standards

- care for no more than the specified number and ages of children

- demonstrate that they adhere to the principles of caring for children, including behaviour management

- provide healthy, well-balanced meals

- keep records as required.

Training and qualifications

Good quality childcare requires training, but what kind of qualification is suitable for family day care providers? This was another difficult issue for the Working Group. Should providers have the same training as childcare centre workers, who work with the under threes? Or should they be trained to the same level as kindergarten teachers, or possibly that of a health visitor? The different forms of child-related training are quite separate (just as the branches of government responsible for the different types of provisions are separate), with each requiring a different level of education. Would prospective providers be willing to study for some years to look after children in their own homes? And if they were, could they afford the costs of becoming qualified? Other issues related to training that the group considered were where it was to be located, and whether schools/colleges could accommodate an influx of mature students. It could be that family day care training would require substantial changes to the education system.

Quality and training were some of the most controversial issues discussed before and during the development of licensing standards. Many believed that family day care could never offer the level of quality found in childcare centres. Concerns were voiced that family day care provision would lower the overall quality of childcare in the country. A vision of unqualified family day care providers looking after children, compared to the high proportion of staff in centres who were qualified (80–90%), prompted some people to speak up against childcare in domestic settings. It could be argued that due to the unmet demand for childcare, informal care would exist with or without regulation, and that some parents from minority groups prefer childcare by members of their own communities. However, this did little to convince the opponents. Nor did the fact that there were not enough qualified childcare workers in Hungary to staff the expected number of family day care homes.

After much debate, a compromise was reached. It was decided that family day care providers should receive some training, but that to legislate for a childcare qualification would at this stage deter people from applying for a license. Thus to become licensed family day care providers must attend an introductory training course but there is no legal requirement for them to have a childcare qualification. The curriculum for the 40-hour course was developed by the National Institute responsible for childcare. It covers a range of topics including issues in child development, care and education; managing children's behaviour; relationships with parents; keeping documentation; relationships with the local authority and running a small business.

Support

It was anticipated that the number of family day care providers would grow quickly and that providing them with support in their work would be necessary. Thought was therefore given to support structures. There were no established family day care providers to learn from and no association to help. Where there were childcare centres, staff could potentially help home-based care providers. However, it was acknowledged that childcare workers might consider they were in competition with the providers of family day care. Family day care could be seen as a threat, since if local authorities supported this new form of childcare they might withdraw support from centres and close them down. The Working Group considered that other professional workers, such as social workers, health workers, kindergarten teachers or psychologists could fulfil the roles of both development officer and inspector.

Status

Perhaps the most difficult challenge was to make sure everyone understood the purpose of family day care. Parents needed to understand that family day care is a service and the provider is a professional. Childcare workers and kindergarten teachers needed to understand that family day care providers offer a different kind of care and environment for the children. They are not competing with centres. Local authorities have to understand that parents have different needs. Some prefer centre-based care, while others prefer home-based care. Local authorities should make the decision which one (or both) to offer based on the assessment of needs in their area and not primarily on predicted short-term savings in the authority's budget.

The family day care model

The working group developed a model for family day care in Hungary. This includes four parties: parents, the local authority, the provider and the inspection and development officers. The duties of each party and the relationships between them are clearly defined. The key element in the model is the inspection and development officer. Their role is to assist and train the provider to ensure a good quality service.

Parents who need childcare may opt for family day care either through personal choice or out of necessity, because there is no alternative. Parents have a duty to respect the care provider, pay for the service and observe the rules of the service. However, parents' requests should be taken into consideration as much as possible. Parents pay the provider for the service directly. Usually, the provider sets a standard daily or hourly rate and charges for additional services, such as working irregular hours or weekends.

The provider cares for children in her home or in some other, suitable, home-like place with or without a helper. Her duty is to make sure children's physical, developmental and emotional needs are met. The local authority can employ her, or she can be self-employed. Each provider has to obtain a license and thus to become registered. It is the local authority's responsibility to issue the license and make regular inspections. The local authority also has a duty to ensure that families within the area who require childcare have access to childcare services – although, as described earlier, they do not necessarily discharge this duty.

The inspection and development officer is professionally trained with a qualification relating to childcare or child development, and is contracted by the local authority to work with family day care providers. Their job is to help the prospective providers to meet the licensing requirements, to visit providers regularly and to help them resolve problems and improve their service. The officers also undertake inspections for the local authority.

Family day care homes usually offer:

- care for children, usually from 7 a.m. until 4 or 5 p.m. although extra hours can be provided if necessary to cover evenings, weekends and even overnight
- four meals a day: breakfast, mid-morning fruit, hot lunch and afternoon snack
- an integrated age group, in contrast to centre-based childcare, where children are usually in same-age groups
- flexibility in meeting parents' needs and requests
- different learning experiences for the children, such as going for trips in the neighbourhood or visiting the local market
- a home-like environment.

Additional features of the service are determined by the providers' interests, knowledge and training. Some offer educational support for children between the ages of three and six, others care for children with special needs.

Piloting the family day care model

Having established the criteria and model for family day care provision, the next step was to see if the model could work in practice. The local authority of Kiskunhalas, a town in the southern part of Hungary with a population of about 30,000, agreed to help pilot the model with the Working Group. Several childcare centres in Kiskunhalas had been closed shortly before the pilot began, and there was a need for childcare for children under the age of three. The pilot phase first established the level of interest in the local authority for family day care before introducing the service and assessing the outcomes of this new form of provision.

Level of interest in family day care

An assessment of needs and interest in providing family day care was made in the town. Two questionnaires together with information about family day care were published in the local authority's monthly paper, delivered free to all households. One questionnaire asked people if they thought there was need for family day care and whether they would use it if it was available. The other questionnaire enquired about people's interest and willingness to provide such a service. The response to the questionnaires suggested that there was a positive interest in using family day care and in providing this service (Korintus *et al.* 1995).

Introducing family day care

The results from the questionnaire survey led to the decision by the local authority of Kiskunhalas to introduce family day care in the town. A psychologist, a paediatrician, a social worker, a health visitor, a lawyer, and a childcare professional were contracted by the local authority to serve as inspection and development officers and trained by the Family Day Care Working Group. This small team was then able to help prospective family day care providers to create a safe and healthy environment for children and meet the licensing criteria. This team also provided the initial training course. The local authority provided financial support with a start-up grant for new providers and subsidies. They also supplied toys and some essential equipment. With this level of support, five family day care homes were eventually set up, some involving more than one provider.

Outcomes

A year after the first family day care home was set up, a second survey was conducted in Kiskunhalas to assess the success of the new service, including the views of parents and providers.

Parents tended to use family day care mostly for children aged between two and five years old. Their reasons for choosing this form of care were the small number of children cared for, the family-like environment, and the flexibility of the service. Parents working non-standard hours were able to leave children in family day care, which would not have been possible in childcare centres or kindergartens. One of the most important factors in choosing a provider was the personality of the carer rather than her qualification. Although the fees for family day care were higher than in centres, because (unlike centres) family day care received no state funding, parents seemed willing to accept the higher fees.

Most providers were about 40 years old. Those who were younger had a childcare qualification because they had previously worked as childcare centre workers and had been made redundant when some centres in Kiskunhalas closed. They saw it as a means of continuing in their profession. Two of the providers were pension-aged women who had decided to look after others' children in their own home together with their own grandchild. Each provider lived in a detached house with a garden. All were self-employed rather than employed by the local authority. According to the providers in Kiskunhalas, taxes were paid as required and family day care provided a reasonable income. They did not, however, expect to gain large profits and to become rich because of this business. Most of them had a member of their family registered as a helper, which meant they could take care of more children and thus generate a higher income.

We noted that some family day care homes in Kiskunhalas operated very much like centres and followed a similar routine. In fact, providers in other parts of the country have often followed this pattern. Two factors seem to be at work here. First, providers who had previously worked in childcare centres or kindergartens set up their homes and cared for children based on their training and experience of centre-based routines. Second, for financial reasons (explained more fully below), providers need to admit the maximum number of children. The home environment is set up to accommodate a higher number of children than is usual for the average family. The frequency of child-sized furniture, outside climbing equipment and multiple sets of toys all suggest a childcare centre-like atmosphere. Nevertheless, these environments are still more family-like than the usual centres and children have much more freedom to wander. Whereas in centres children stay in the group room or go out to the garden, in family day care homes it is possible for them to explore the kitchen, take part in preparing the food or in gardening. In Hungary even the smallest centres have places for 20–40 children, while groups in family day care homes, even with the maximum number of 14 children with 2 adults, are smaller and therefore more flexible.

The inspection and development officers were under contract to the local authority to undertake licensing duties and to support family day care providers. They did this work in addition to their regular job, but the small number of providers they had to license and support made this possible. They thought their initial licensing tasks were well defined, but the process of continuous inspection and support after licensing was less developed. In their assessment of the service, inspection officers cited the support of the local authority, proper preparation of prospective providers and continuous monitoring and evaluation, as key to a successful, good quality service.

Today, Kiskunhalas has the largest number of family day care providers in Hungary. Building on their success, the local authority has for several years been operating an information service for interested people and other local authorities in the country. However, family day care has been slow to develop in Hungary as a whole. According to data available to the staff of the National Institute for Family and Social Policy, there are approximately 38 family day care homes in total, though official statistics give a total of 31 (Ministry of Social and Family Affairs, 2000). The exact number is not known, since family day care providers are not required to provide information to the office of statistics. What are the reasons for this slow development?

Reasons for the slow development of a family day care service

Family day care is one of the services for which there is no state funding (normative support). This is the main reason for the small number of providers. Local authorities can choose whether to financially support a family day care provider or not and the level of funding. Although most of the current providers receive some local authority funding, it does not cover the full cost of childcare. Parents still have to pay about three to four times more than for other childcare services. In those cases where the local authority does not support the provider, parents have to cover the full cost. Most household incomes in Hungary are insufficient to pay this amount. Thus family day care homes exist only where there is local authority financial support. Since most local authorities have restricted budgets, many feel unable to support childcare provision although they have a statutory duty to do so.

Although the local authority can employ providers, in practice so far they are all self-employed. As small entrepreneurs, they have to run a business and make an adequate income. However, without national or local authority support, providers are forced to take as many children as possible to generate a larger income. In unofficial estimates, a provider and helper need to care for approximately 15 children to cover their salaries and the indirect costs of providing care. Those providers who had only two or three children for a period of time, experienced difficulties and considered giving up. Operating as a small business means that providers have to possess at least some knowledge of accounting and other business-related activities. However, we have found that those people who want to work with children are usually not business-oriented, and those people who are do not want to provide family day care because it is not profitable.

In addition to funding, support and quality assurance remain the other obstacles to development. As we have seen, inspection and development officers are a key component of the family day care model. Yet with the exception of Kiskunhalas, no local authority has contracted people to undertake this work. This is mainly due to the fact that the numbers of providers are usually low, sometimes only one, and until recently there was no legal requirement for monitoring them. Thus initial concerns that family day care providers may be isolated seem to have been proved true. Although attempts have been made to support these providers, geographical distance makes this difficult. Changes in the law, which now require family day care providers to be monitored, may resolve this situation.

Conclusions

This chapter has described the reasons for developing a family day care service in Hungary and the process involved. Hungary now has a legal framework for the provision of family day care. Parents are showing increased interest in this type of childcare, as indeed are many local authorities. There also seems to be a growing interest from people who want to become family day care providers. However, there has not been a rapid increase in the number of family day care homes. Development of the service has been restricted by lack of funding and support. The problem of funding is a serious one that somehow needs to be addressed. It is hoped that the government will introduce normative support for family day care in 2003, which will go some way to improving the situation. Steps could also be taken to support providers and ensure a high quality service.

For example, family day care providers and childcare centre staff have much to offer each other in terms of sharing experience and discovering different ways of working with children. Yet staff in childcare centres feel threatened by family day care. Many are convinced that when local authorities realize the financial advantages of supporting family day care rather than centres, centres will be closed. Most family day care providers are former childcare workers or kindergarten teachers who have lost their jobs. So, where centres have closed, former staff have taken the opportunity to take up work as family day care providers. However, this is not a rationale for closing centres. Rather than pit one form of provision against another, it would appear preferable to offer a range of services and let parents decide which suits them best.

Given these reservations and concerns, a better understanding of each other's work is essential. At the introductory training for family day care providers and at meetings of centre-based staff, co-operation and collaboration between childcare workers is emphasized. Exchanging and sharing experiences is useful in learning about the difficulties and achievements of each type of provision. On the one hand, centre staff have much professional knowledge and experience to offer, while on the other, family day care providers represent a different perspective and so can contribute to achieving more flexibility in centre-based services.

It would help to establish and develop family day care if providers were able to support one another and become organized as a group with some influence. Up until now providers have had little energy to take the initiative. In 2002, however, a national organization of family day care providers was set up, run by family day care providers themselves. Through sharing information and experience and organizing regular events for providers, it is hoped that this will be a further step towards professionalization. As the number of members grows, equipment and toy libraries can be set up and further training courses can be organized with the active participation of the association.

In conclusion, despite the obvious difficulties of developing family day care in Hungary, it nevertheless appears to have a future here. There is an unmet demand for affordable, accessible childcare; there are women who want to become family day care providers and there are parents who prefer home-based childcare. Generally, there is the political will to see the service grow. Against such a canvas it is impossible not to feel confident that these difficulties will be overcome.

References

Korintus, M., Kálló, É., Mátay, K. and Vigassy, J. (1995) 'Családi napközi modell-kísérlet' [Family day care piloting]. *Család, gyermek ifjúság, 6.*

Papp, K. (1977) 'Bölcsődei ellátás a szülők szemszögéből' [Childcare as parents see it]. *BOMINFO*, Hirlevel *33.*

Notes

1   One of the predecessors of the National Institute for Family and Social Policy.

CHAPTER THREE

Carving out a Niche?

The Work of a *Tagesmutter* in the New Germany

Ulrike Gelder

Like Hungary, the former East Germany had a high level of publicly-funded childcare centres, but economic and political changes have created a need for new forms of childcare and led to the development of a family day care service. This chapter by Ulrike Gelder draws on her research with family day care providers in one town in the north-east of Germany, to explore how the service has developed and some of the tensions created by combining the public role of childcare worker with the private sphere of home and family.

Introduction

This chapter examines the development of family day care in one town in the north-east of Germany eight years after unification. It describes who becomes a family day care provider (*Tagesmutter*, plural *Tagesmütter*), the daily routine they develop in their work, and the business opportunities that arise from providing such care. Intended and unintended effects of policies regulating family day care and the need to take the wider economic and cultural context into account are identified as central issues for family day care providers and policy makers alike.

Family day care was not part of the extensive provision of public childcare in the former socialist German Democratic Republic (GDR). The unification of West and East Germany and the changes to the organization of economy and social life as established in the former West Germany had a dramatic effect on the new *Länder*[1]. It set off a spiral of female un-employment, a sharp decline in the birth rate, a decline of demand for childcare provision due to the introduction of fees for day care and the closure of day care centres (Pettinger 1996; Bundesministerium für Familie Senioren Frauen und Jugend[2] 1998). One consequence of unification and the merging of the new Länder into the West German political system was that family day care (not officially acknowledged in East Germany before unification) in the new Länder came under the legal framework of the *Kinder-und Jugendhilfegesetz* (*KJHG* – Children and Youth Service Act, Social Code Book VIII). Since then the number of family day care providers and children looked after in this form of day care has steadily risen in the new Länder (Trimpin 1996).

In 1993, the German government financed a pilot scheme, 'Qualification of Tagesmütter in rural areas', with a focus on the new Länder. The scheme aimed to fill the emerging gaps in day care provision to enable mothers to go out to work and to establish a new form of income source for women, although the limitations on generating substantial income with this form of self-employment were acknowledged (Nolte 1995). The courses offered were taken up eagerly by women, particularly unemployed trained childcare workers, or workers who feared impending redundancy. At the same time the introduction of family day care provision into the childcare landscape was seen as competition to day care centres providing for children under three, possibly leading to further closures and redundancies (Trimpin 1996). At first, the new legal framework for family day care simply meant that women who had provided these services before unification continued providing childcare in their homes. Initially family day care was seen as an acceptable choice for children who for medical reasons were unable to attend a day care centre or where the working hours of parents were not covered by the opening hours of day care centres (Trimpin 1996). In general, parents in the new Länder approve of sending their children to day care centres (Bundesministerium für Familie Senioren Frauen und Jugend 1996), but family day care may widen their choices (Hauser et al. 1996).

As well as bringing women who were already caring for children in their own homes within a legal framework, it has been claimed that formal recognition of family day care provision has created new opportunities for work, allowing providers to earn an income (Nolte 1995). This claim needs closer examination. It is important to consider who becomes a Tagesmutter, what the work entails and the level of earnings. Another issue is whether it is possible to develop a career. In this chapter, I consider how family day care operates, women's pathways into this form of self-employment, their work routines and the business opportunities that are provided. While there has been research on family day care in the former West Germany (e.g. Blüml *et al.* 1980; Geenen, Strangmeier and Fröhlich 1992; Tietze, Roßbach and Roitsch 1993; Wingerter 1995) and internationally (e.g. Bryant, Harris and Newton 1980; Salmi 1996; Thomson 1995) it is difficult to apply the findings to the situation of Tagesmütter in the new Länder due to the different legal frameworks and to differences in the social, cultural and economic context.

Tagesmütter find themselves at the interface of the public and the private domains. By definition, family day care takes place on domestic (private) premises and, according to the Children and Youth Services Act, the business of family day care can take place entirely in the private market. Its advantages may be seen in the similarity to the family and with it a context that is easier to handle for small children (Pettinger 1996). The colloquial name 'Tagesmutter' (literally, day mother) also expresses a private, intimate relationship between family day care provider and child. On the other hand there is now legislation in place that, under certain circumstances, prescribes an assessment of the suitability of the Tagesmutter by the *Jugendamt* (youth office providing statutory youth services). There is also a longstanding demand for the qualification and integration of Tagesmütter into the childcare workers' qualification system (e.g. Schumann 1996) and there are efforts to promote a businesslike approach by Tagesmütter (Arbeitsgemeinschaft tagesmütter – Bundesverband für Eltern Pflegeeltern und Tagesmütter e.V. 1992; Kurth 1997).

An examination of family day care that recognizes the closeness of providers, place and activity to the activities of housewives and mothers has to deal with the difficulties presented when attempting to disentangle these two roles. Previous research focusing on women's experience of housework (Oakley 1974) or on women's experience as mothers (Boulton 1983; Piachaud 1984; Richardson 1993) has shown on one hand, the extensive overlap of both roles, and on the other hand, inevitable conflicts. A clear separation of roles between that of a housewife and that of a mother is not possible. There is also a danger that in examining domestic activities through the lens of (public) work, the relational aspects are lost (Boulton 1983; Himmelweit 1995). An emphasis on one role seems to push the other into the background. An emphasis on the work role runs the risk of commodifying care, while an emphasis on the role of mother risks using biological explanations to account for women's care of children. This dilemma becomes even more extreme when the third role, that of a family day care provider is introduced, caring for *other people's* children.

The research study

This chapter draws on data collected for a comparative study of family day care providers in the north-east of England and Rostock in the north-east of Germany.[3] One of the reasons for choosing Rostock in Mecklenburg-Vorpommern – a 'new' *Land* – as a location was that there the numbers of family day care providers and children looked after by Tagesmütter was steadily rising. Information was collected through a postal questionnaire sent out to all 40 Tagesmütter who had been registered with the Jugendamt Rostock in January 1999 (no men were registered). Twenty replied, a response rate of 50 per cent.

The survey showed that the average age of the Tagesmütter was 37, ranging from 21 to 60. They had worked as a Tagesmutter for an average of 3 years, ranging from 6 months to 20 years. Ninety per cent (18) lived with their husband or partner, and 70 per cent (14) with at least one of their children. Three of the 20 Tagesmütter were not mothers.

Ten of the Tagesmütter were interviewed. The sampling frame for the in-depth interviews included the length of time worked as a Tagesmutter, the number and age of her own children, the length of the working week, level of income from family day care and whether she had childcare training.

Legal framework in Germany and childcare provision in Rostock

The German Children and Youth Services Act states that family day care providers do not have to seek permission from the Jugendamt as long as they do not look after four children or more, excluding their own. A registered Tagesmutter can look after up to six children. When the family day care provider is subsidized with public money, the Jugendamt has to be satisfied that the Tagesmutter is suitable and register her. Land laws have the power to specify and regulate childcare services within the framework of the Act, for example to set the circumstances that warrant eligibility for subsidy and also the amount, which is paid directly to the childcare provider rather than the parents. Practice varies considerably among the 16 Länder (Walter-Smets 1996). The Jugendamt also has a duty to advise and support Tagesmütter groups. This may take the form of personal contact with staff of the Jugendamt or of training provided by the German family day care association, jointly commissioned by the federal state and individual Länder.

Some of the extensive full-time childcare provision established before unification has been maintained. In Rostock day care centres cater for just under a third of the children under three and for 93 per cent of pre-school children between three and six years (Hansestadt Rostock Amt für Statistik und Wahlen 2000). Tagesmütter provide for only a very small proportion of children. However, the number of children placed in the care of a Tagesmutter has risen more than threefold to 67 between March 1997 and December 1998 (Hansestadt Rostock Amt für Statistik und Wahlen 2000).

The Tagesmütter included in the study were all registered with the local Jugendamt. It would be very unlikely to find unregistered Tagesmütter in Rostock, since the local Jugendamt subsidizes places for up to three children with registered Tagesmütter (with parents contributing up to 30 per cent of the cost), but does not subsidize places with unregistered Tagesmütter.

The path into family day care

None of the women in the study had chosen family day care provider as a lifetime career. As in other European countries, the economic activity rate of mothers is lower than that of men or fathers (Statistisches Bundesamt 1999). Mothers in the new Länder show a clear commitment to work despite increasing difficulties in combining work and family (Meise 1995; Schulze Buschoff 1996). Most of the women in the sample belong to the age brackets where 90 per cent had obtained vocational qualifications, or further or higher education. They had grown up in a socialist society where it was the norm for women and mothers to work full-time (Miethe *et al.* 1990; Trappe 1995). Women's path into family day care work followed two distinctive steps. First they left the labour force, or rather were pushed out of the labour market, and then they became Tagesmütter. For the majority of the respondents, the path out of the labour market was the effect of economic restructuring after unification. Twelve of the twenty respondents stated that they were unemployed before they became a Tagesmutter.

Seven respondents had completed a three-year full-time training course in childcare and had lost employment in one of the public day care facilities.

Two Tagesmütter did not seek employment. Another two were still on parental leave, however, one woman's workplace had closed before she was due to return. Two Tagesmütter had not entered the labour market before taking up family day care. They were students increasing their income. Three women had to leave the labour force when one of their children was not able to attend a day care centre due to medical reasons. Two of these women had tried to work at night, when their partner could look after the children, but did not feel able to cope after a while.

The attitudes expressed by Tagesmütter in the questionnaires and the interviews reflected the fact that they had access to maternity and parental leave up to the third birthday of the child, as well as their commitment to work. Women who had grown up in the former GDR were likely to have a positive attitude towards combining employment and raising children and a positive attitude towards public childcare (Bundesministerium für Familie Senioren Frauen und Jugend 1996).

Just under half of the respondents had known another Tagesmutter. Just over half had heard that the Jugendamt was looking for family day care providers or gained their information from the local press or regional television. This happened at a time when the German family day care association was particularly active in Rostock. The association helped to set up the first two courses for Tagesmütter, which began in December 1997 and were free of charge to participants. One comprised 100 hours for trained childcare workers, the other 180 hours for people without formal childcare training. Thirteen of the respondents had participated in one of these courses. The focus of the course was pedagogic work with children in this particular framework, and the relationship between Tagesmutter and parents.

Most of the interviewees described the next step as a careful consideration of whether this kind of work would suit them and could be reconciled with their families. For example, some decided just to start with one child in order to find out if it worked, while another waited until she and her family had moved from a rented flat to their own bungalow before taking on other people's children. The two women who, before unification, could not make use of available childcare facilities for their own children saw a possibility to help out parents in a similar situation and also earn some money. Just two women describe how they became a Tagesmutter as a kind of coincidence, from having been asked to engage in this kind of work at the right time with no good reason to decline.

The questionnaires asked the respondents to note down in a few words their reasons for becoming a Tagesmutter. Half stated that it was important to be able to look after their own children. Liking children and enjoying working with children were also a strong motivation. Earning money was the least frequently mentioned reason. The high incidence of women who said they became Tagesmütter because they wanted to work in their occupation reflected the situation of trained childcare workers in the new Länder, who had often lost their jobs when centres closed, but wanted to continue working with children.

Daily routines and practices

The Tagesmütter's organization of their daily work strongly reflected cultural views of the needs of children. Children in Germany, particularly young children, are perceived to need regular meals, activities in the fresh air and regular sleeping times (Table 3.1).

Table 3.1 The daily routine of Tagesmütter	
7 a.m.	Children arrive
8 a.m.	Joint breakfast Nappies, potty etc.
9 a.m.	Playground, walk etc. or
10 a.m.	Activities inside, painting, reading, singing Some gymnastics or dancing
11 a.m.	Tagesmutter prepares lunch while children play
Noon	Lunch Nappies, etc. Children sleep
1 p.m.	Dishes, prepare afternoon snack, some housework, break
2 p.m.	'Coffee' (drink and snack) Nappies etc.
3 p.m.	Playing outside in the back yard, garden or nearby playground until collection time
4 p.m.	

Nevertheless, all Tagesmütter have to juggle commitments arising from their work as family day care provider and from their role as mother and housewife. Where the work takes place – most of the time in the home of the Tagesmutter – does not distract from a conceptualization of her daily routine as her work routine. Her job is to look after children and she is paid to do so. Yet at the same time she does not cease to be a mother and – working at home – housework tasks may lurk in every corner as she goes through the day.

When Tagesmütter were asked in the survey to describe their previous working day, they produced working routines, which were remarkably similar. The social and cultural context produces a hierarchy of determinants of the daily routine, which are listed in Figure 3.1. These can be used to compare working conditions of Tagesmütter and family day care providers in other countries (Gelder 2002).

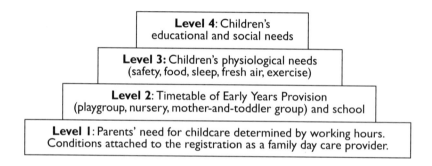

Figure 3.1 The hierarchy of determinants of routines

On Level 1 are the determinants that cannot (or only in extreme circumstances) be altered by the day care provider. Level 2 consists of the timetable of other early years provision. Level 3 is what Maslow (1970) has labelled as physiological needs, the basic level in the hierarchy of needs. Family day care providers have to keep children safe, fed and able to rest. These requirements have a direct impact on the daily routine. Level 4 addresses needs higher up in Maslow's hierarchy of needs, particularly 'love and belongingness' and 'cognitive needs' (Maslow 1970). Each ascending level has to fit into the pattern developed in the previous level.

For the Tagesmütter, parents' need for childcare at given times is the most compelling determinant of their daily routine (Level 1). Parents seek family day care that covers their working hours. It means family day care providers have to be in a certain place at a certain time for children to be delivered and collected. Usually that is the home of the Tagesmutter, although for some it is the home of the child.

Level 2 is the context of other childcare provision in which family day care takes place. For example, family day care may be sought in addition to other childcare provision. Then the family day care provider has to tailor her daily work practices to the opening hours of these. The daily routine of the Tagesmütter in Rostock was not affected by determinants on Level 2. None of the children in their care attended other childcare facilities without the Tagesmutter. None of the respondents filling in the questionnaire looked after school children. However, children in Germany start school when they are six and then they are perceived as being able to walk to and from school without adult supervision. Therefore, none of the respondents took her own children to school or had to meet them at the school gate. This makes early years provision less fragmented and better suited to meet parents' need to cover working hours.

When routines are not prescribed by circumstances beyond the control of the Tagesmutter, it is up to her how and to what extent to structure the day. Housework may be organized following certain routines and standards in order to keep to acceptable standards (Oakley 1974). Mothers gain the feeling of being in control and having some time and space for themselves by establishing routines or rhythms in the day (Boulton 1983). The Tagesmütter who had been working in a day care centre explained that they continued to use this pattern for their work with children at home.

The argument that children need routine – perhaps better called rhythm – is strong in Germany. It is an issue in textbooks for childcare workers and parents (e.g. Bachmann *et al.* 1986; Beu *et al.* 1971; Neubert 1967) The physical and emotional development process of children is seen to demand structure and it is believed that learning is supported by routines. The Tagesmütter interviewed agreed that a daily repeated routine allowed children to 'get their bearings' and gave them a sense of security. A particularly strong influence on the organization of daily routines was the perceived needs of children concerning food and sleep.

German Tagesmütter emphasized that they offer a well-balanced diet. One explained why she was considering increasing the amount parents were asked to pay for food.

I only buy good things. I don't want to buy any cheap juice, or something. Fruit and yoghurt every day, and muesli. There is always everything there. …I do not buy any kind of meat. We do not like to eat pork. We prefer turkey. And that is slightly more expensive. However, the parents agree. One of the mothers wants everything fresh. I do not cook any instant foods or use tins. (Ursula, worked as a Tagesmutter for 8 months)

This attitude, and the knowledge shown about nutrition, seems to be shared by most Tagesmütter. Women who did not wish to cook lunch ordered meals. Two Tagesmütter used a company that provides cooked meals for day care centres, while a third used the 'meals-on-wheels' service provided by the German Red Cross.

Sleep, like food, is a basic physiological need of human beings. In children, this need takes a different form compared to adults and changes over time, particularly during the first year of their life. Very young infants fall asleep almost anywhere when they are tired (e.g. Leach 1997). However, this ability vanishes over time. On the diary sheets of the Tagesmütter, the after-lunch sleep or after-lunch rest took a central position. The absence of Level 2 determinants of the daily routine (school runs or similar) in Germany enabled this to happen. Tagesmütter were convinced of the necessity and the benefits of an after-lunch sleep.

If you know a bit about psychology, then you know that a child needs to switch off, that she needs this break for her body [and] for her development …My Xaver…this lad really loves to go to bed. At midday he is looking forward to it. Next week he is going to be two [years old]. Well, that would be the worst I could do to him if I would not lay him down. (Almut, worked as a Tagesmutter for 4 years)

Activities connected to food and sleep were seen as important and a useful way of improving children's skills in everyday activities and in social situations. For example, in order to enjoy a meal together the table has to be set and children can be involved. The after-lunch sleep provides daily practice in getting undressed and dressed. Making use of these learning opportunities situated in daily activities requires time and patience from the carer. The time left over was filled with activities geared to furthering children's development. It was seen as important that children played outside to get fresh air and to develop their gross motor skills. Other activities, like painting and the use of scissors, were geared towards developing fine motor skills. The interviewed Tagesmütter also brought up the benefits of playing with and learning from other children. When asked what they viewed as essential personal attributes for family day care providers, the Tagesmütter mentioned loving and respecting children, perseverance and flexibility, being able to stay calm, and the ability to create a cheerful atmosphere. It was also obvious from their accounts that they saw good care as requiring knowledge of child development and organizational skills.

Restricted business opportunities

The tasks of running a business run parallel to the daily work of looking after children for the Tagesmutter. This involves negotiating terms and conditions, setting up contracts with parents, handling income and expenses, and completing paperwork for the tax office and the Jugendamt. Some of these tasks become routine; others have to be undertaken infrequently. The main actors are the Tagesmutter, the child's parents and the officer in the Jugendamt.

When setting up in business as a Tagesmutter, restrictions and regulations fixed by the legal framework immediately come to the fore. Business practices and opportunities are determined by legislation, as well as by the availability of other childcare provision and the general attitude of parents towards childcare.

Tagesmütter assume that parents take up their services exclusively in order to go out to work. In Rostock the condition for receiving a public subsidy is that parents work or study.[4] Of the 46 children cared for by the Tagesmütter in the study, over half stayed longer than 40 hours a week and none spent less than 11 hours a week in the household of the Tagesmutter. The oldest child being looked after was four years old, but over three-quarters were under the age of three. Children in Germany are expected to attend a kindergarten when they are three years old, as every child has a right to a kindergarten place. Since children arrive and are collected at different times, the working hours of a Tagesmutter are extremely long. Eighty-five per cent of the Tagesmütter worked longer than 40 hours a week, and the longest working week was 69 hours. Extremely long working days and weeks were the result of looking after at least one child with a shift-working mother or parents.

The average number of children cared for by a Tagesmutter was 2.3, and this rose only slightly (to 2.5) when their own children under the age of 8 were taken into account. Most looked after one, two or three children. All appeared to be happy with their workload. The women who had only one child on their roll looked after this particular child as a favour to their parents, or felt that their other commitments, to their own family or study, did not allow taking on any more. The two Tagesmütter who each cared for four children were also happy with this number, arguing for example that four children play better together and that one child is less likely to be left out than in a group of three. Tagesmütter with childcare training felt better able to cope easily with more children, as they had the training and experience of providing childcare for large groups of children. The family day carers hoped that the Jugendamt would increase the number of children receiving public subsidy to be looked after by a Tagesmutter with childcare training from three to four.

The income a Tagesmutter receives depends on the number of children on her roll, whether these children attend full-time or part-time, the amount of money charged for food and whether the Tagesmutter waives the parents' contribution. The median income per month of the twenty Tagesmütter was the equivalent of £602.84, ranging from £118.56 to £946.56. Out of this money all expenses have to be paid. This compares unfavourably to the 1999 salary of trained childcare workers in day care centres or kindergartens, who would have earned between £1053 and £1338 a month gross, depending on their training. Yet, in the light of high unemployment rates of trained childcare workers and of women, Tagesmütter put forward a positive evaluation of their income. Some of them were clearly taking a long-term perspective.

> A Tagesmutter these days – this [the money] is sometimes not earned by women going out to work all day …Now that I am self-employed – I knew that before: self-employment means that I would need at least one-and-a-half years to make a profit. (Monika, worked as a Tagesmutter for 2 years)

Looking only at the business potential also ignores other possible advantages.

> Certainly, financially, this in not the way to earn a golden nose. However, considering your health – you haven't got stress, you are calm, you are balanced. And you are here for your family. (Almut, worked as a Tagesmutter for 4 years)

The wish when setting up as a Tagesmutter – being there for one's family – seems to have come true. However, Almut's lack of stress may not be typical. She works jointly with another Tagesmutter, she has childcare training and the financial survival of her household does not depend on her income.

Career opportunities in childminding

Whether or not a Tagesmutter had formal childcare training did not appear to affect the amount of income earned. A stronger restriction on business expansion was the maximum number of children who could receive a subsidy with one Tagesmutter, which varies from region to region in Germany. One possibility for overcoming this constraint to some extent is to work jointly with another Tagesmutter. However, that may entail the opening of one family home not only to other people's children and their parents, but also to another adult on a daily basis. It is not an option at all if there is not the space to take more children. Although some of the Tagesmütter liked the idea of working with a colleague, they found it difficult to envisage this taking place in a family home. Tagesmütter reported that their husbands in particular did not like the idea of another adult in the family home. Monika described her husband's reasoning:

> He said, 'then she [the other Tagesmutter] is already there when I get up and then I can't walk around in my underpants'. He also does not like the idea that she could use our cooker. (Monika, worked as a Tagesmutter for 2 years)

Two sets of Tagesmütter had in fact teamed up. In both instances a room and bathroom were set aside solely for the purpose of day care provision. Here the income situation of both women working jointly together had to reflect the expenses of the owner of the premises. Also, a working relationship had to be developed. According to the Tagesmütter already working jointly together and those who had plans to do so, this form of day care was popular with parents. Yet this way of organizing their work was criticized by the officer in the Jugendamt, who viewed this as a move towards becoming a 'mini-nursery' and defying the ethos of family day care.

Some of the Tagesmütter saw their work clearly as a stopgap. Those who treated this kind of work as a stopgap were either students or older women who looked after the children of neighbours or friends as a favour. These differing intentions created potential problems for integrating family day care providers into existing training and occupational structures (Melchert 1992; Schumann 1996). When there is no aspiration to a long-term commitment, it remains unlikely that these women (or men) will attend extensive training or pursue qualifications. Without qualifications, payment within the pay structures negotiated for childcare workers by trade unions and employers cannot be justified, although Tagesmütter are not members of a trade union.

Conclusion

The establishment of family day care in Rostock, a town in one of the new Länder in the unified Germany, has the potential to ease some of the problems thrown up for women by the profound economic and social restructuring. At the same time, the rapid increase of women working as Tagesmütter has to be seen in the context of these structural changes.

The women who had been working as Tagesmütter before unification have now become self-employed within the legal framework of the Children and Youth Service Act. The advantage is that formal support from the Jugendamt and the German family day care association is available. This may be beneficial for the business side and for their daily work. Yet the application of the legal framework intended to encourage good quality childcare provision also means a restriction on the number of children, and a constraint on earning power. It is true that the availability of subsidies for childcare costs, payable to the provider, constitutes some kind of income security, albeit limited, as well as official recognition of the family day care provider. Yet compared to the situation before unification, the main beneficiaries appear to be those parents who would have used private arrangements anyway, whether due to preference, child ill health or shift work. Their use of family day care, like centre care, is now eligible for a subsidy.

The motivation to become a Tagesmutter also has to be examined against the background of economic and political restructuring. Many of the women did not want to leave their work, but were made redundant. Their options were unemployment, retraining or participation in a job-creation scheme. For the women with childcare training the only way to work with children – a work they loved – was to become a Tagesmutter. For others, the provision of family day care seemed to offer a way of reconciling looking after their own children with earning an income. Effective publicity by the local Tagesmütter association had been instrumental in leading these women to consider the option of becoming a Tagesmutter.

A significant consequence of the way women entered family day care in the new Germany is how they envisage their future. This can take one of two opposing directions. One direction is to treat this kind of self-employment as a stopgap. Some women were looking after one child of a neighbour as a favour and intended to stop working as a Tagesmutter once the child had outgrown the need for their care. Others financed their studies with family day care. These women were less responsive to the offer of training or other more formal support measures. The other direction is women's attempt to team up with another Tagesmutter and to re-interpret family day care as mini-nurseries, loosely connected to the private space of their family home. This entails a careful consideration of the working relationship between the women involved, financial planning and a long-term commitment. Advantages are seen in the possibility of offering better, more reliable care, less isolation and more flexibility. One of the most interesting aspects of the attempts to move family day care closer to the set-up of a mini-nursery is that it shows what the 'experts', the women working as Tagesmütter, view as the disadvantages of looking after other people's children in their family home. These include having sole responsibility for a group of children, the difficulties of leaving the house with an increasing number of children in their care, and the isolation of Tagesmutter and children, to mention a few. An advantage of working jointly with another Tagesmutter is that it allows women to engage in childcare work who do not have the space in their own homes or whose husband or children oppose the opening of the family home to other people's children.

Whether the provision of family day care continues to expand, and how stable the arrangements between parents and family day care provider will be, depends on several factors. Demand for family day care and supply of Tagesmütter will be influenced by the general development of the labour market and particularly women's position in it. A change in policies concerning the subsidy of childcare provision may boost the opportunity for Tagesmütter to find work, if subsidies are increased, or may push family day care in to the private market, if subsidies are cut or the criteria for subsidies are changed to reduce eligibility. Yet if Tagesmütter succeed in establishing mini-nurseries, they may also be able to demand better support, financially and in kind, from the Jugendamt. Further research into the development of family day care provision in the new Länder and an analysis of the quality of the service, including that of Tagesmütter who have teamed up, would surely provide interesting information. It would extend the general knowledge of the opportunities and limitations of family day care for women and children.

References

Arbeitsgemeinschaft tagesmütter – Bundesverband für Eltern Pflegeeltern und Tagesmütter e.V. (1992) *Grundlagenpapier zur Familientagespflege* [Basic thesis of family day care]. Meerbusch: Arbeitsgemeinschaft tagesmütter, Bundesverband für Eltern, Pflegeeltern und Tagesmütter e.V.

Bachmann, F., Berger, I., Besse, M., Hoffmann, R., Regel, G., Weber, C. and Weigl, I. (1986) *Programm für die Erziehungsarbeit in Kinderkrippen, 2. Auflage* [Curriculum for care and educational work in day nurseries]. Berlin: VEB Verlag Volk und Gesundheit.

Beu, W., Dumke, I., Freese, I., Jürgens, A., Krase, E., Michaelis, H., Michaelis, S., Müller, L., Rösler, J. and Rosenbaum, U. (eds) (1971) *Pädagogische Studientexte zur Vorschulerziehung* [Pedagogical texts for pre-school education]. Berlin: Volk und Wissen, Volkseigener Verlag.

Blüml, H., Erler, G., Frauenknecht, B., Gudat, U., Permien, H., Rommelspacher, B., Schumann, M. and Stich, J. (1980) *Das Modellprojekt 'Tagesmütter' – Abschlußbericht der wissenschaftlichen Begleitung* [The pilot scheme 'Tagesmütter' – concluding report of the scientific observation]. Stuttgart: W. Kohlhammer.

Boulton, M.G. (1983) *On Being a Mother: A Study of Women with Pre-School Children*. London: Tavistock.

Bryant, B., Harris, M. and Newton, D. (1980) *Children and Minders*. London: Grant McIntyre.

Bundesministerium für Familie Senioren Frauen und Jugend (ed) (1996) *Gleichberechtigung von Frauen und Männern: Wirklichkeit und Einstellung in der Bevölkerung 1996* [Equality of women and men: reality and attitudes of the population 1996]. Stuttgart, Berlin, Cologne: Kohlhammer.

Bundesministerium für Familie Senioren Frauen und Jugend (ed) (1998) *Zehnter Kinder- und Jugendbericht: Bericht über die Lebenssituation von Kindern und die Leistungen der Kinderhilfen in Deutschland* [Tenth children and youth report], 13/11368. Bonn: Bundestagsdrucksache.

Geenen, E.M., Strangmeier, R. and Fröhlich, W. (1992) *Kindertageseinrichtungen und Tagepflege* [Day care providers and family day care]. Kiel: Die Frauenministerin der Landes Schleswig-Holstein.

Gelder, U. (2002) 'Working for women? Family day care providers' social and economic experience in England and Germany.' Unpublished PhD thesis. Newcastle upon Tyne: University of Newcastle, Department of Sociology and Social Policy.

Hansestadt Rostock Amt für Statistik und Wahlen (2000) *Statistisches Jahrbuch 1999* [Statistical yearbook]. Rostock: Hansestadt Rostock, Amt für Pressearbeit und Stadtmarketing.

Hauser, R., Glatzer, W., Hradil, S., Kleinhenz, G., Olk, T. and Pankoke, E. (1996) *Ungleichheit und Sozialpolitik* [Inequality and social policy]. Opladen: Leske and Budrich.

Himmelweit, S. (1995) 'The discovery of "unpaid work": The social consequences of the expansion of "work"'. *Feminist Economics 1*, 2, 1–19.

Kurth, T. (1997) *Tagesmutter, Kinderbetreuung mit Familienanschluß: Ein Ratgeber für Eltern und Tagesmütter* [Tagesmutter, childcare within a family: a guide for parents and Tagesmütter]. Munich: SYM Verlag.

Leach, P. (1997) *Your Baby and Child: The Essential Guide for Every Parent.* Third edition. London: Penguin.

Maslow, A. H. (1970) *Motivation and Personality.* Second edition. New York: Harper and Row.

Meise, S. (1995) 'Rabenmamas und Superfrauen: Mütter in Ost und West' [Uncaring mother or superwoman: Mothers in East and West]. *Psychologie Heute* September, 32–37.

Melchert, H. (1992) *Gutachten: Möglichkeiten und Grenzen von öffentlichen Maßnahmen in der Tagespflege.* Göttingen: Eigenverlag.

Miethe, H., Radtke, H., Sallmon, S., Lötsch, I. and Ebert, E. (1990) 'Berufstätigkeit' [Work]. In G. Winkler (ed) *Frauenreport 90* [Women report 90]. Berlin: Die Wirtschaft.

Neubert, R. (1967) *Das Kleinkind: Zur Erziehung in der Familie* [The small child: upbringing within the family]. Berlin: Volk und Wissen, Volkseigener Verlag.

Nolte, C. (1995) 'Kinderbetreuung in der Tagespflege' [Childcare in the form of family day care], paper presented to the conference 'Fachtagung: Kinderbetreuung in der Tagespflege', Magdeburg.

Oakley, A. (1974) *Housewife.* London: Penguin.

Pettinger, R. (1996) 'Zum gesellschaftlichen Wandel von Familien – Konsequenzen für die Kinderbetreuung.' In Bundesministerium für Familie Senioren Frauen und Jugend (ed) *Kinderbetreuung in Tagespflege: Tagesmütter-Handbuch* [Childcare in the form of family day care: Tagesmütter handbook] Stuttgart, Berlin, Cologne: Kohlhammer.

Piachaud, D. (1984) *Round About Fifty Hours a Week.* London: Child Poverty Action Group.

Richardson, D. (1993) *Women, Motherhood and Childrearing.* Basingstoke: Macmillan.

Salmi, M. (1996) 'Finland is another world: The gendered time of homework.' In E. Boris and E. Prügl (eds) *Homeworkers in Global Perspective: Invisible no more.* New York: Routledge.

Schulze Buschoff, K. (1996) 'Der Konflikt Familie und Erwerbsarbeit – die Situation in West- und Ostdeutschland' [The conflict of family and work – the situation in West and East Germany]. *Zeitschrift für Frauenforschung:* 1 and 2: 115–127.

Schumann, M. (1996) 'Qualifizierung von Tagespflegepersonen durch Aus- und Fortbildung' [The qualification of family day care providers by training and further education]. In Bundesministerium für Familie Senioren Frauen und Jugend (ed) *Kinderbetreuung in Tagespflege: Tagesmütter-Handbuch* [Childcare in the form of family day care: Tagesmütter handbook] Stuttgart, Berlin, Cologne: Kohlhammer.

Statistisches Bundesamt (1999) *Statistisches Jahrbuch für die Bundesrepublik Deutschland* [Statistical yearbook of the Federal Republic of Germany]. Stuttgart: Metzler-Poeschel.

Thomson, K. (1995) 'Working mothers: Choice or circumstance?' In R. Jowell, J. Curtice, L. Brook and D. Ahrendt (eds) *British Social Attitudes, the 12th Report.* Aldershot: Dartmouth.

Tietze, W., Roßbach, H.-G. and Roitsch, K. (1993) *Betreuungsangebote für Kinder im vorschulischen Alter* [Care provision for children of pre-school age]. Stuttgart: Kohlhammer.

Trappe, H. (1995) *Emanzipation oder Zwang? Frauen in der DDR zwischen Beruf, Familie und Sozialpolitik* [Emancipation or coercion? Women in the GDR between occupation, family and social policy]. Berlin: Akademie Verlag.

Trimpin, U. (1996) 'Entwicklung der Tagespflege in den neuen Bundesländern' [Development of family day care in the new Länder]. *Tagesmütter 3,* 3–6.

Walter-Smets, L. (1996) 'Zur Situation der Familientagespflege in der Bundesrepublik Deutschland' [The situation of family day care in the Federal Republic of Germany]. In Bundesministerium für Familie Senioren Frauen und Jugend (ed) *Kinderbetreuung in Tagespflege: Tagesmütter-Handbuch* [Childcare in the form of family day care: Tagesmütter handbook]. Stuttgart, Berlin, Cologne: Kohlhammer.

Wingerter, M. (1995) 'Tagespflege – eine Herausforderung für betroffene Familien?' [Family day care – a challenge for concerned families?]. Unpublished *Diplomarbeit,* Landau: Universität Koblenz-Landau, Erziehungswissenschaft.

Notes

1   Germany is a federal state, it consists of 16 Länder.
2   Ministry for Family, Senior Citizens, Women and Youth.
3   It was funded by an ESRC research studentship (R 00429734466).
4   Childcare for children 'in need' is regulated by a different part of the KJHG and is financed out of a different public account.

CHAPTER FOUR

Family Day Care in New Zealand
Training, Quality and Professional Status
Elizabeth Everiss and Carmen Dalli

In the late 1980s New Zealand embarked on a significant reform to its provision and regulation of early childhood services. One result was that family day care has been transformed from a charitable welfare provision and repositioned within the mainstream of formally organized early childhood services. It is funded and regulated on a par with other services and governed by the same early years curriculum. However, this new positioning has been accompanied by challenges, especially that of how to enhance training. Liz Everiss and Carmen Dalli describe in this chapter how these challenges have arisen and suggest how they could be addressed.

Introduction

Family day care is the fastest growing early childhood service in Aotearoa-New Zealand. Between 1990 and 2000, the number of children enrolled in licensed home-based early childhood services rose from 1611 to 8937, an increase of 450 per cent. This is a large expansion, but licensed family day care still only accounts for just over 5 per cent of the 87 per cent of pre-school age children who are enrolled in formal early childhood services (Ministry of Education 2002; Education Review Office 2001). An informal and unregulated home-based care sector also exists, but remains hidden from the domain of public policy. The first comprehensive national survey of users of early childhood services, the *New Zealand Childcare Survey* (Department of Labour and National Advisory Council on the Employment of Women 1999), found that 27 per cent (some 45,000) of all pre-school age children experienced some form of informal (and non-familial) childcare arrangement.

This chapter outlines the development of family day care in Aotearoa-New Zealand from its emergence onto the formally organized early childhood scene in the mid-seventies to its current status within the overall regulatory framework that governs all Aotearoa-New Zealand early childhood services. It argues that the formal family day care sector in this country is at a crucial time in its history. Its unprecedented growth and its position within the new regulatory framework of early childhood services make it a strong player in the early childhood policy arena. At the same time, the new regulatory framework challenges family day care services to stake their place more firmly in ongoing discussions about quality, within the broader early childhood sector. The issue of training for work in family day care is central to these discussions. This chapter positions this issue as the major challenge that family day care providers must engage with if they are to move closer to the aim of the broader early childhood sector, of enhancing quality of provision and its professional status.

Early beginnings: family day care as welfare

The history of formally organized family day care networks in Aotearoa-New Zealand can be traced back to the 1970s when the increasing participation of mothers in the paid workforce was accompanied by a shortage of childcare places (Cook 1983). The pioneering days of family day care were characterized by localized initiatives developed by community groups in response to an identified need for childcare. These initiatives were often supported by local councils or by childcare associations (St Johanser 1980) and many were able to receive an establishment grant from the Department of Social Welfare. Continuing to generate enough funding to ensure their ongoing operations was, however, often problematic and the need to survive led these groups to seek other sources of financial support.

It was from this base that family day care in Aotearoa-New Zealand became inextricably linked with the welfare system of child and family support provided by Barnardos (Aotearoa-New Zealand). Barnardos had a track record of generating significant Government funding. As an organization, it was eligible to apply for the childcare fees subsidy, known as the capitation grant. Introduced by government in 1973, the subsidy was intended to provide fees relief for parents who met financial and/or welfare criteria, and was paid directly to childcare services.

St Johanser (1980) argued that the capitation grant provided a powerful attraction for family day care initiatives to align themselves with a voluntary organization eligible for this grant. By 1985 there were 33 family day care schemes nationwide and only two were not connected to Barnardos (Smith and Swain 1988). From Barnardos' point of view, the provision of family day care services was an ideal vehicle for developing their role as a significant charitable organization. Family day care was also a cost-effective alternative to centre-based childcare, which Barnardos also organized and which had relatively high establishment costs (Collie-Holmes 1991).

The prospect that family day care might become a convenient alternative to centre-based childcare was not universally acclaimed. Proponents of the service argued the merits of providing a 'family, not institution, for [the] child who needs care' (McCarthy 1975), and the merits of a provision that 'extended' the family into the community (Le Grice 1976) and helped to build communities (Stewart 1980). However, others, feminists in particular, opposed the expansion of family day care services on the grounds it was 'not in the best interests of women or children' (Coney 1980, p.7). According to Coney, family day care exploited women who were already trapped at home with a pittance of a wage, and added the potentially conflicting role of paid caregiver to a woman's role as wife/mother/housewife. The isolation of women who cared for other people's children in their own homes was also seen as potentially harmful to children. Coney argued that without the scrutiny of fellow workers or supervisor and without any regulations to ensure their well-being, children's rights could easily be abused.

In defence of these criticisms, organizations providing family day care services pointed out that they did have strategies in place to support caregivers, such as network co-ordinators, group meetings for caregivers, equipment support and advice and referral to appropriate social services (Duurloo 1980–81; McKinlay and Cameron 1980). The organizers of family day care also had to meet specified conditions in return for the childcare fees subsidy (capitation grant). These focused largely on safety issues and required the providers to:

- accept responsibility for the child while s/he was in care

- make placement in the best interest of the child

- supervise the placement by visiting

- contribute to the cost of the child's care from their own funds.

While these conditions were minimal in comparison to current requirements, they nonetheless made organizations providing home-based care responsible for the supervision and welfare of the children they placed and as such represent the first Government intervention in home-based provision (Everiss 1998, 1999).

In the last two decades, significant changes have occurred within the field of early childhood policy in Aotearoa-New Zealand, which have impacted significantly on the development of family day care services. The following sections outline these changes and their implications.

The move from welfare to education: the 1980s

In 1986, after many years of lobbying by childcare activists, administrative responsibility for all childcare services moved from the Department of Social Welfare to the Department of Education, making international history. This break from the welfare principle was intended to bring about 'equitable funding for childcare' (State Services Commission 1980, p.91) and was also in line with the increasing acceptance within the local early childhood community that it is very difficult to separate care from education (e.g. Smith 1988). Other policy initiatives that supported this approach included the introduction, in 1988, of three-year integrated training for work in centre-based early childhood services. In the late 1980s early childhood policy in Aotearoa-New Zealand was breaking down the traditional boundaries between care and education services, a move consolidated by the amalgamation, in 1991, of the Early Childhood Workers Union and the Kindergarten Teachers' Association into the Combined Early Childhood Union of Aotearoa. Since many family day care caregivers are paid as 'volunteers' rather than as waged earners, they were not eligible for membership of this organization and have not collaborated to develop their own collective 'industrial' voice.

The move to integrate childcare services within Education was not supported by Barnardos, the biggest arranger of family day care, whose welfare model was seen as more compatible with the policies of the Department of Social Welfare (Department of Education, archival material, October 1985). However, for many individual family day care schemes, the new administrative structure provided the opportunity to access funding from the Department of Education in their own right as childcare services. This led some schemes to sever their relationship with Barnardos, with some justifying their action on the grounds of philosophical differences related to the transfer of childcare administration to the Department of Education (Department of Education correspondence 1986; Collie-Holmes 1991).

New schemes also started applying for funding recognition through the Department of Education. By 1986 the Department moved to clarify procedures for applying for funding recognition, particularly in relation to requirements about the qualifications of the network co-ordinators and about caregiver training. It also identified a need for regulations for family day care (Department of Education, archival material, 14 October 1986). It took a further six years for this to be achieved. However, its discussion as a policy 'need' firmly placed family day care on the early childhood policy agenda.

In the meantime, changes were afoot at the grass-roots level of the national family day care scene. In 1987 the New Zealand Family Day Care Association (NZFDCA) was launched. This new group aimed to provide a forum for collaborative action by the increasing numbers of non-Barnardos family day care schemes, and to advocate for more education and support for all facets of family day care. The main strengths of the association were that:

- it opened up channels of communication nationally; parents, providers and practitioners were brought together

- it triggered a 'purist' approach to family day care

- issues related to the provision of family day care could be addressed separately from the goals and philosophies of the organization to which its members were affiliated (Everiss 1999).

To this day the NZFDCA continues to play a key advocacy role for family day care in Aotearoa-New Zealand. The higher profile created by the NZFDCA for family day care, and the increasing attention being paid to it by the Department of Education (Department of Education correspondence to the Dunedin Community Child Care Association, December 1987), resulted in the convening of a Department of Education working group in 1988 to consider issues related to quality family day care provision.

In another significant step, a report commissioned by government in 1988 (Meade 1988) to review the state of early childhood services generally and to make recommendations for policy development, included family day care in its terms of reference. The Meade Report highlighted the need for more equitable access to funding and funding processes across the childcare sector and for a balance between costs and benefits for early childhood education. It also made recommendations for a quality assurance system that linked higher levels of funding to the achievement of higher quality standards of provision.

The report resulted in two major policy changes. First, all children under school age were to receive the same hourly entitlement to Government subsidies based on their age, not on the service they attended, and with rates for children under two being substantially higher than for over-twos. Second, a quality assurance framework was developed which included a range of linked regulatory and policy instruments to enhance quality provision.

The impact of these two policies on family day care was remarkable. From an underfunded poor relation within a poorly funded sector, family day care, with its high enrolment of under-two-year-olds, suddenly found itself at the wealthier end of the spectrum of early childhood services. At the same time, it became subject to a similar quality assurance system as other early childhood services. This positioning established family day care as an integral part of the 'professional' early childhood education sector. At the same time, the fast pace of change left scant time for this newly 'mandated' and diverse group to clearly define its place in its new world. It was faced with major challenges: the challenge of defining standards of practice; the challenge of training for caregivers and the challenge of defining future training options towards enhancing quality.

Family day care in the 1990s: change and challenge

The change in status for family day care services was consolidated throughout the 1990s. It became clear that Government was leaning towards a professional conceptualization of quality for family day care.

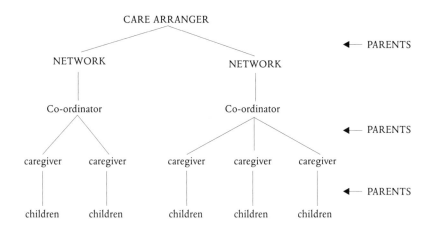

SCHEME
- A scheme is the term used to describe the networks that are the responsibility of a specific care arranger.

CARE ARRANGER
- An agency, body or person who or that arranges or agrees to arrange home-based care for children under six years, either in their own home or the home of a person who provides such care and education.

NETWORKS/PROJECTS
- A network is the responsibility of the co-ordinators.
- A network is a group of premises and caregivers where children receive home-based care and education.
- An unlimited number of networks may operate within a scheme.
- The total number or children receiving home-based care at one time must usually be no more than 80.
- Every network must have at least one co-ordinator with a recognised early childhood qualification.

Co-ordinators
- A co-ordinator is the employee of a care arranger.
- A co-ordinator is responsible for the selection and support of caregivers, and appropriate placement of children.
- A co-ordinator must contact every caregiver in her/his network at least once a fortnight and must visit all caregivers at least once a month.

Caregivers
- A caregiver is a person who provides education and care for children in either his/her own home or the home of the child.
- Every caregiver must be 20 years of age or older.
- No more than one caregiver is usually allowed per home.
- A caregiver may care for no more than four children under six years at one time. No more than two children are allowed to attend if the children are under two years unless they are siblings. Caregivers' own children who are under six years of age, and being looked after, must be included in these numbers.

Figure 4.1. Structure of home-based services in Aortearoa-New Zealand

The challenge of defining standards of practice

The first step in meeting the challenges posed by this conceptualization was taken through the development of the *Education (Home-based Care) Order 1992* (hereafter referred to as the Order). In the development of the Order, the government undertook extensive consultation with the organizers of family day care. The Order has a 'safety' emphasis and strong focus on what Doherty (1997, cited in Taylor, Dunster and Pollard 1999) describes as the concrete, objective, quantifiable components of quality believed to be associated with positive outcomes for children. These typically include caregiver:child ratios, network size, co-ordinator qualifications and requirements for visiting caregivers' homes.

The Order was viewed as a key achievement towards providing assurance that quality experiences would be provided for children in family day care. The development of the Order was a long and arduous process involving reconciling contradictory views as to what components should be included. For example, discussions about the maximum number of children to a network were particularly contentious. These differences emanated from the tension inherent in crafting a regulatory policy driven by a traditional professional perspective (Boisvert 1997 cited in Taylor *et al.* 1999), which was simultaneously seeking to retain and legitimize the uniqueness of the family day care setting. The Order formalized the existing structures of family day care schemes, consisting of networks of caregivers supported by paid co-ordinators who are employed by an organization or individual acting as a care arranger (see Figure 4.1).

Beyond meeting the requirements of the Order, family day care services which aspired to government funding also became bound by the requirements of the *Statement of Desirable Objectives and Practices (DOPs) for Chartered Early Childhood Services* issued in 1990 and reissued in 1996 (Ministry of Education 1996b). By nature, the DOPs are less specific than the Order. While the Order tends to focus on the areas of regulation that are easier to prescribe, such as standards for premises and record-keeping practices, the DOPs also have a strong focus on process aspects of quality provision. The requirements are broad in scope to ensure that they are achievable by the diverse early childhood services of Aotearoa-New Zealand. The Education Review Office monitors all chartered early childhood services. Thus family day care homes affiliated to a chartered family day care arranger also became subject to the reviews of this Office.

In 1996 chartered early childhood services also became bound by the requirement to adhere to the 'Principles, Strands and Goals' of *Te Whaariki*, the early childhood curriculum framework. This document has itself contributed significantly to transforming the status of family day care into that of a legitimate early childhood education service, and the status of family day care 'caregivers' into that of 'educators'. The framework is designed to be applicable in all early childhood settings including the home-based one. The draft version of Te Whaariki described home-based programmes as a specialist context 'with a specific identity and curriculum needs' (Ministry of Education 1993, p.10) and as providing a 'rich but different style of learning and development' (p.12). In the final version of Te Whaariki (Ministry of Education 1996a) specific examples relating to the home-based situation were dropped but family day care remained included as an early childhood education setting.

One of the writers of Te Whaariki, Helen May (2001), has noted that transforming the national curriculum into practice has been complex and challenging for all early childhood services. May saw a number of reasons for this:

- The assumption that early childhood services would have the funding and trained staff capacity to operate quality programmes.

- The holistic and bi-cultural approach to curriculum of Te Whaariki.

- A political climate of accountability that made increasing demands on early childhood staff in relation to assessment and evaluation.

Within the family day care scene, these challenges have been compounded by the fact that no statutory requirements have existed for home-based caregivers to be trained. This issue remains at the core of current concerns about the future of a quality family day care service.

The challenge of training for family day care caregivers

In the rest of this chapter we explore the challenge of developing an appropriate training programme for family day care caregivers, drawing on results from a postal survey of caregivers working in chartered home-based schemes across Aotearoa-New Zealand (Everiss 1998). Issues of caregiver training are not a new phenomenon for family day care in Aotearoa-New Zealand. During the early 1980s, the momentum for training and support for caregivers came from individual co-ordinators within schemes. By 1988 most networks were operating an amalgam of formal and informal training programmes for caregivers as a way of encouraging training. Some schemes were supporting caregivers to attend courses run by training providers outside of the family day care scene. As Jill Cameron of the Dunedin Community Childcare Association noted (Department of Education, archival material), a major problem was that courses containing elements specific to family day care were generally unavailable. There was also little incentive for caregivers to undertake formal training.

Acknowledging the problems, a nationally recognized training programme for family day care was developed and in 1994 the New Zealand Qualifications Authority approved the 'New Zealand Certificate in Family Day Care: Caregiver'. This comprised a two-year programme made up of six modules involving 50 hours of course work and 50 hours practical work, and one module of 20 hours of course work and 20 hours of practical work. For the first time too, family-day-care-specific training was now available through tertiary training institutions. However, this period of rapid expansion was followed by one of steady decline. In 2002 only two tertiary institutions are understood to still be offering the Certificate programme. Although there are no recorded studies on the reasons for this fast decline, issues of access and affordability for caregivers are generally seen as responsible (Education Review Office 2001).

A number of tertiary institutions also offer a higher level certificate course in early childhood education which builds on the family day care certificate and can take students with home-based training into training for centre-based settings. While this poses a potential problem for the retention of trained caregivers in the family day care sector, it provides an empowering adult education programme for caregivers who may choose to move out of the home-based setting and obtain positions in the wider early childhood sector. The desire for access to higher level qualifications by caregivers was supported at a family day care conference held in September 2001.[1]

In March 1996, the Aotearoa-New Zealand government introduced a higher rate of funding for early childhood services meeting higher standards for staff qualifications and staff:child ratios than those required by the regulations. The higher rate was expected to act as an incentive for early childhood services to improve existing standards. This policy was intended to place a new emphasis on family day care training because it promised additional funding for chartered home-based networks in which all caregivers had completed at least the first module of the 'New Zealand Certificate in Family Day Care: Caregiver', or another approved qualification. However, most home-based networks already required new caregivers to have completed the introductory module. Thus, the initiative had no real effect in providing an incentive to train. Instead, it simply acted to confirm the established practice of family day care arrangers to require pre-entry training for caregivers. As a result many family day care networks experienced this policy simply as an increase in funding rather than as an impetus to support their caregivers to undergo further training. The failure of this policy is disappointing because it contributed nothing to enhancing the quality of family day care provision, nor to improving the professional profile of caregivers.

More recently, a working group convened by the Minister of Education to develop a strategic plan for all early childhood services for the next ten years (Early Childhood Education Strategic Plan Working Group 2001), recommended that a long-term goal for all home-based 'educators' should be that they have an 'appropriate qualification' (p.21). Unfortunately 'long-term' was not defined, resulting in a continuing lack of clarity about which future training options might be reasonable for home-based caregivers/educators. The document does however replace the term 'caregivers' by the more inclusive term of 'educators', reflecting the changed perception of family day care work as an educational as well as a custodial/care endeavour.

Towards enhancing quality: the challenge of defining future training options

There have been few studies in Aotearoa-New Zealand concerned with family day care provision. To explore the issue of training a national postal survey of family day care caregivers was undertaken (Everiss 1998). The survey focused on caregivers' views about training, their perceived training needs, and factors that they felt were likely to encourage them to become involved in, and to value, specialized training. The survey also sought to compile a profile of family day care caregivers to provide an insight into what could reasonably be expected from caregivers working at home in terms of their training intentions and professional aspirations. Nearly 400 caregivers working in chartered home-based schemes were sent the questionnaire, and 230 replied (a response rate of 59%). The survey findings suggest possible responses to the training challenges facing the family day care scene in Aotearoa-New Zealand over the next decade.

Who are the home-based caregivers? A profile

The caregivers in the study were a heterogeneous group, though a large number share similar characteristics. The typical caregiver is a married female of Pakeha[2] New Zealand descent who is in her thirties. She is likely to be an experienced parent with dependent children living at home, although these children may not be of pre-school age. She probably has some level of informal early childhood training and three years of secondary school education. She is unlikely to have a tertiary qualification, and any paid work undertaken prior to family day care caregiving is unlikely to be related to working with children. She is likely to view home-based caregiving as a temporary occupation.

Caregivers' training backgrounds and their views about training

The majority of survey respondents said that they had participated in informal training provided by their home-based networks (80%), and considered training necessary for working with young children. The majority also said that they were likely to participate in training if it was appropriately supported and rewarded. Only a small number of respondents had no training (9%). The remaining respondents (11%) had New Zealand Qualifications Authority training points; a few had a Diploma of Teaching (ECE) or its equivalent.

The high levels of participation in at least a modicum of training can be attributed to the mandatory pre-entry training for caregivers adopted by home-based networks (Everiss 1998). The willingness of caregivers to undertake further training if properly supported and rewarded is supported by the findings of other non-Aotearoa-New Zealand studies, which suggest that the effects of training are cumulative and that the successful completion of initial training instils in learners a desire for more (e.g. Eheart and Leavitt 1986; Modigliani 1991 as cited in De Bord 1994). With the majority of caregivers already favourably disposed towards training, it should be possible to design appropriate training programmes to increase caregivers' skills, and also to encourage the concept of caregiving as an early childhood career option rather than a temporary occupation.

So far, however, providers of family day care training and of family day care services have not picked up the challenge of responding to this training opportunity. Statistics provided by the Education Review Office (Education Review Office 2001, p.6) show that, at 1 July 2000, three-quarters of caregivers had completed at least one module of the 'New Zealand Certificate in Family Day Care: Caregiver', which is likely to be the introductory module utilized for government funding purposes. However of these, only 11 per cent had gone on to complete additional modules. Recognized qualifications (nanny or playcentre qualifications) are held by a further 16 per cent of caregivers, while 17 per cent had no recognized qualifications. Scope clearly exists for a concerted effort to rise to the challenge of providing training opportunities for family day care caregivers/educators.

What would attract family day care caregivers to do training?

A number of international studies (e.g., De Bord 1994; Kontos, Howes and Galinsky 1996; Stonehouse 1994; Taylor et al. 1999) have noted that the key to involving caregivers in early childhood training is careful programme design that involves caregivers. They argue that training should:

- be sensitive to caregivers' needs both as caregivers and as adult learners

- acknowledge and build on their experiential knowledge base

- provide them with a range of training options at different levels

- include appropriate support systems and training incentives.

Just over half (54.6%) of the survey respondents indicated that lack of time, course costs and the accessibility of courses were major obstacles to training participation. These barriers applied across all groups of caregivers, regardless of their levels of previous training. Not unexpectedly, preferred training incentives chosen by the respondents included organizational features associated with course access, such as childcare and assistance with course fees; the ability to work towards an early childhood qualification and rewards for training achievements. These findings suggest that appropriate policy interventions to address the challenge of encouraging family day care caregivers to undertake further training would include enabling arrangers of home-based services to implement training systems which incorporate support and reward structures and give recognition for prior experience, education and training.

Furthermore, these findings raise another important issue. To date the prevalent model of caregiver reimbursement has been based on the notion that caregivers are volunteers and not paid employees. Reimbursement has been based solely on the number of children cared for irrespective of training and experience. The findings suggest that this system creates a powerful disincentive for training and retention in family day care. It seems appropriate for family day care schemes to consider ways to develop a career path for caregivers, and to pay them accordingly.

What forms of training delivery are likely to be effective?

The survey showed that caregivers, particularly those with higher levels of previous training, were keen to participate in training with staff from other early childhood settings. This could be facilitated either through training collaboration with other early childhood services, or by supporting caregivers to access more broad-based early childhood courses. One positive spin-off of training collaboration between centre-based and home-based services could be the strengthening of early childhood community networks in a given area. Links of this nature are important, given Pence and Goelman's (1991) belief that the involvement of caregivers in neighbourhood support networks acts to create a form of peer regulation, peer education and peer support, all of which can be supportive of better levels of home-based care.

Some survey respondents would also prefer more widely available distance education programmes. This was particularly evident among caregivers who were undertaking a recognized early childhood qualification, and those who had not participated in any training. Distance education can overcome problems related to training accessibility and gives caregivers the flexibility to work at home in their own time and at their own pace. Kontos' (1992) review of international family day care research provided evidence that it is possible to solicit a high degree of caregiver participation in distance education programmes if appropriate teaching methods are adopted, including the use of videos and printed materials.

International research indicates that individualized support is important for successful training outcomes, although such tailored support is more expensive and time–intensive than a more broad-based approach (Kontos 1992; Kontos *et al.* 1996). However, the survey did not find this was a preferred training option. Perhaps this is because caregivers do not see the network co-ordinators, who are responsible for caregivers' professional development, currently fulfilling this role. One reason could be that some caregivers are only being visited by co-ordinators every one or two months (Education Review Office 2001).

These findings have a number of policy implications. First, family day care schemes need to give attention to the effectiveness of the professional development part of their operations, including ensuring that co-ordinators have appropriate qualifications and training and are adequately resourced for this role. Second, schemes need to consider the introduction of buddy and mentoring systems where caregivers, and particularly those with recognized early childhood qualifications, assist other caregivers. Incentives, such as increased pay, would be desirable in order to encourage caregivers with early childhood qualifications to become mentors, and for the scheme to succeed. Training and support would also need to be provided to assist them in this role. The benefits of adopting a mentoring system would be that caregivers receive assistance additional to that provided by co-ordinators and training providers. This would also create an opportunity for the development of a career path in family day care, which could result in higher retention rates for the more highly trained caregivers within the family day care sector. The quality and stability of the caregiver workforce would also be likely to increase.

What content should be included in training programmes?

It has been noted (e.g., Kontos 1992; Kontos *et al.* 1996; Stonehouse 1994; Wattenberg 1977) that caregivers' participation in training is encouraged only if the content of home-based training programmes is highly relevant to the caregiving task. For caregivers in Aotearoa-New Zealand, their work is strongly affected by the requirements contained in the *Revised Statement of Desirable Objectives and Practices* (Ministry of Education 1996b) and Te Whaariki, the early childhood curriculum statement (Ministry of Education 1996a). The survey showed that while many caregivers were being introduced to Te Whaariki during orientation training, they were keen for more practical input on how to meaningfully link the goals and objectives of Te Whaariki to practice.

A particular characteristic of Te Whaariki is its bi-cultural framework, rooted in both Maori and Pakeha traditions. This poses a specific requirement for practical training input. Te Whaariki supports the cultural identity of all children, affirms and celebrates cultural differences, and aims to help children gain a positive awareness of their own and other cultures. The mono-cultural and predominantly Pakeha background of the majority of caregivers, the fact that training in the areas of bi-culturalism and multi-culturalism did not appear to be of major interest to them in the survey, and the finding by the Education Review Office that training in these areas is not a priority within the training currently provided by networks (Education Review Office 2001), all suggest that the majority of home-based caregivers may struggle to meet the cultural needs of Maori and of other ethnic minority children and families. They may also find it difficult to encourage an understanding of Aotearoa-New Zealand as a bi-cultural and multi-cultural society among other children in their care. This suggests that there is need for policy intervention that would support a training stream which focuses on Maori language and culture, as well as on responding to the increasing cultural diversity in Aotearoa-New Zealand.

The results of the survey, combined with the findings of the Education Review Office's report on quality in home-based settings (Education Review Office 2001), can provide a useful starting point for coherent planning to develop appropriate training programmes that would meet the challenges currently facing the family day care sector in Aotearoa-New Zealand.

Concluding comments

We have argued in this chapter that family day care in Aotearoa-New Zealand is at a crucial point in its history. Over the last two decades there has been growth in the participation rates of children in family day care, growth in the funding base of these services and growth in the regulatory framework within which they operate. We have argued that this growth has transformed the traditional status of family day care from that of a charitable welfare provision, and positioned it within the mainstream part of the formally organized early childhood education sector. This new positioning has been accompanied by new challenges. These include the challenge of defining standards of practice; the challenge of enhancing training levels among its caregivers and the challenge of identifying reasonable training options that would enhance quality provision.

Our view is that these challenges need to be urgently addressed. Despite the growth of the sector in terms of participation rates, and in terms of its overall status within the early childhood policy environment, there has not been a corresponding growth in training opportunities and incentives. Failure to address this gap would hinder the enhancement of quality in family day care. Given the focus on enhancing quality as a major goal of the Early Childhood Strategic Plan, failure by the family day care sector to address the issue of caregiver/educator training would also jeopardize the sector's newly attained status as an emerging professional service within the range of formally organized early childhood services. The likely result of this failure would be the reinforcement of the public perception that home-based care is primarily custodial, that specialized knowledge and skills to work in this area are not necessary, and that caregiving is an extension of women's work and thus not worthy of professional reward.

References

Collie-Holmes, M. (1991) *Where the heart is: A history of Barnardo's in New Zealand 1866–1991.* Wellington: Barnardo's.

Cook, H.M. (1983) *The politics of childcare: An analysis of growth and constraint.* Unpublished MA thesis, Victoria University, Wellington.

Coney, S. (1980) 'Family day care – why is it a bad idea?' *Broadsheet 79*, 6–7.

De Bord, K. (1994) 'A little respect and eight more hours in the day: family childcare providers have special needs.' *Young Children 48*, 4, 21–26.

Department of Labour and National Advisory Council on the Employment of Women (1999) *The New Zealand childcare survey 1998: A survey of early childhood education and care arrangements for children.* Wellington: Department of Labour.

Duurloo, L. (1980–81) 'Family day care – the realities.' *Early Childhood Quarterly 3*, 4, 17–18.

Early Childhood Education Strategic Plan Working Group (2001) *Final report of the strategic plan working group to the Minister of Education.* Wellington: Ministry of Education: New Zealand.

Education (Early Childhood Centres) Regulations 1990 S.R. 1990/261. New Zealand.

Education (Home-based Care) Order 1992 S.R. 1992/238. New Zealand.

Education Review Office (2001) *What counts as Quality in Home-based Care.* Wellington: Education Review Office, New Zealand. http://www.ero.org.nz/Publications/pubs2001/HomeBasedCare

Eheart, B. and Leavitt, R. (1986) 'Training day care home providers: Implications for policy and research.' *Early Childhood Research Quarterly 1*, 119–132.

Everiss, E.A. (1998) 'Time to move on? A study of training participation by caregivers working in chartered home-based schemes in Aotearoa/New Zealand.' Unpublished MA thesis, Victoria University, Wellington.

Everiss, E. (1999) *Bringing it back to mind: Two decades of family day care development in Aotearoa/New Zealand.* Occasional Paper No. 5. Institute for Early Childhood Studies, Victoria University, Wellington and Wellington College of Education.

Kontos, S. (1992) *Family Day Care: Out of the Shadows and Into the Limelight.* Washington DC: National Association for the Education of Young Children.

Kontos. S., Howes. C. and Galinsky, E. (1996) 'Does training make a difference to quality in family child care?' *Early Childhood Research Quarterly 11*, 427–445.

Le Grice, B. (1976) 'Extended family care.' *Early Childhood Quarterly 1*, 3, 4–5.

May, H. (2001) *Politics in the Playground.* Wellington: Bridget Williams Books and New Zealand Council for Educational Research.

McCarthy, P.F. (1975) 'Family, not institution, for child who needs care.' *New Zealand Herald*, 24 October.

McKinlay, P. and Cameron, J. (1980) 'Family day care defended.' *Broadsheet*, September 1980, 2.

Meade, A. (1988) *Education to be more. Report of the Early Childhood Care and Education Working Group.* Wellington: Department of Education.

Ministry of Education (1993) *Te Whaariki: Draft Guidelines for Developmentally appropriate programmes.* Wellington: Learning Media.

Ministry of Education (1996a) *Te Whaariki. He Whariki mo nga mokopuna o Aotearoa. Early Childhood Curriculum.* Wellington: Learning Media.

Ministry of Education (1996b) *Revised Statement of Desirable Objectives and Practices (DOPs) for Early Childhood Services in New Zealand.* Wellington: Ministry of Education, New Zealand.

Ministry of Education (2002) *Early Childhood Education Statistics 2001.* www.minedu.govt.nz

Pence, A.R and Goelman, H. (1991) 'The relationship of regulation, training, and motivation to quality of care in family day care.' *Child and Youth Care Forum 20*, 2, 83–101.

St Johanser, C. (1980) 'Family day care in New Zealand 1980.' Unpublished MA thesis, Victoria University, Wellington.

Smith, A.B. (1988) 'Education and care components in New Zealand childcare centres and kindergartens.' *Australian Journal of Early Childhood, 13*, 3, 31–36.

Smith, A. B. and Swain, D. (1988) 'Family daycare.' In A. B. Smith and D. Swain (eds) *Childcare in New Zealand.* Wellington: Allen & Unwin/Port Nicholson Press.

State Services Commission Working Group (1980) *Early Childhood Care and Education. A Report of the State Services Commission Working Group.* Wellington: States Services Commission.

Stewart, J. (1980) 'Family Day Care.' *Early Childhood Quarterly 3*, 1, 11–13.

Stonehouse, A. (1994) *Not Just Nice Ladies: A Book of Readings on Early Childhood Care and Education.* New South Wales: Pademelon Press.

Taylor, A.R., Dunster, L. and Pollard, J. (1999) '...And this helps me how? Family child care providers discuss training.' *Early Childhood Research Quarterly 14*, 3, 285–312.

Wattenberg, E. (1977) 'Characteristics of family day care providers: Implications for training.' *Child Welfare 56*, 4, 211–228.

Notes

1   Teachers' Refresher Course Committee (TRCC) on family day care, 27–29 September 2001.

2   'Pakeha' is the Maori word for all people of European-origin in Aotearoa-New Zealand.

CHAPTER FIVE

The Development of Childminding Networks in Britain

Sharing the Caring

Sue Owen

Childminding, as family day care is commonly known in the UK, has been regulated by the state since 1948 but has traditionally been an individualized and isolated form of childcare. In this chapter, Sue Owen provides a brief history of family day care in Britain and charts the development of childminding networks, which aim to support home-based care providers and to raise their standards of care. She draws on her evaluation of the new childminding networks set up in one English town in response to the National Childcare Strategy, and considers how networks may be altering the profile of family day care in Britain.

Introduction

In the United Kingdom childminding has traditionally been an individualized and isolated form of childcare in which individual providers, working in their own homes, have negotiated arrangements with individual parents. Quality has been controlled since 1948 by a process of registration augmented, since 1989, by annual inspections. Registration and inspections were carried out by local authorities first under the Nurseries and Childminders Regulation Act and, since 1989, under the Children Act. They were taken over in 2001 by the Office for Standards in Education (OFSTED) which, for the first time, will work to national standards rather than to local interpretation of national legislation. It has always been accepted, however, that the legislative framework sets only minimum standards and that improvements in quality are the responsibility of the childminders themselves, the parents who use them and the local authorities whose areas they live in. As a result of this, the development of structures to facilitate improvements in the care and education of children and in support for childminders has been piecemeal. The 'childminding networks' discussed in this chapter have been the major national response to the issue of quality assurance.

Since the introduction of the National Childcare Strategy in 1997 there has been a gradual growth in the organization of networks designed to link childminders in a locality together as an efficient way of providing resources, support and training, and of ensuring consistently higher standards than could be expected under normal circumstances. The Strategy also brought with it considerable amounts of central government funding for initiatives such as this, channelled through Early Years Development and Childcare Partnerships (EYDCPs) in each local authority area. These are multi-agency bodies which represent all the relevant early years interests in the area and their job is to plan and deliver a massive increase in co-ordinated early years services. In the planning guidance issued for 2001–2 (Department for Education and Employment 2001) it was announced that every Partnership in England was expected to put in place at least 3 childminding networks by March 2004 (450 in total) with a minimum of 20 childminders per network. Twenty-five thousand pounds was made available for the first year costs of each of these networks. The government also indicated that it expected total childminder registrations to rise by 15,000 over the three years, an increase of 145,000 places (Early Years National Training Organization 2001). Childminding's professional body, the National Childminding Association (NCMA), has promoted networks as the way forward for childminding since 1990 and, with the government, has agreed a structure for networks which can be put in place, with local variations, by any sponsoring body (National Childminding Association 1998a).

The organization of childminders in this way appears at first sight to be a radical departure from the way in which the service has operated historically and it has added a new dimension to the debate in Britain. Childminding seems set to become a more highly structured profession with more demanding educational standards, more standardized quality assurance and huge recruitment targets. How might this alter its traditional flexibility, affordability and attraction as an occupation?

In this chapter the aim is to chart the history of network development in Britain, to look at how networks are altering the profile of family day care in Britain and to suggest some issues for future development and study. I also draw on work done for my own current study of childminders moving from traditional childminding into organized networks, which involves evaluation of new childminding networks set up in response to the National Childcare Strategy.

The development of childminding networks in the UK

I would argue that the type of networks now being organized in Britain are not radical departures but are logical developments of the kind of work which has been done with childminders since the 1960s.

At that time some of the essential factors about childminding were seen to be that:

- between them childminders catered for large numbers of children
- the children were very young and therefore vulnerable
- the provision was often in economically disadvantaged areas
- childminders were isolated within their own homes
- childminders' practice was invisible within their own homes
- the sector was largely unregulated
- childminders often lacked formal childcare training and qualifications
- there were few resources for support.

Some types of childminding had been required to register under the Nurseries and Childminders Regulation Act since 1948, but in 1968 the legislation was updated to include more categories of childminders and, in the early 1970s, newly created social services departments took over the registration of childcare services from health authorities. Many of these departments appointed specialists for day care registration who highlighted support issues. People began to look at ways of improving the work situation for childminders in order to improve the quality of care for children. Mostly these strategies were focused on developing support groups because an obvious way around many of the perceived problems was to form connections and bring childminders together. The benefits of groups for tackling the above issues were seen to be their potential for:

- cutting down isolation
- providing group play and better play spaces for children
- providing forums in which to share knowledge
- providing a location for support outside the home
- providing cost effective resources and support workers.

Some projects were initiated by local authority workers, some by childminders themselves and some by voluntary organizations which saw childminding support as a valuable community service to offer.

The most high profile work done on childminding at this time was initiated by Brian Jackson who set up the Childminding Research Unit in 1973 with funding designed to research the incidence of 'illegal' (unregistered) childminding in two cities in the north of England (Huddersfield and Manchester). His 'dawn watches' to see where parents were taking their young children highlighted complex local patterns of informal childcare which were unknown or ignored by the authorities (Jackson and Jackson 1979). The project also instigated a huge press campaign about the dangers of unregulated and unsupported childcare which was to adversely affect the image of childminding for many years to come.

This interest in home-based day care was shared by other countries. In Australia voluntary organizations were specifically requested by the federal government to establish full-time day care schemes (networks) following the passage of the Child Care Act in 1972. This followed the model of a pioneering scheme set up by the Brotherhood of St Laurence in Melbourne, and full-time day care schemes were formally endorsed by the government as one of the main services in its childcare programme in 1974 (Brennan and O'Donnell 1986). This initiated a national model in which all official childminding in Australia was provided by networked childminders linked by co-ordinators who acted as a resource for providers as well as taking referrals for places and administering the fee subsidies which supported parents to pay for childcare.

In contrast the early organization of networks in Britain was very piecemeal. A noted example was that of the Groveway scheme in Lambeth in the mid 1970s in which a group of salaried childminders was attached to the council's Groveway Day Nursery for support and training. Although salaried childminding was a recommendation of a number of research studies into childminding at the time (Bryant, Harris and Newton 1980; Jackson and Jackson 1979; Mayall and Petrie 1977 and 1983) this was the only scheme in which local authorities actually employed childminders as opposed to simply subsidizing places or paying retainers in order to keep places free for local authority use, and it was never replicated elsewhere (Willmott and Challis 1977).

Most other schemes consisted of community development models in which childminders were supported to meet together for informal learning, group play for the children and resource sharing. These were often supported by services such as a paid support worker, a playgroup worker for the children, toy libraries, equipment loan schemes and outings. One example is the childminding project established in 1975 by the Save the Children Fund's UK Department. Impressed by Brian Jackson's research, they funded development workers for Manchester and Huddersfield to work with the unregistered childminders identified by the research study in order to improve practice and encourage them to register with the local authority. The project specifically assisted childminders to form groups in which they could meet regularly, run training sessions and set up toy and equipment loan schemes.

A BBC Television series *Other People's Children* in 1977 was a televisual equivalent of this type of development. A free handbook was made available to every registered childminder in the country and BBC Education organized a scheme by which existing groups got together to watch the programmes and their responses were then monitored. The last programme in the series was used by a group of development workers, childminders and parents to advertise a new national network for all the childminders' groups which had grown up locally; hundreds wrote in and the National Childminding Association was born in 1977.

This new national organization used a cell structure in which local groups could link into regional and national groupings in order to represent their interests. So local childminders now did more than just get together for support; they also worked on fundraising, managing the organization, lobbying politicians, representing childminding on other bodies, raising the status of the occupation and attracting new members.

Alongside this, support for individual childminders continued to be developed as a way of improving quality for children, and the more formalized models of support from overseas started to attract the interest of policy makers at both national and local government levels. In addition to the Australian model there was that of employer-supported schemes in the United States such as the highly organized procedures of the United States military's worldwide family day care system (Owen 1991).

In Britain, as a result of the NCMA structure, childminding groups were more common than in most other countries but they were usually self-selecting support groups rather than organized systems for the delivery of specific standards of childcare. It is the latter which has come to be recognized as the definition of a 'childminding network'.

The emerging network model grew out of work done by local authority social services departments to set up sponsored childminding schemes as a way of ensuring consistent quality of care for children seen to be at risk (the current operation of such schemes is described in Chapter Eleven). Social workers were often involved in the registration and support of childminders and recognized that networking, training and resources could improve quality. Childminding also offered a relatively inexpensive means of providing respite care for parents and children on their case loads. Many such schemes stretched back to the 1970s but their development had been patchy, relying on the individual initiative of social services managers or childminding workers, varying political priorities and the fluctuating availability of funds (Statham, Dillon and Moss 2001; Novak *et al.* 1997).

In 1988, with support from the Department of Health, NCMA developed a 'Community Childminding' model which aimed to codify some of the best principles of sponsored childminding and provide a national model which local authorities could adopt with the support of NCMA development workers.

Following this, in 1989 NCMA developed *Childminding in Business*, a charitable company which allowed the organization to market the same type of network model to employers at a time when there was increasing interest from companies in supporting childcare for their employees. Central government was encouraging industry to take on more of the costs associated with family responsibilities and some companies, following the United States lead, were coming to recognize the benefits of 'family friendly' policies for recruitment and retention of workers.

The first company to contract with *Childminding In Business* in September 1990 was Allied Dunbar, an insurance multi-national. The company developed a model of employer-supported childcare which included an on-site day nursery and a childminding network with a full-time co-ordinator. Since then only a handful of additional employers have developed childminding networks for their workforce, partly because British taxation legislation penalizes employees receiving financial support for childcare not run directly by their employers. This has contributed to a difficulty in sustaining such networks over the long term. As mentioned above, Planning Guidance issued to EYDCPs by the government in 2001 indicated that funding for new networks had been calculated at £25,000 each and such high costs cannot be met from parental fees alone.

The impact of the National Childcare Strategy

The original two NCMA network models were developed largely to tap the only two sources of subsidy for the costs of places and of support, namely social work budgets and employer subsidies. However, in 1995 the Conservative government announced a voucher scheme to pay for nursery education for all four-year-olds. This was to consist of a voucher for part-time nursery education (i.e. 2.5 hours per day during term times) available to all parents on their child's fourth birthday, and redeemable at a range of settings offering nursery education which met government criteria. These criteria included meeting the requirements of a new system of nursery education inspection carried out by OFSTED and applied to all settings receiving this public funding, namely state and private schools, playgroups and day nurseries. The inspection would assess the setting's ability to provide a curriculum which would enable children to meet a set of specific learning outcomes (the 'Desirable Learning Outcomes') on entering formal schooling, usually at the age of five.

Childminding was conspicuously absent from the list of nursery education providers and the NCMA immediately made representations to the Department for Education and Employment for childminders to be included in the scheme. The possibility that childminders might be capable of educating, as opposed to caring for, children had clearly never entered the minds of the scheme's architects and so civil servants had to choose their words carefully at this point. One explanation offered was that childminders only had two or three children at a time and so could not engage in the group activities that were essential to the successful delivery of a nursery curriculum.

NCMA very quickly produced a guide to the 'Desirable Learning Outcomes' (NCMA 1998a) which explained how they could be met within a home setting. By the time the scheme was due to commence full operation in 1996, it had been accepted that childminders could be funded. However, a mechanism had to be found to make it feasible for individual childminders to be inspected and quality-assured for nursery education in the same way as group settings. This development work took place in 1997–8 and resulted in a national model for networks called *Children Come First*. By this time, the Labour government had come to power and replaced the voucher scheme with the National Childcare Strategy, which included the nursery education initiative within a planning model for local childcare services. Under the government's agreement with NCMA only childminders who were part of an 'accredited' network which could be inspected by OFSTED were eligible for government funding to provide nursery education (Department of Health and Department for Education and Employment 1997). This did not solve the problem of group size, as childminders would still be operating individually in their own homes, but it did allow for standardized support procedures, regular contact with other childminders, group play and learning opportunities and training leading to qualifications. It had taken 20 years of lobbying by the NCMA to gain the level of recognition which had been legislated for in Australia in 1974.

NCMA's two original models, *Community Childminding* and *Childminding in Business*, were incorporated in *Children Come First* into a system of support designed to provide quality assurance for anyone funding childcare places with childminders, be they individual parents, employers, social workers or central government (NCMA 1998b). Networks may adopt one of three models:

- core (a network with its own co-ordinator)
- cluster (a group of networks with a co-ordinator for a geographical area)
- attached (a core network linked to a group setting).

Networks can be either NCMA approved or can be inspected against additional criteria in order to be accredited for nursery education funding. Many childminders had argued that the nursery education grant was of minimal interest to them because the four-year-olds who were eligible for such funding were usually in school. In 2000, however, the entitlement was extended to three-year-olds and this had a much larger effect on childminders. At the time of writing (2002) there are 65 approved networks in England, of which all but 9 have opted to become accredited. However, government guidance to EYDCPs does not stipulate that networks have to be either NCMA approved or accredited, it simply states a timetable for network development. This is because the government has indicated that it does not want to limit the traditional flexibility of childminding and its responsiveness to local circumstances by prescribing a particular network model or requiring childminders to be part of such a network before they can operate.

NCMA has marketed the network model actively with EYDCPs as a way in which they can improve the recruitment and retention of childminders in their areas and, consequently, meet the very high targets set by central government for new day care places. In theory, childminding is the most easily expandable of all childcare options because it requires very little in the way of capital expenditure or planning. It has always been the largest provider of full day care and, up to 1999, had maintained a steady increase in numbers. Women with their own young children have traditionally seen childminding as an attractive employment option which allows them to stay at home, practise and extend their childcare skills and stay involved in the world of work (Mooney, Knight, Moss and Owen 2001) However, it has always been difficult to plan levels and standards for childminding services, because childminders come directly from local communities and so respond closely to the patterns of demand in those communities and to other economic factors such as the availability of alternative jobs. A study of women moving into childcare, including childminders, by Miles *et al.* (1999) showed that women stay in childcare for shorter periods than in other jobs and that this can be related to the difficulty of balancing the rewards and the demands of the job. When other pressures intervene, such as family responsibilities, or when there are opportunities for more lucrative employment, the intrinsic satisfaction of childcare work is often not strong enough to keep them in the job. Consequently, it has always been difficult to ensure a childminding service that meets the overall needs of a local authority area, especially in more disadvantaged communities where there might not be enough demand from working parents.

Networks offered a way of tackling this problem and allowing partnerships to plan where new childminding places would be located, to set higher than minimum standards for them, and to intervene in supply and demand to ensure the sustainability of services in any area. It was also stressed that sharing the same basic criteria for operation would still allow local variations to be developed. Although the government has no policy stating that networks are a future model for childminding, funding via the National Childcare Strategy is focused on network development and this, twinned with NCMA's emphasis on networks has resulted in a de facto policy. NCMA's Business Plan for 2000–2003 states that it should be an entitlement for all registered childminders to 'have the opportunity to join an approved *Children Come First* network' (NCMA 2000).

Paradoxically, however, since the advent of the National Childcare Strategy, childminding numbers have been in decline (Department for Education and Employment 1999). Although local authority registration officers were used to a regular turnover in childminders, for the first time recruitment was not outstripping loss. In response to the decline in numbers the government introduced start-up grants for childminders, and there is some anecdotal evidence that this is having a positive effect on recruitment. However, Mooney, Moss and Owen (2001) investigated the reasons why childminders have left the occupation and found that the most usual reasons were actively wanting to do something different and changes in family circumstances. Better working conditions, especially pay, greater satisfaction and the chance to interact with other adults were usually seen as the reasons for finding alternative employment. Any policy which makes childminding networks central to the development of sustained neighbourhood childcare services will need to be able to respond to these issues.

It will also be important to address the difficulty of developing services in areas of disadvantage. Although childminding originated in working class communities (Owen 1988) the demands of the job now make it difficult to sustain in areas with poor facilities and without a demand from working families with reasonable incomes. Government policy is to concentrate funding on just such disadvantaged areas but, to date, development has been patchy with some geographical areas meeting targets much more easily than others.

Little evaluation has been done in Britain on the success factors which help to develop services in 'difficult' areas, but one study from the United States looks specifically at how childminding can be organized to deal with local constraints (Larner 1994). After considering ten different programmes in nine states, the study identified four 'keys to success':

- funds: financial and material resources tailored to the needs of the community

- people: hiring 'friendly, familiar and trustworthy' local people to work with providers

- co-operation: innovative models of co-operation between community organizations and childcare experts in order to deliver high quality but appropriate programmes

- time: allowing for the time it takes to make changes in public policy, organizational relationships and human behaviour.

The study concluded that 'short term efforts will not suffice to develop a supply of care. Instead, on-going commitment and investment offer the greatest potential for raising the standard and supply of care in low income neighbourhoods.' (Larner 1994, p.44)

Networks and the debate on quality in childminding

The above quotation from Larner highlights the twin imperatives of the current policy to develop childminding along networked lines: standards and supply. These two aspects can, of course, work both for and against each other. Higher standards and procedures that are more systematic can deter the very type of recruit which childminding has traditionally relied on, particularly if they are not twinned with substantially improved pay and conditions. On the other hand, there is evidence that low status and lack of respect are some of the most important reasons why people leave childminding for other work or do not find it attractive in the first place (Mooney, Moss and Owen 2001). Network elements such as training and qualifications will have an effect on this and might, in the long run, also lead to higher levels of pay.

During the period described in this chapter there has been increased research interest in quality in childminding both in Britain and overseas, particularly the United States. Overviews of this research have consistently pointed to the importance of group activity and support as indicators of quality, thus reinforcing the beliefs of network pioneers. The literature also pinpoints training, involvement in professional bodies, general educational level and the possession of childcare specific qualifications as indicators for higher standards (Galinsky *et al.* 1994; Mooney and Munton 1998; Owen 2000; Peters and Pence 1992; Phillips 1987). The current network model addresses most of these aspects of quality in its content and its methods. Indeed, interviewees in my own study (in progress) on the development of organized forms of childminding have, without exception, placed improved standards as the primary reason for network development.

In order to meet current targets childminding will need to continue to attract its traditional recruits: people who want to work in their own homes and to use home-grown childcare skills. NCMA staff have identified that, although the same groups of people are being attracted to childminding, their attitudes to and expectations of the work have now changed. However, it will still be vital for networks to explore methods that will nurture such people to identify and meet higher standards and to enjoy the work enough to stay in it. Childminding is a very specific form of childcare meeting particular community and individual needs and, in order for it to find its place within a more planned and extended childcare system, its distinctiveness needs to be recognized and developed. One way of doing this is through the creation of quality measures which relate specifically to the characteristics of childminding, rather than arising from models of group care.

During 2002 NCMA are publishing a childminding-specific quality assurance scheme. However this is a national framework, and it can be argued that one of the important developmental roles for networks is, as Larner learnt from the United States examples, the ability to create a local debate on childcare needs which has meaning for people's individual circumstances. Evaluation of the development of a childminding network in Great Yarmouth, Norfolk, which is part of a study I am currently involved in, specifically included discussions with potential network members on their views of quality in childminding which were then contrasted with views collected from the professionals involved in planning the project. The aim of this exercise was to develop an agreed baseline of views and areas of interest relating specifically to childminding in a particular locality. This could then form a jumping-off point for continuous reflection on practice and evaluation of quality for all the parties involved – individual providers, network staff, childcare planners and families.

In this exercise, childminders interviewed placed emphasis on elements of practice which related to individual children's needs and to the ways in which childcare practice was mediated by their home environments. For instance, when asked to rate quality indicators for importance they were more likely than project planners to pick the ones which described childcare elements in very practical terms relating to individual children and families e.g. 'providing a safe environment for children' rather than 'knowing health and safety guidelines'.

In a discussion of childcare quality, Dahlberg, Moss and Pence develop a model in which group childcare settings can become 'forums' for supporting improved practice based on community needs:

> ...we believe in the importance of an education based on relationships. These relationships are diverse and complex, not only between children themselves and between children and adults, but also between adults. A distinctive feature of centre-based settings is that they offer possibilities for members of staff to work together, as a group providing mutual support and engaging with each other, as well as others, in the process of documentation and more general dialogue. (Dahlberg *et al.* 1999, p.11)

Networks can offer this type of forum for childminders who do not work in centre-based settings. Larner's study suggests that they will be most successful when they are allowed to develop a local debate which then controls a flexible approach to support and funding. The Great Yarmouth evaluation was based on the assumption that, at a time when the nature of childminding is changing and numbers are reducing, this would be one of the best ways of addressing issues of recruitment and retention: to engage childminders more in the development of their practice (job satisfaction and interaction with other adults) and to raise their status in the community by involving the community in the debate (pay, conditions and status). 'Drivers for change' like this need to be identified in order to interest people in the occupation as it changes into a more structured, educational activity. This is particularly true as research shows that family-related reasons for entering childminding still take precedence over career-based decisions and that pay and conditions in childminding seem unlikely to improve significantly over the short term (Mooney, Knight, Moss and Owen 2001).

On reviewing an earlier collection of research papers on family day care in the United States and Canada, Emlen and Prescott said:

> Throughout these chapters we have sometimes felt that caregivers were not given much credit for the knowledge that they might have. The vocabulary in common use for child rearing is not precise. When mothers want a homelike atmosphere or when caregivers say that they are like mothers or that the experience of mothering is valuable, there may be more precise meanings behind this. (Emlen and Prescott 1992, p.275)

The current policy on childminding networks has grown organically from a tradition of community-based support and development. Childminding networks offer the potential for providers to discuss what these 'precise meanings' might be, and through debate and the sharing of ideas to improve the quality of care and education which children receive. If networks can accommodate a flexible agenda based on community needs, they appear to offer an excellent vehicle for the further development of childminding in Britain and to integrate a more standardized quality with the occupation's traditional flexibility.

References

Bryant, B., Harris, M. and Newton, D. (1980) *Children and Minders.* Oxford: Oxford Pre-School Research Project.

Brennan, D. and O'Donnell, C. (1986) *Caring for Australia's Children.* Sydney: Allen and Unwin.

Dahlberg, G., Moss, P. and Pence, A. (1999) *Beyond Quality in Early Childhood Education and Care: Postmodern Perspectives.* Brighton: Falmer Press.

Department for Education and Employment (1999) *Statistics of Education: Children's Day Care Facilities at 31 March 1998.* England. London: Stationery Office.

Department for Education and Employment (2001) *Early Years Development and Childcare Partnerships: Planning Guidance 2001–2002.* Nottingham: Department for Education and Employment, UK.

Department of Health and Department for Education and Employment (1997) *Guidance on the implications of the nursery education voucher scheme for four year olds for providers registered under the Children Act 1989 and for Social Services Departments [and] Guidance on the Nursery Education Voucher Scheme.* London: Department of Health and Department for Education and Employment, UK.

Early Years National Training Organisation (2001) *Workforce Development Plan for the Early Years Sector.* St Albans: Early Years National Training Organisation, UK.

Emlen, A. and Prescott, E. (1992) 'Future policy and research needs.' In D. Peters and A. Pence (eds) *Family Day Care: Current Research for Informed Public Policy,* 266–278. New York: Columbia University, Teachers College Press.

Galinsky, E., Howes, C., Kontos, S. and Shin, M. (1994) *The Study of Children in Family Child Care and Relative Care: Highlights of Findings.* New York: Families and Work Institute.

Jackson, B. and Jackson, S. (1979) *Childminder: A Study in Action Research.* London: RKP.

Larner, M. (1994) *In the Neighborhood: Programs that Strengthen Family Day Care for Low Income Families.* New York, NY: National Center for Children in Poverty.

Mayall, B. and Petrie, P. (1977) *Minder, Mother and Child.* London: Institute of Education.

Mayall, B. and Petrie, P. (1983) *Childminding and Day Nurseries: What Kind of Care?* London: Heinemann Educational Books.

Miles, R., Hall, B., Cordeaux, C. and Owen, S. (1999) *Women's Progression through Training to Employment: Childcare Workers in Suffolk.* Ipswich: Suffolk County Council.

Mooney, A., Knight, A., Moss, P. and Owen, C. (2001) *Who Cares? Childminding in the 1990s.* Bristol: Policy Press.

Mooney, A., Moss, P. and Owen, C. (2001) *A Survey of Former Childminders. Research Report 300.* London: Department for Education and Skills, UK.

Mooney, A. and Munton, A. (1998) 'Quality in early childhood services: Parent, provider and policy perspectives.' *Children and Society 12,* 2, 101–112.

National Childminding Association (1998a) *Children Come First: NCMA approved childminding networks.* Bromley: National Childminding Association, UK.

National Childminding Association (1998b) *Children's Learning: the NCMA Framework for delivering Desirable Learning Outcomes.* Bromley: National Childminding Association, UK.

National Childminding Association (2000) *NCMA's Vision, Values and Plans.* Bromley: National Childminding Association, UK.

Novak, T., Owen, S., Petrie, S. and Sennett, H. (1997) *Children's Day Care and Welfare Markets.* Kingston upon Hull: School of Policy Studies, University of Lincolnshire and Humberside.

Owen, S. (1988) 'The unobjectionable service: a legislative history of childminding.' *Children and Society 4,* 367–382.

Owen, S. (1991) 'The advantages and disadvantages of an organised system of family day care.' In J. Peeters, J. Braam and R. Van den Heede (eds) *Family Day Care Provider: Teacher or Substitute Mother?* Gent: VBJK.

Owen, S. (2000) 'Assessing quality in childminding.' *Children and Society 14,* 2, 147–153.

Peters, D. and Pence, A. (eds) (1992) *Family Day Care: Current Research for Informed Public Policy.* New York, NY: Columbia University Teachers College Press.

Phillips, D.A. (1987) *Quality in Child Care: What Does Research Tell Us?* Washington DC: NAEYC.

Statham, J., Dillon, J. and Moss, P. (2001) *Placed and Paid For: Supporting families through sponsored day care.* London: The Stationery Office.

Willmott, P. and Challis, L. (1977) *The Groveway Project: an Experiment in Salaried Childminding.* Lambeth Inner Area Study 17. London: The Department of the Environment, UK.

CHAPTER SIX

Family Day Care in Israel
Policy, Quality and the Daily Experiences of Children
Miriam K. Rosenthal

Family day care in Israel exists both as an unregulated, informal arrangement between parents and individual caregivers and, since 1977, also as an organized and regulated childcare service. It complements the extensive provision of day care centres in both town and kibbutz settings. This chapter by Miriam Rosenthal describes how the organized family day care service operates, and summarizes findings from various research studies that she and colleagues at the Hebrew University of Israel have carried out over the past 15 years, investigating factors that affect children's experience in family day care homes. The studies show that structural standards and regulation do indeed have an effect on the quality of children's life in these settings, and highlight the importance of individual, in-service training/supervision and support. However, the chapter concludes with a cautionary reminder of the difficulties of ensuring that research findings are translated into policy and practice.

Introduction

Multiple caregiving and shared care responsibility among family and community members has been an integral part of child rearing in most cultural communities throughout history (Harkness and Super 1992; Nsamenang and Lamb 1995; Tronick, Morelli and Ivy 1992; Weisner and Gallimore 1977). Modern, industrial western societies continue this tradition of out-of-home care in a variety of forms. Family day care, or childminding, is probably one of the oldest forms of such out-of-home care.

Family day care in Israel exists in two forms. One is as an unregulated, informal, private, arrangement between parents and individual caregivers. The other is as a regulated, organized, social service sponsored both by the Israeli Association of Community Centres (IACC), who initiated the service, and by the Ministry of Labour and Social Affairs. The organized family day care service in Israel has grown very rapidly, from 25 homes opened in 1977 by the IACC to 2300 in 2001.

This chapter draws upon nine research studies which we have carried out over the past 15 years, as part of the Graduate Program in Early Childhood Studies at the Hebrew University, on the organized family day care system in Israel. Our exploration of factors which affect children's experiences in family day care homes was guided by Bronfenbrenner's (1979) ecological model. This led us to consider factors at the level of the individual child, their immediate environment, and the wider social and political context in which childcare services operate. The studies involved interviews with over 120 providers and observations of over 180 children in different family day care homes, as well as of 20 children and 20 caregivers in other childcare settings. They also involved informal interviews with family day care co-ordinators, trainers and policy makers in the Ministry of Labour and Social Affairs and IACC.

The chapter begins with a description of policies related to the provision of family day care services and standards aimed at regulating quality of care in these settings. We then summarize the findings from the various research studies. These explored the influence of aspects of the children's immediate environment (such as the physical setting, the peer social context and caregivers' attitudes and behaviour) on their emotional state, peer interaction and play behaviour. The studies also explored the effects of standards set by policy, such as caregivers' training and support or requirements of group composition, on the behaviour of caregivers as well as the experiences of children in their family day care homes.

Provision, standards and regulation of quality of family day care services

The organized family day care service is available throughout Israel to parents with children under the age of three. It complements day care centres providing for children of the same age. Eleven thousand children under three years of age attend the organized family day care services, compared to 59,000 who attend publicly organized day care centres. Today family day care serves approximately 10 per cent of Israeli children aged between 6 and 36 months, who attend some form of a group setting outside their home (including private and public nursery schools). It is interesting to note that over 40 per cent of the family day care homes operate in Arab, Bedouin and Druze communities (Attia 2001; Israel's Central Bureau of Statistics 2000).

Local community centres or local Social Welfare departments operate family day care services in each town or region. Parents of 'children in need' are referred to the service co-ordinator by the Social Welfare department. Other parents register with the same co-ordinator either through the municipality or the local community centre. The co-ordinators set up placements, allowing parents some choice among providers in their neighbourhood. The Ministry of Labour and Social Affairs subsidizes fees for the service according to a sliding scale based on parents' income level, area of residence, employment, status as new immigrants, family size and the presence of risk factors for the child's development. In addition to the subsidy, the same Ministry pays the salary of the family day care co-ordinators and provides an infrastructure for training, supervision and linkage to other social services.

The organized family day care system evolved out of a growing public and professional dissatisfaction with the quality of care for infants and toddlers offered by the large and poorly staffed day care centres. A public steering committee, with inter-ministerial representation, recommended the establishment of the subsidized family day care service in 1977 as an alternative model of care for a population served until then by day care centres only. One of the committee's major objectives was to provide and maintain quality care for infants and toddlers, and to offer stable and continuous care from one caregiver in the intimacy of a home environment. The establishment of family day care in Israel in 1977 was accompanied by development of specific policies and standards aiming to provide and maintain quality care for infants and toddlers.

Unfortunately, some of the standards have changed over the years. Regular weekly individual supervision-consultation sessions by a university-trained professional early childhood co-ordinator, and a mix of ages in the group, are no longer part of the standard requirements. The standards prevailing today require that:

- Each family day care home can serve no more than 5 children ranging in age between 6 and 36 months.

- Each caregiver and her home (including physical space and equipment and domestic conditions) have to be approved by a local steering committee that includes the family day care co-ordinator of the area, a representative of the Ministry of Labour and Social Affairs, a supervisor of the local Children and Youth Service, a public health nurse and either the director of the local social welfare department or the local community centre.

- The caregiver has to have successfully completed at least 12 years of education and an intensive 3-month pre-service course provided by the Ministry of Labour and Social Affairs.

- The family day care homes are supervised regularly by the service co-ordinator, who is a qualified social worker or a professional with a graduate degree in early childhood studies. The caregiver is obliged to receive individual and group supervision/training, at least on a bi-weekly basis, and two intensive in-service training days each year.

- Each family day care co-ordinator participates in ongoing regional training and supervision meetings.

The Ministry of Labour and Social Affairs is confident that adherence to these standards ensures the quality of care offered in family day care. According to the Ministry, the organized family day care service has acquired such a high reputation among parents of infants and toddlers that many caregivers in the private sector are seeking recognition by the organizing agencies, hoping to get on their referral lists (Attia 2001).

Assessment of quality of care in the Israeli family day care service

There is an ongoing debate in the research literature as to the appropriate definition of 'quality of care' in early childhood settings and the extent to which it is culturally constructed (Moss 1994; Rosenthal 1999; Woodhead 1996). Family day care services are always embedded in socio-cultural contexts, current regimes and political systems, and so is the definition of their quality.

The definition employed in our studies is based on developmental goals valued by western cultures and the assumptions underlying western research concerning the relationship between the nature of children's early experiences and their development (Rosenthal 1999). We assessed the quality of care offered in family day care by observing and evaluating the daily experiences of children in these homes. Our focus was on experiences that indicate the current well-being of the child, as well as experiences that contribute to the child's development. This includes experiences generated by the children as well as by the behaviour of others. Our studies documented a wide range of daily experiences of infants and toddlers attending the Israeli family day care settings. We recorded children's emotional states, the quality and level of their engagement with the physical environment, the quality and level of their interactions with other children in the group, and the quality of their interactions with the caregiver.

As was expected, we found that family day care homes vary in the quality of experiences offered in a number of ways. First, the amount of time children spend relaxed and actively engaged in interaction, or alternatively being upset or wandering about aimlessly, is quite different in different homes. Second, in some homes children spend more time interacting with toys and objects in the physical environment (non-social play) while in others they spend more time in social interaction with peers and/or with the caregiver. The level of play with peers and the quality of these interactions also varies greatly between homes. Finally, differences were found in caregivers' responsiveness to children and the educational activities in which they engaged the children.

Factors affecting children's daily experiences in family day care homes

One of the major goals of our studies was to explore factors that influence the daily experiences of young children in family day care homes. Based on Bronfenbrenner's (1979) ecological approach, our studies investigated different systems that are likely to have an effect on these experiences as well as possible interactions among these systems (Rosenthal 1990; 1991a; 1991b; 1994a).

We examined the influence of children's age, gender and any difficulties separating from their mothers on their daily experiences. On what Bronfenbrenner terms the 'micro–system' level, we examined the influence of various aspects of the family day care setting, including features of the physical environment, such as equipment, toys, space organization, and peer social context, such as the age and gender composition of the group as well as the number of 'socially at-risk' children participating in the group. Additionally we investigated caregiver's behaviour, particularly the frequency and quality of her responsiveness to children in general and during peer interaction in particular, as well as the educational program she offered. We further assumed that children's experiences are likely to be influenced by their family background, such as their parents' level of education, expectations and attitudes towards their child's development. In addition, we examined the influence of the caregivers' level of education, developmental expectations and role perception.

Following Bronfenbrenner's model we also explored the influence of some aspects of the exo- and macro-systems in which childcare in Israel operates. Specifically, we were interested in examining the effect of policy. Social policy sets childcare standards and strategies for their regulation, which determine the structural aspects of childcare settings. Research has shown that structural features affect processes that in turn influence children's daily experiences and hence their well-being and development (Vandell and Wolfe 2000). Since family day care services in Israel vary in their adherence to criteria and standards set by policy makers, we were able to compare the impact of these variations on children's daily experiences. We were particularly interested in the influence of standards that determine group composition, training and supervision requirements and the relative autonomy of the caregivers. Furthermore, as the policy-determined standards of family day care differ considerably from those of other childcare settings, we were able to examine the effect of these differences on the daily experiences of children in different childcare settings. Employing a series of multiple regression analyses we examined the relative contribution of various aspects of family day care ecology to children's daily experiences in these settings. The rest of this chapter summarizes some of the main findings. The results of the earlier studies are discussed more fully in Rosenthal (1994a).

Social policy and children's daily experiences

Two of our studies focused on the influence of standards regulated by policy on the daily experiences of children. One study (Rosenthal 1991a) compared children's daily experiences in family day care with those of children in two other types of settings, which have different guiding policies and standards. The other settings were town and kibbutz-based day care centres. The three settings differed greatly in a number of structural aspects determined by their respective policies and standards. Until recently kibbutz childcare policy encouraged substantial investment in early childhood education (Aviezer and Rosenthal 1997). As a result, kibbutz settings rated higher than family day care settings on many structural indicators of quality, such as a high adult-to-child ratio (1:3), more educational activities/programs, more extensive training of caregivers, and a more spacious and better equipped physical environment. The policy decisions guiding the procedures of town day care centres are made by the same government ministry that sets the standards for family day care. Parents in both systems benefit from the same subsidies, and caregivers in both systems have a similarly low level of education and training. Most centres have equipment and facilities adapted to care for young children. The systems differ, however, in the size of the groups and their adult-to-child ratios. While the family day care caregiver works with 5 infants and toddlers, we find in town day care centres up to 27 children in infant groups and 35 in toddler groups, with 2–3 caregivers to a group.

Although this study found no differences between kibbutz and family day care in specifically recorded behaviours of caregivers, kibbutz children engaged more frequently in both positive learning experiences and social behaviour compared to children in family day care. It seems that the investment in the training of caregivers, in the educational program and the educationally designed environment has enabled children in the kibbutz settings to have better daily experiences.

Again, although no differences were found between centres and family day care (both in town) in their educational program and in the educational quality of the physical environment, interaction with the caregivers in the centre settings was of a poorer quality (frequent use of negative control methods). The emotional tone of the program was also much more negative than in family day care. This difference may be due to group size. In contrast to the small groups in family day care homes, the very large groups in town day care centres increase the tension of both caregivers and children, leading the caregiver to more frequent expressions of anger towards the children. Frequent negative methods of control, such as reprimanding and scolding children in an angry tone, were also reported in a study by Sagi and his associates (Koren-Karie *et al.* 1998) during meal time with infants in town day care centres in the north of Israel.

A second study (Rosenthal 1990; 1991b) examined differences in the behaviour of caregivers in family day care homes, which varied in their adherence to standards set by policy makers. Group composition was supposed at the time to be regulated, to ensure an adequate mix of children's ages and socio-economic backgrounds. Some services, however, are less heterogeneous than policy intended. Some family day care services are located in very poor neighbourhoods. The groups in these homes are likely to be more homogeneous than those in socio-economically mixed neighbourhoods. Furthermore, some services yield to demands of parents, or caregivers, requesting age-homogenous groups.

Our findings showed that the quality of the educational program a caregiver provides relates to the mean age and social background of the children in the group. Caregivers working with groups of relatively older children (i.e. most of them between 24 and 36 months) and with children of better educated parents, offered more frequent educational activity. Contrary to the intent of the social policy-makers, the results suggest that children who should have benefited from a more intensive educational program were in fact getting less frequent educational activity.

Other standards set by policy are those that determine the criteria for selecting caregivers, the availability and frequency of individual supervision and in-service training, as well as those determining the degree of caregivers' autonomy in their work. In this study we found that caregiver selection criteria and frequency of in-service training had relatively little effect on children's daily experiences. This finding could be an artefact resulting from insufficient variability among family day care caregivers on these criteria. However, caregivers who met with their supervisor for individual supervision-consultation sessions every week, and caregivers who had greater autonomy in decisions concerning furnishing, toys or the daily program, were more responsive and provided children with better quality spontaneous interactions. It has been suggested that relative autonomy in daily decisions as well as in the provision of individual supervision by an early childhood professional conveys an organizational trust and support to these generally untrained and somewhat poorly educated caregivers working alone in their homes.

Overall, our analyses support the contention that a policy designed to ensure a high quality educational environment, as well as certain structural aspects such as group size, determines both the quality of children's emotional well-being as well as their daily learning experiences.

Impact of video-aided supervision on caregivers in family day care

In view of the findings concerning the positive influence of regular, individual supervision-consultation sessions on caregivers' interaction with children, and the fact that such supervision is no longer part of the standards of operating family day care services, we began exploring ways in which to reintroduce effective supervision into the family day care system. One of our more recent studies focused on the role of video-aided individual supervision-consultation in facilitating caregivers' sensitive responsiveness to infants and toddlers in family day care settings (Gatt 2000). The use of a video to analyze interactions between adults and children is regularly found in research, but is rarely used in supervision of early childhood staff. This study aimed to ascertain whether this type of training could be used with 'para-professionals' in family day care settings, and whether it could enhance sensitive and responsive behaviour and promote positive interaction with the children in their care. The video-aided supervision-consultation model allows for highly intensive guided observation of children's behaviours, as well as caregivers' interactions with the children and their understanding of these interactions.

A sample of family day care caregivers was divided into two groups, who each received different types of supervision (intervention): regular supervision or video-aided supervision. Pre-intervention and post-intervention observations were conducted in both groups to assess change in the quality of caregivers' behaviours. The results showed improvements in the responsiveness patterns of caregivers who participated in the video-aided supervision program, including:

- diminished use of restraints and prohibitions, and the incorporation of positive behaviour when controlling children (such as sensitive touch, positive speech, mutual affect, cognitive and social stimulation)

- an increase in positive caregiving practices in response to a greater variety of children's behaviours

- enhanced differentiated responsiveness to different distress behaviours of the child

- a more attentive and sensitive approach to children when they are occupied and playful, when they seem satisfied and do not signal an urgent need for an adult

- more developmentally appropriate behaviour in response to peer relations and conflicts.

The results of this study indicate the significance of this visual medium for early childhood education and care services in general, and specifically for the training of those working in family day care settings. Video observation may facilitate an improved insight into children's behaviour, intentions and emotions, as well as providing an opportunity for the caregiver to observe her own patterns of interaction. Other investigators (Kontos *et al.* 1992) have noted the importance of joint observation by the supervisor and supervisee. The video-aided supervision model enables adults working with infants and toddlers to focus on observable behaviours that represent sensitive and responsive care for children.

Influence of the family day care environment on young children's play and social interactions

In other studies, we focused on two specific aspects of toddlers' engagement with their environment: play with objects and play with peers (Rosenthal 1994b). We examined the relationship between these play behaviours and a number of different factors, including children's family background, the age composition of the family day care group, and the caregivers' attitudes and behaviour. We found that family background had very little effect on the children's play behaviour, and that the age mix of the group affected play only for young children (under two). In groups with a moderate age mix (13 to 24 months between the youngest and oldest child), young children played more competently with both toys and peers than they did in groups where children were either closer in age or further apart. This suggests that in moderately heterogeneous groups, while the presence of older children facilitates a high level of play in younger children, the presence of younger children does not affect the competence of older children's play.

The family day care caregiver's developmental expectations influenced the nature of children's play. Children cared for in the homes of caregivers with expectations of early achievement in the *cognitive* domain spent more time in fine-motor play with objects, and less time in gross motor play or alone. It is likely that caregivers' expectations indirectly affect children's play with objects by mediating the physical environment and the daily program. Conversely, it seems that caregivers with expectations of early achievement in the *social* domain believe that young infants and toddlers are competent enough socially to 'manage on their own'. The children in these homes actually spent more time alone and less time in social play or in fine-motor play with objects. Presumably, caregivers' attitudes influence their interactions with children through the activities they offer children and some of the physical conditions they create in their homes. We also found that children cared for by caregivers who frequently engaged in positive interactions with them, spent more time in positive interactions with their peers compared to children cared for in homes where there was less frequent positive interaction with caregivers.

The findings of these studies led us to conduct a series of workshops with supervisors and trainers of family day care caregivers, to discuss the implications for caregivers' practice. These discussions led to a greater appreciation of the need to understand the perceptions and ideas of family day care caregivers concerning pro-social and conflictual interactions among toddlers. In an exploratory study based on in-depth interviews with 11 family day care caregivers, we have been investigating the caregivers perceptions and understanding of social behaviours of toddlers in their care, as well as their understanding of what influences these behaviours. Most perceive their responsibility as being to 'set the stage' for the development of group cohesion. They describe avoiding intervention, perceived as interference, in peer interaction, so that children can develop skills of adjustment and survival in a group. Such skills are seen as necessary for survival in school and adult society. They are seen as best acquired without adult mediation or intervention. The themes of adaptation and survival permeate through the interviews. The caregivers attribute their knowledge and beliefs concerning social development to their 'life experiences' and their own socialization, rather than to their training. They see their beliefs as reflecting values, beliefs and child rearing ideology characteristic of Israeli society at large.

Conclusion

Our studies highlight a number of issues related to the quality of care young children receive in family day care. Policy that determines structural standards and regulation does indeed have an effect on the quality of children's life in these settings. Family day care services, however, differ in their adherence to regulations. Since group size was identical, and level of pre-service training was similarly low in all settings, we could not find any significant effects of these factors. They emerged as important factors only when we compared the daily experiences of children in family day care with those of children in other childcare settings. The most important feature emerging from our studies of quality of care in family day care is that of individual, in-service training/supervision and support. The use of video recording in the caregivers' home, as part of the training/supervision, was very effective in increasing their sensitive responsiveness to individual children. Our studies reveal, however, that the professional socialization of the family day care caregivers tends to emphasize 'educational activities' that enrich cognitive development rather than the acquisition of social competence and skills of pro-social peer interaction.

The research studies described above have evolved over the years as part of our continuous concern with, and efforts to improve, the quality of care offered to children under three years of age in Israel. As part of these efforts we have been involved, both directly and indirectly, in training those who work with these young children, consulting with organizations operating childcare and holding discussions with various committees in government ministries that set the social policy for childcare and education. Two of our field-based training programs are described above in the context of our research. These, as well as other projects, are having a slow yet cumulative effect on family day care services throughout the country. While we might have been relatively successful in our university-based and field-based training programs, we did not have much impact on policy that determines the structure, standards and regulation of quality in childcare.

Our studies of the effect of social policy on children's daily experiences in family day care (Rosenthal 1990; 1991a) were conducted in collaboration with a steering committee in which all relevant government ministries were represented. Committee members considered issues of structure and practices of family day care and their effects on the quality of care that children receive in these settings. It was intended that members of this committee would implement, through their ministries, the policy-related implications of these studies (Rosenthal, Shimoni and Simon 1986). The only members of the steering committee who never attended its meetings were the appointed representatives of the Ministry of Finance. A report of the study was published highlighting, for example, the importance of weekly training/supervision of the caregiver in family day care by an expert professional in the field of early childhood. Following the report's publication the Ministry of Finance, through budget cuts, pressured the Ministry of Labour and Social Affairs to change the work load and role definition of the family day care co-ordinator. The changes that were made virtually eliminated that form of supervision-consultation by an early childhood expert. Furthermore, most co-ordinators are now social workers without any professional training in early childhood development and education and/or in methods of supervision.

Previous and current assessments of both structural and process aspects of quality of care in Israeli family day care make it clear that within the existing social policy framework it is impossible to achieve the goals of providing care of a satisfactory quality. This can be understood in light of the conflict between the drive to meet public demand and provide large numbers of affordable and relatively safe childcare programs, and the simultaneous demand of professionals to offer quality care and provide children with the kind of early experiences that contribute to their well-being, as well as to the development of their academic and social competence. The public policy concerning childcare seems to pay lip service to the latter goal (quality) while pursuing the former (quantity).

These pressures and conflicts represent familiar dilemmas in the field of social policy relating to childcare in many western societies (Melhuish and Moss 1991; Lamb *et al.* 1992). These dilemmas are likely to stay with us as long as the perception of day care by policy makers and society at large remains that of a system designed to meet the economic goals of increased maternal employment and more childcare places, rather than the needs of parents and children for good quality childcare services.

References

Attia, I. (2001) Personal communication. Ministry of Labour and Social Affairs. Tel Aviv, Israel.

Aviezer, O. and Rosenthal, M. K. (1997) 'A comparison of early childhood education settings in the Kibbutz and Israeli towns.' In Y. Dror (ed) *Kibbutz Education in its Environment*, 37–58. Tel Aviv: 'Ramot' Tel Aviv University Press (Hebrew).

Bronfenbrenner, U. (1979) *The Ecology of Human Development*. Cambridge MA: Harvard University Press.

Gatt, L. (2000) 'The effect of video-aided supervision on caregivers' quality of care and on infants and toddlers' experiences.' MA thesis, Early Childhood Studies, Hebrew University, Jerusalem, Israel.

Harkness, S. and Super, C. (1992) 'Shared child care in East Africa.' In M. Lamb, K. Sternberg, C. Hwang and A. Broberg (eds) *Child Care in Context: Cross-Cultural Perspectives*, 441–462. Hillsdale, NJ: Lawrence Erlbaum Associates.

Israel's Central Bureau of Statistics (2000) *Statistical Yearbook*. Jerusalem, Israel (Hebrew).

Kontos, S., Machida, S., Griffin, S. and Read, M. (1992) 'Training and professionalism in family day care.' In D.C. Peters and A.R. Pence (eds) *Family Day Care*, 188–208. New York: Teachers College Press.

Koren-Karie, N., Egoz, N., Sagi, A., Joels, T., Gini, M. and Ziv, Y. (1998) *The Emotional Climate of Center Care in Israel*. Paper presented at the ISSBD meetings in Bern, Switzerland.

Lamb, M.E., Sternberg, K.J., Hwang, C. and Broberg A.G. (1992) *Child Care in Context: Cross-Cultural Perspectives*. Hillsdale, NJ: Lawrence Erlbaum Associates.

Melhuish, E.C. and Moss, P. (1991) *Day Care for Young Children: International Perspectives*. London: Routledge.

Moss, P. (1994) 'Defining quality: Values, stakeholders and processes.' In P. Moss and A. Pence (eds) *Valuing Quality in Early Childhood Services*. London: Paul Chapman Publishing.

Nsamenang, A.B. and Lamb, M. (1995) 'The force of beliefs: How the parental values of the NSO of Northwest Cameroon shape children's progress toward adult models.' *Journal of Applied Developmental Psychology 16*, 4, 613–627.

Rosenthal, M.K. (1990) 'Social policy and its effects on the daily experiences of infants and toddlers in Family Day Care in Israel.' *Journal of Applied Developmental Psychology 11*, 1, 85–103.

Rosenthal, M.K. (1991a) 'Daily experiences of toddlers in three child care settings in Israel.' *Child and Youth Care Forum 20*, 1, 39–60.

Rosenthal, M.K. (1991b) 'Behaviours and beliefs of caregivers in family daycare: The effects of background and work environment.' *Early Childhood Research Quarterly 6*, 263–283.

Rosenthal, M. K. (1994a) *An Ecological Approach to the Study of Child Care: Family Day Care in Israel*. Hillsdale, NJ: Lawrence Erlbaum Associates.

Rosenthal, M.K. (1994b) 'Social and non-social play of infants and toddlers in family day care.' In H. Goelman and E. Jacobs (eds) *Children's Play in Child Care Settings*, 163–192. Albany, NY: SUNY Press.

Rosenthal, M.K. (1999) 'Out-of-home child-care research: A cultural perspective.' *International Journal of Behaviour Development 23*, 477–518.

Rosenthal M.K., Shimoni R. and Simon Z. (1986) *Family Daycare in Israel: Social Policy and its Implication*. Jerusalem: Akademon, Hebrew University (Hebrew).

Tronick, E.Z., Morelli, G. and Ivy, P.K. (1992) 'The Efe forager infant and toddler's pattern of social relationships: Multiple and simultaneous.' *Developmental Psychology 28*, 568–577.

Vandell, D.L. and Wolfe, B. (2000) *Child Care Quality: Does it Matter and Does it Need to be Improved?* Report available at http://aspe.hhs.gov/hsp/ccquality00/ccqaul.htm.

Weisner, T.S. and Gallimore, R. (1977) 'My brother's keeper: child and sibling caretaking.' *Current Anthropology 18*, 2, 169–190.

Woodhead, M. (1996) *In Search of the Rainbow: Pathways to Quality in Large Scale Programs for Young Disadvantaged Children.* The Hague: Bernard Van Leer Foundation.

Part II

Understandings of Family Day Care

CHAPTER SEVEN

What it Means to be a Childminder

Work or Love?

Ann Mooney

This chapter by Ann Mooney considers the distinct features of family day care or childminding, in particular its close relationship with the task of mothering and the blurring of boundaries between the public and private domains of work and home. It draws on evidence from a study of current and former childminders in England to explore why they undertake this work and their understanding of the service they aim to provide. The chapter considers the implications of these findings for the future development of the childminding service.

Introduction

The expansion of childcare provision to meet increasing demand for non-parental childcare and to tackle child poverty is high on the political agenda in the UK. Following an inter-departmental Childcare Review, the Government has recently announced increased spending on childcare. In a press release, Baronness Ashton, chair of the Childcare Review, stated:

> These spending plans provide the resources, together with important reforms, that will allow us to deliver an expansion of childcare across the country, particularly in disadvantaged areas, and enhance opportunities and services for families and children everywhere. This will allow us to progress towards our longer term vision of a childcare market, in which

every parent can access affordable, good quality childcare (Department for Education and Skills 2002).

An essential factor in achieving this vision is the recruitment and retention of a well-motivated, well-trained workforce. Childminders are one group of the childcare workforce. They are self-employed, working from home looking after other people's children (the development of this service is described in Chapter Five). There are a number of reasons why providing childcare in one's own home is different to childcare provided in an institution such as a crèche or nursery (Saggers and Grant 1999). Not only is there less visibility, but the public and private domains of work and home are blurred. Unlike childminders, other care workers, such as nurses and nursery (centre) workers, can achieve a physical if not emotional separation between their private lives and their paid employment (Nelson 1994). Furthermore, childminders are often caring for their own children while at the same time caring for other people's. What they do for their own children, which is unpaid, is similar to what they do for other children in their care, for which they are paid. The roles of mother and childcare provider are therefore closely intertwined. This chapter considers how these distinct features of this type of childcare may affect how childminders come to understand their work and attitudes towards training and the work itself. But first we turn to the demand for childcare, the role childminders play in the childcare landscape and the regulatory framework under which they operate.

The demand for childcare and the role childminders play

With more women returning to the labour market when their children are young, the demand for childcare has significantly increased. Between 1984 and 2000, the employment rate for women with a child under five doubled from 27 to 54 per cent, with the growth in full-time employment recently outstripping the growth in part-time employment (Twomey 2001). Over the last two decades the proportion of women working full-time within one year of having a baby increased from 5 to 24 per cent (Twomey 2002). The strongest growth in full-time employment has been among women with higher qualifications and who are married with employed partners (Brannen et al. 1997; Holtermann et al. 1999). It is this group of parents, couples working full-time, in higher status and therefore better paid jobs, who are more likely to use formal childcare, such as childminders and nurseries (centres) rather than informal care such as relatives (Mooney, Knight, Moss and Owen 2001; Woodland, Miller and Tipping 2002). Parents using informal care are less likely to be in managerial or professional jobs, and mothers are more likely to be working part-time (Mooney, Knight, Moss and Owen 2001).

These demographic changes, combined with policies designed to encourage more parents in to employment, suggest that the demand for childcare is likely to continue. Yet, childcare provision varies in terms of type, cost, and availability. In 2000 there was one childcare place for every seven children under the age of eight in England (Daycare Trust 2002). Most provision is in the private sector with little provision that is publicly funded. Most working parents needing childcare rely on informal care such as relatives and friends, or formal provision within the private sector, such as nurseries, pre-school play groups and childminders.

In recognizing the need for more childcare provision, the government launched a National Childcare Strategy in 1998. The strategy aims to make childcare more accessible by increasing the number of places available, raising the quality of childcare and making it more affordable. By 2004 the aim is to create new childcare places for 1.6 million children with a minimum of 145,000 new places with childminders. To meet this expansion in provision it is estimated that at least 150,000 new people will need to be recruited.

Childminders have an important role to play in this expansion. After relatives and friends, childminders are a major provider of formal childcare (Mooney, Knight, Moss and Owen 2001; Woodland *et al.* 2002). A recent survey of parents' use of childcare found that among couples where both parents work full-time the use of childminders and nurseries/crèches was the same at 17 per cent each. However, lone parents working full-time were more likely to use childminders rather than nurseries/crèches (Woodland *et al.* 2002).

Not only does childminding provide a valuable service for working parents, but it is also a source of employment. However, between 1996 and 2001 the number of childminders has dropped by 30 per cent to 72,300 (Department for Education and Employment 2001). At a time when the government wants to expand childcare provision, this decline in the number of registered childminders is worrying, and we return to this issue in the conclusion.

Regulation

Before the implementation of the Children Act, in 1991, childminding was subject to minimal regulation. Now anyone caring for a child under the age of eight for more than two hours a day for reward must be registered with the Office for Standards in Education (OFSTED). People wishing to become childminders apply to OFSTED and pay a registration fee (set at £14 in 2002). During the registration assessment, prospective childminders are visited at home and interviewed. OFSTED assesses the suitability of the person to provide childcare and the suitability of the premises to be used for childminding against national standards introduced in 2001 (Department for Education and Skills 2001). Health, safety and police checks are carried out on all household members over the age of 16. Conditions of registration include limits on the numbers and ages of children who may be looked after. For example, childminders can care for no more than three children under the age of five including their own children. Although a childcare qualification is not mandatory for registration, all childminders must attend an approved training course within six months of registration. This training is usually no more than six to twelve hours and covers topics such as health and safety, child development and childminding as a business. Following registration, childminders are annually inspected by OFSTED.

The 'Who Cares' Study

This chapter is based on data from a study of childminding undertaken at Thomas Coram Research Unit, Institute of Education, University of London between January 1999 and November 2000 (Mooney, Knight, Moss and Owen 2001). The study was funded by the Joseph Rowntree Foundation under their Work and Family Life Programme. The aim was to look at childminders as a distinct occupational group within the childcare workforce. It included a large postal survey and 30 case studies. The survey involved a representative national sample of 1050 childminders in England and achieved a response rate of 62 per cent, although of these nearly a quarter were not childminding. They had either stopped childminding altogether or were taking a break from this work. This left 497 respondents who were currently working as childminders.

The survey collected information about their education, training, past employment, working conditions and commitment to childminding. It also explored their views about a childminder's role and about employed parents and the care needs of young children. The case studies were drawn from an inner London and outer London suburban area and included new childminders, established childminders and childminders who had recently stopped childminding. Each childminder was interviewed using a semi-structured interview schedule, which covered similar topics to the survey. In addition, shorter telephone interviews were conducted with 21 parents of children cared for by new and established childminders.

Sample characteristics

Only 2 of the 497 childminders in the survey were men. Over three-quarters were aged between 25 and 44, with almost half in the age group 35 to 44. Almost all were white with children of their own. Of those with children, two-fifths had a child under five. Most were living as a couple with partners who were working full-time. How does this sample of childminders compare with other childcare workers such as nursery nurses (centre-based workers)? Nursery nurses are predominately female, as is the childcare workforce as a whole, white, on average younger than childminders (33% aged under 26) and almost a third are single (Cameron, Owen and Moss 2001).

On average, survey childminders had been childminding for six years, though more than a half had worked for less than five years and less than a fifth had been childminding for over ten years. The survey found that childminders do not necessarily childmind continuously. A quarter had taken a break in their childminding career. The case study childminders had a similar demographic profile to those in the survey, although there were more lone parent households and childminders from ethnic minority groups.

Why take up childminding?

Most childminders in the study (95%) were mothers when they started childminding, with three-quarters having at least one pre-school child (under five) when they began. Although some childminders (15%) took up childminding because they wanted to work with children, the majority said it was because they wanted to be at home with their own children.

> I wanted to stay with my children. I still wanted to work, but I wanted to do a job that provided time with the children. Quality time with the

children as well as earning money. And the only way, really, to do it was to become a childminder.

Other surveys also report the main reason why workers choose to work at home is to be at home with their children whilst earning an income (e.g. Felstead and Jewson 1996).

In choosing to work from home and avoid the need for childcare, childminders would appear to be subscribing to the belief that young children need to be in the full-time care of their mothers. As one provider explained: 'I can't hand my child out to somebody else.' Yet, although the majority had themselves not worked outside the home when they had children, half of the childminders we surveyed thought it acceptable for mothers with a child under one to work either full-time or part-time. This rose to two thirds for a child aged between one and three. This suggests a disparity between their views and their behaviour. While they are accepting of maternal employment, they do not want their own children looked after by others, unless it is unavoidable. There was, however, less acceptance of women who worked through choice rather than necessity: 'Fine, I had to do it. It's part of necessity these days. And I just thought, you don't have to go back to work. To me, people like that don't need to do it.' It would appear that mothers who exercise a choice not to stay at home with their children are not conforming to the normative image of motherhood.

The desire to be at home with their own children was a strong influence on the decision to childmind, but it was not the only motivating factor. Because of childminders' older age profile, they have usually worked in other jobs before childminding, generally before having children. Previous employment for childminders in the study was often in the service industries (e.g. shop assistant, cook, bank clerk) and less likely to be professional or managerial. Their previous employment is probably a reflection of their lower level of education. Almost a quarter had no formal educational qualification and few had a university degree or its equivalent (5%). The lack of intrinsic rewards and financial benefits offered by potential alternative employment are likely to be factors in the decision to become a childminder. This was reinforced by the experience of the group of childminders (a third of the sample) who had worked outside the home after having children. They commented on the lack of affordable and suitable childcare, little job satisfaction, and the difficulties of balancing work and family life:

By the time I'd paid for travel and childcare costs, I was bringing in less than I earn now, working two and a half days from home as a childminder.

I'd been doing shop work, which I got fed up with.

I was tired. The housework wasn't getting done – it's time to rush around to get her to school, and get her to my mum's, and get to work. And it was just a nightmare.

How the work is understood

If the motivation to become a childminder is primarily driven by wanting to be at home to care for one's own children, how do women who take up this work feel about it? The fact that childminders are looking after their own children as well as getting paid to look after other people's children, is likely to influence the way in which they understand their work (Nelson 1994). Much of the work they do as a childminder is similar to what they do for their own children. For example, providing a safe environment in which children feel secure, can establish close, warm relationships and where a variety of activities are provided both for enjoyment and to facilitate development. This may make it difficult to differentiate between the care provided as a mother and the care provided as a childminder, particularly as both take place in the childminder's home.

Survey respondents were asked to rate the importance of a number of possible objectives for childminding work. Most thought it very important for children to be safe, shown affection and helped in their development (Table 7.1).

Three-quarters considered providing 'a home away from home' to be very important. Providing a service for families, preparing children for school and allowing mothers to work were seen as less important. During the interviews, childminders talked about the many and varied activities they provided for children, but it was the close affective relationship that they emphasized, with frequent mention of the love given to children, the hugs and cuddles.

Table 7.1 Childminders' ratings on the importance of these goals in their work

	Importance				
	No	Somewhat	Very	Total	
	%	%	%	%	Number
Provide safe physical environment	0	2	98	100	495
Make children feel loved	0	7	93	100	494
Help children develop and learn	0	12	88	100	492
Help child like self	1	19	80	100	488
Provide fun-filled activities	0	20	80	100	489
Home away from home	1	23	76	100	487
Social contacts for children	2	27	71	100	492
Service for families	2	42	56	100	491
Prepare children for school	2	45	53	100	489
Allow mothers to work	5	47	48	100	487

Source: TCRU survey data

The in-depth interviews revealed that childminders often think of childminding as an extension of mothering, making frequent reference to being a substitute or second mum, treating the children like their own and as extended members of their family. In fact, being a good childminder was often seen in terms of being a parent, treating all children – your own and the minded children – the same:

> Someone who's just willing to make the child one of their own. Because our aims for our children are that they get the best possible of your time, your attention, of the things that are out there. And I think, if as a childminder, you keep that attitude with a minded child, that minded child becomes as your flesh. So that's the best thing.

The success of the childcare arrangement often rested on how well childminded children were integrated within the childminder's family. Here a childminder talks about a child who did not settle: 'She wasn't as much family, even though I tried hard to make her part of the family... But she just somehow never got the – I never was as relaxed as with [other child].' Another interviewee explains how successfully caring for a child means the child being one of her family: 'I think this is what's wrong with some childminders – the child isn't part of a family. And I think if you're looking after a child, that child has to be part of your family.'

But the accounts reveal ambiguities about what childminding is. On the one hand, childminders interpret what they do as being close to mothering but, on the other hand, they recognize that what they are doing is not the same as mothering:

> I feel like his second mum. Because he is like having one of mine. You don't feel the same, because they're not yours. But he's very loving. He loves being cuddled and kissed. And it just feels like having your own child, but you give him away at the end of the day, and you get paid for it.

Nelson (1994) suggests that by emphasizing the way in which they treat childminded children and their own children in the same way, childminders want to imply that an intense bond with their own children will not stand in the way of fairness. In publicly denying that their feelings differ between children of their own and of others, they do not have to deal with the way in which childcare is different from mothering. There was also evidence from our study that childminders struggled to define what their role was, perhaps because of a lack of terminology, other than that associated with mothering, which adequately embraces the close relationships childminders have with children they care for. One childminder summed it up as 'you're like mum, but you're not mum – you're more like an auntie, rather than just the childminder'.

Implications of understanding childminding as mothering

If childminders construct their work around the ideal of mothering, emphasizing the importance of a home environment and treating children as their own, does this influence the way in which they think about training and being qualified as a childcare worker? Does it affect how they perceive childminding as work and as a business?

	Importance				
	No	Somewhat	Very	Total	
	%	%	%	%	Number
See themselves as professionals	5	32	63	100	486
Views on child rearing similar to parents	3	41	57	100	477
Be parents themselves	17	31	52	100	484
Opportunities to develop their childcare career	9	57	35	100	479
Attend childcare training courses	13	56	31	100	484
Hold a childcare qualification	32	45	23	100	488

Table 7.2 Childminders' ratings on the importance of particular aspects associated with their work as childminders

Source: TCRU survey data

Training and qualifications

Just as Kyle (2000) reported in her study, we found that childminders drew on their maternal values to guide them in their care of children. They based their ideas of what was good for children in their care on their ideas about what they thought was good for their own children: 'The children I look after, I take round to friends' houses, which – I take them as if they were my own. All the things that I would do with my own children, I do with child-minded children – they all call my mum nanny and my sisters auntie exactly the same as my children do.'

Whereas childminders wanted to see themselves as professional childcare workers, they felt that their experience as a parent was more important than training and having a childcare qualification (Table 7.2). Over half thought it very important that childminders should be parents themselves, while having a childcare qualification and training were rated this highly by only a quarter and a third respectively. Less than a quarter had a qualification related to childcare. In a recent survey of childcare centre workers, 78 per cent of managers and 67 per cent of other staff had a childcare or early years qualification (Cameron *et al.* 2001). That care is

WHAT IT MEANS TO BE A CHILDMINDER: WORK OR LOVE? / 121

understood in terms of mother care may explain the greater importance attached to the experience of parenting over qualifications and training, as suggested by this childminder: 'Childminding is like – it just needs me being a mother. And I don't really know what sort of qualification you really need.'

The experience of parenting is elevated in importance and value, providing feelings and insights that those who are not mothers are deemed to be lacking. This was implied by a childminder who commented 'I think you only can understand children and have any love for children once you're a mum. Because you can read it in a book and learn how to do it. But the feeling isn't going to be there.' From this perspective, suggesting that childminders should be trained or qualified may be understood by childminders to mean that their parenting skills are inadequate. The absence of a registration requirement for childminders to be trained or qualified may also reinforce rather than challenge this emphasis on parenting experience. Training and becoming qualified (often paid for by the childminder herself) does not result in increased status or the ability to command higher rates of pay, unlike in most other occupations. Childminders are at the mercy of the market place and if they raise their fees above the going rate for their area may well find that they have no business. Finally, the design, content and delivery of training courses may not adequately meet the needs of childminders since they often fail to build on the knowledge and skills that childminders bring to the work.

Not all childminders endorsed the view that having one's own children was adequate preparation for childminding. Those with a childcare qualification were much more likely to say it is training rather than the experience of parenting that is important. Those with childcare qualifications were more likely to have worked with children, usually in a nursery, before having children themselves.

Childminding as an occupation

Childcare is an occupation notable for its extreme gender segregation: less than two per cent of the workforce are men (Cameron *et al.* 2001). That it is a largely female workforce contributes to the low pay found in childcare work, well below national average earnings. Home workers comprise some of the lowest paid workers in the labour force (Felstead and Jewson 2000) and childminders are particularly low paid among the childcare workforce. Childminders' average earnings in 1999 were around £5000 per annum, with an average hourly rate per child of £2 (Mooney, Knight, Moss and Owen 2001). This compares with average earnings in private childcare centres in 2000 of £13,400 for managers and £7800 for other workers (Cameron *et al.* 2001). Moreover, childminders' income is not guaranteed or reliable since when childcare arrangements end they have no idea when they will find new business and restore income levels.

Poor rates of pay affect how the work is valued. Survey respondents were most dissatisfied with society's lack of recognition for their work. This sense of low status also emerged when they were asked what could be done to improve childminding as a job or career. Positive publicity was placed before better pay and financial support from the government:

> So I think just that the whole image of it needs a make-over. It needs to be an ongoing thing. Just to reinforce the message. Because it's going to take time before the whole culture, the whole way of looking at it is improved – where people can walk around and say 'Yeah. Actually, I'm a childminder.' 'Wow! Really? You've such a gift. I couldn't survive without you.' But we're not, as a nation, I don't think we're very good at valuing people that do the most important jobs.

It was difficult for some to see the job as 'real' work: 'It's not that I can't be bothered to go out to work. I couldn't get a job.' Poor pay, low status and the fact that, as childminders pointed out, childcare experience counts for very little in the wider labour market, contributes to this view. But also because childminding is seen as similar to being at home and caring for one's own children, it seems hard to see it in terms of a career: 'I suppose it is a career in a way. I don't know. It's just something you do. I suppose it's like – you know, a mother at home, bringing up their children.'

But the reasons why these women become childminders may also influence their attitudes to it as 'real' work. Two in five said that child-minding was convenient while their children were young and still at home. While about a third in the study saw childminding as their chosen career, for the majority childminding would seem to be a passing phase in their employment, although some will move on to other jobs working with children. For example, in a survey of former childminders, a third had moved to other childcare related jobs such as classroom assistants in primary schools and assistants in centre-based provision (Mooney, Moss and Owen 2001). While women on average spend six years working as a childminder, as many as a quarter quit the job within two years (Mooney, Moss and Owen 2001).

Yet, despite the poor pay and devaluation of the work, childminders express a high level of satisfaction with their work. In fact, among different groups of workers, childcare workers have been found to be the most satisfied with their jobs (Rose 1999). The intrinsic enjoyment of working with children seems to outweigh the negative aspects associated with poor wages and low status work. Childcare workers clearly do enjoy interacting with children and find this aspect of their work meaningful. However, other reasons may be contributing to job satisfaction for childminders, such as working from home, which they said was one of the most satisfying aspects of the work, and the control and autonomy they exercise.

Childminding as a business

Being self-employed, childminders are in effect running small businesses. In the in-depth interviews, childminders were asked their views on this. Interestingly, their accounts reveal tensions between being committed to childcare and wanting to earn a reasonable income. While some saw it as a business, others were unable to do so since it seemed to suggest a child-minder who was more interested in money than in caring for children. Although the principal reason for childminding was wanting to stay at home while working, there was strong disapproval of a financial motivation for childminding. 'Good childminders' were described by childminders and parents alike as entering the occupation because they liked children and wanted to care for them and not for financial reasons: 'A good childminder has to love children, and not just do it for the money.' Criticism was levelled at childminders who appeared to put money before children: 'She's bringing in far too many children to actually be able to look after properly. Just to earn more money. That's wrong. Because then it's not about childcare, is it? It's about the money going in your pocket, and who cares about what's happening to the children.' The authors of another study about parents' childcare arrangements reported how parents felt uneasy about leaving their babies or young children with childminders who see childminding as just a job and a way of earning money (Vincent and Ball 2001).

Nelson (1989) refers to the cultural taboo against redefining care as a commodity. Suggesting that one is motivated by financial gain rather than by caring about children appears to suggest that one cannot care enough. Parents want reassurance that the childminder really does care about their child and is not providing care just for financial reward. Increasing fees, charging for extra services or imposing overtime rates interferes with the notion of 'really' caring. Many childminders left their fees unchanged even with a contract detailing increases. A strong sense of commitment to the child and their family made it difficult to ask for more money. A childminder who felt justified in charging a particular amount for her services, began to have doubts when she became attached to the child: 'Because I think if you ask for less than that [£4.00 an hour], it's kind of saying it's not very good care. I decided I wasn't doing it for any less…but then when I got him…he's so nice, I started feeling guilty.'

Parents look for a childminder who is affectionate, loving, and good with children. It is these characteristics which were most frequently mentioned by the parents we interviewed. Around two-fifths of parents in a national survey based their choice of a childcare provider on the affection the provider would show their child. This reason was more common where an individual, such as a childminder, was looking after the child (Woodland *et al.* 2002). In turn, childminders who view care as an extension of mothering cannot easily equate childminding as a business transaction: 'I don't really treat it as work, as such, to me. It's just they're part of the family unit when they're here. And I just treat them as part of a family.'

Conclusion

We have seen in this chapter how childminding in the UK (England) is mainly undertaken by women as a means of enabling them to combine paid work and care for their own children. Mothering and childminding are therefore closely linked, not only at this practical level, but also at a conceptual level because the work is often understood in terms of substitute mothering and providing a home-like environment. Childminders want to be seen as professional childcare workers, yet the need for training and qualification is less strongly felt. Many see their experience of being a mother as the most important requirement. The low status of the work, poor pay and close links to mothering make it difficult to see childminding as a career. In fact, there is some ambivalence among some childminders as to whether it is a 'real job'. There are also tensions between being a carer with its emphasis on commitment and affective engagement with children, and operating as a small business in a private childcare market.

Our understandings of early childhood work are limited, not only within childminding but across the childcare and early years sector. There are currently two dominant concepts: the worker as substitute mother and the worker as school teacher. Neither is an appropriate or useful concept either for childminding or for other types of early childhood work. The current understanding of the work of a school teacher involves a narrow educational role confined to work with children over the age of three years. This contrasts with the more holistic approach to the needs of children both under and over three that is expected of childminders. The concept of substitute mother is equally inappropriate. Not only are the relationships and roles different, it is in contradiction with the increasing expectations placed on childminders. First, childminders are taking on much more of a 'formal' educational role and can now become accredited to provide nursery education for three- and four year-olds for which they receive a government grant. Second, there is a greater emphasis on their welfare role and providing places sponsored by the local authority for children in need (Statham, Dillon and Moss 2001). Third, childminders are being encouraged to see their work in professional terms and their service as a small business. Furthermore, the concept of substitute mother is based on a misconception that any woman, or at least any mother, is naturally capable of working with children.

How might childminding be understood in a way that is not substitute mothering and not centre-based? Changes in the role of childminders, as described above, may influence how the work is seen and understood, as may the growth of childminder networks. The establishment of formal local networks of childminders, via an approved scheme organized by the National Childminding Association, is a recent development in the UK (England). Childminders, who are assessed, recruited and monitored by a network co-ordinator, enjoy certain benefits for being a network member. They have greater access to training opportunities, the chance to use network resources, the help and advice of the network co-ordinator and the possibility of becoming accredited to provide nursery education.

More support and training may help towards changing the status of the work and the way it is understood. However, there are other fundamental issues which have to be addressed, including low pay, the low status of the work and the tension between intimate, close relationships associated with caregiving and operating a small business. Some form of salaried childminding as used in several other European countries, with pay and conditions linked to training may be a way forward. Under this system, childminders are assessed, recruited, supported and paid by an agency, which might be a local authority or private organization. Parents pay the agency and the agency pays the childminders, usually with a substantial subsidy from public funds. Applied in the UK, this option would involve a shift in public policy from subsidizing some parents through tax credits, to subsidizing all providers through the payment of salaries. Furthermore, such an option would require childminders to cede their independence and assume employee status.

The childcare sector, as with other care sectors such as nursing, is currently facing difficulties in the recruitment and retention of childcare workers, which threatens the targets set by Government for the expansion of childcare provision. The number of registered childminders, for example, has fallen by 30 per cent over the last five years. A number of reasons have been put forward to explain the decline in the numbers of childminders including demographic changes (Mooney, Moss and Owen 2001). For many women, childminding is seen as convenient while their children are young. When their children are older and at school, they are likely to look for alternative employment and are unlikely to return to childminding. This situation is sustainable only while there are sufficient numbers of women willing to become childminders while their children are young and replace those that leave. There is evidence to suggest that the pool of women from which childminders have been traditionally drawn is shrinking, a point to which Peter Moss returns in the concluding chapter. In the past, childminders have tended to have lower levels of education and possibly be less well placed to return to work after childbirth. For example, childminders in our study were less likely to be in managerial or professional posts before taking up childminding: a reflection of their lower levels of education. However, the level of education has been rising and women are having fewer children and having them later. Consequently, more women are now in a position to pursue a career and pay for childcare. At the same time, there is increasing competition for female labour. Alternative employment opportunities with greater flexibility in working patterns, which often avoid the need for non-parental childcare, are more common. Childminding with its low pay and status may therefore be seen as a less attractive employment option.

A number of initiatives have been implemented, including a national recruitment campaign, aimed at addressing the problems of recruitment. It remains to be seen whether these initiatives will be successful. But a transformation of the way in which we think about work with young children is needed, away from the idea that care work is low paid, low skilled and substituting for mother care. This is a challenging task, but desirable not least for the reason that the workforce may be drawn from a wider and increasing pool of women and men.

References

Brannen, J., Moss, P., Owen, C. and Wale, C. (1997) *Mothers, Fathers and Employment. Research Report 10.* London: Department for Education and Employment, UK.

Cameron, C., Owen, C. and Moss, P (2001) *Entry, Retention and Loss: A Study of Childcare Students and Workers. Research Report 275.* London: Department for Education and Employment.

Daycare Trust (2002) *Childcare's Changing: Raising Expectations.* London: Daycare Trust.

Department for Education and Employment (2001) *Statistics of Education: Children's Day Care Facilities at 31 March 2001, England. DfEE Bulletin 08/01.* London: Department for Education and Employment, UK.

Department for Education and Skills (2001) *National Standards for Day Care and Childminding.* London: Department for Education and Skills, UK.

Department for Education and Skills (2002) *Delivering on the Vision for Accessible and Affordable Childcare.* DfES Press Release, 15 July.

Felstead, A. And Jewson, N. (1996) *Homeworkers in Britain.* London: HMSO.

Felstead, A. and Jewson, N. (2000) *In Work at Home: Towards an Understanding of Homeworking.* London: Routledge.

Holtermann, S., Brannen, J., Moss, P. and Owen, C. (1999) *Lone Parents and the Labour Market: Results from the 1997 Labour Force Survey and Review of Research (ESR23).* Sheffield: Employment Service.

Kyle, I. (2000) *Quality in Home Child Care Settings: A Critical Review of Current Theory and Research.* Toronto: Family Day Care Services.

Twomey B. (2002) 'Women in the Labour Market.' *Labour Market Trends 110,* 3, 109–128.

Mooney, A., Knight, A., Moss, P. and Owen, C. (2001) *Who Cares? Childminding in the 1990s.* Bristol: The Policy Press.

Mooney, A., Moss, P. and Owen, C. (2001) *A Survey of Former Childminders. Research Report 300.* London: Department for Education and Skills, UK.

Nelson, M.K. (1989) 'Negotiating care: Relationships between family day care providers and mothers.' *Feminist Studies 15,* 1, 7–33.

Nelson, M.K. (1994) 'Family day care providers: Dilemmas of daily practice.' In E. Nakano (ed) *Mothering: Ideology, Experience, Agency.* New York: Routledge.

Rose, M. (1999) *Explaining and Forecasting Job Satisfaction: The Contribution of Occupational Profiling.* Bath: University of Bath.

Saggers, S. and Grant, J. (1999) 'I love children, and four-pence a week is four-pence!: Contradictions of caring in family day care.' *Journal of Family Studies 5,* 1, 69–83.

Statham, J., Dillon, J. and Moss, P. (2001) *Placed and Paid For: Supporting Families through Sponsored Day Care.* London: Stationery Office.

Twomey, B. (2001) 'Women in the labour market: results from the spring 2000 LFS.' *Labour Market Trends*, February, 93–106.

Vincent, C. and Ball, S.J. (2001) 'A market in love? Choosing pre-school child care.' *British Educational Research Journal 27*, 5, 633–651.

Woodland, S., Miller, M. and Tipping, S. (2002) *Repeat Study of Parents' Demand for Childcare. Research Report 348.* London: Department for Education and Skills.

CHAPTER EIGHT

Agency and Ethics
Family Day Care Providers' Perspectives on Quality
Irene J. Kyle

This chapter by Irene J. Kyle takes as its starting point the experience of a sample of family day care providers in Ontario, Canada, and explores how they think about quality and what they identify as the necessary conditions to enable them to provide high quality care. Although many described negative, stressful aspects of care work, such as the long hours, differences of opinion with parents and lack of back-up when they were ill, their comments suggested that an overlooked aspect of quality is the extent to which family day care providers take pride in and responsibility for their work and seek ways of overcoming such difficulties. The factors that providers identified as important for quality care included intentionality, pride in their work, responsiveness, seeking learning opportunities, and social support. Irene suggests that these extend our notions of quality beyond children's experiences, to consider what working conditions and supports carers need to be able to access in order to offer quality care.

Introduction

This chapter explores the discrepancy between family day care providers' reports of what constitutes 'good' caregiving with the public construction of quality caregiving as reflected in the model of family day care developed in Ontario, Canada. This qualitative research grew out of a concern that, with some exceptions (e.g. Ferri 1992; Nelson 1990; Tuominen 1994), many earlier studies generally did not consult providers about their knowledge and experience and often ignored their needs as care workers. This has meant that carers' ideas about the nature of their work and how best to carry it out have generally been given little attention or credence. In writing about English childminders, Owen has remarked on this problem:

> Anyone reading the literature on childminding until very recently comes away with an overwhelming impression of objectification. Childminders and the work they do are talked about, often in highly critical terms by journalists, academics and politicians just as if they are not there, or do not have the ability to understand the discussion (Owen 1989, p.368).

Recent critiques of childcare research on quality have similarly noted how this work has been dominated by positivist, psychologically oriented approaches that are decontextualized, child-centred, and narrowly focused on child outcomes (Dahlberg, Moss and Pence 1999, Pence and McCallum 1994).

Rather than taking providers and their work for granted, the present study took providers' experiences as the starting point. Providers were viewed not as objects for study and objective measurement, but as persons who actively participate in the defining and practice of quality on a daily basis. By shifting the research focus from the impact of care on children's development to the provider and her work, it became possible to explore how providers thought about quality and what they identified as the necessary conditions to enable them to nurture children. The study also incorporated an ecological perspective by considering providers' care work in the context of their homes, family life, neighbourhoods and community settings.

The public construction of Ontario family day care

In Ontario, policy and legislation have placed responsibility for ensuring quality not with the provider, but with a *public* agency that is held responsible for monitoring carers. Providers are not licensed directly, but may choose to work with a licensed agency that monitors their compliance with minimum provincial standards, offers them training and support and arranges the contract between provider and parents. Many providers, however, work independently of agencies, and are not required to meet any standards beyond that of caring for fewer than six children (not including their own). The Childcare Resource and Research Unit (2000) estimated that there were 18,143 supervised family day care spaces in Ontario in 1998, making up about 11 per cent of all regulated home and centre spaces.

The agency model, led by social workers, originated in the late 1960s. It adopted a child welfare approach similar to that used in foster care (Willner 1967), due to concerns that childcare was 'bad' for children, and fears that mothers were making informal arrangements that offered inadequate care. In the interest of protecting children, the agency model assumed that a high standard of care could be achieved through an initial assessment of providers' homes and families' needs, careful placement of children, ongoing contact with providers and parents, supplemented by various support and training opportunities (Kyle 1992).

This child welfare construction treated providers as clients to be supervised, rather than as autonomous, responsible agents. The agency home visitor was seen as the expert. Family day care providers were viewed not as co-workers and colleagues but as 'surrogate parents' in need of professional supervision and education. Independent providers who were not affiliated with a licensed agency were generally considered even less competent. This deficit view of providers made its way into various public documents and public policy. The Ontario government guidelines explained, for example:

> ...The day care mother will need a good deal of assistance and encouragement in programme planning, because by and large the notions of childcare which prevail in the average home in the community are custodial rather than developmental...care is concentrated upon the feeding and safety of the child with not much awareness of the cognitive social and physical needs... (Ministry of Community and Social Services, c. 1973, para. 7.23).

A subsequent report by the Advisory Council on Day Care (Ministry of Community and Social Services 1975) continued in this vein, stating that 'the quality of Private-Home Day Care programs depends largely on the capability of the home visitor and the workload assigned' (p.6). There was also a tendency to treat providers as if they belonged in a single care worker category. Consequently, there has been little recognition of the skills and knowledge individual providers may bring to their work through prior education and training, their actual caregiving experiences, or participation in community support programs.

Methodology

A cross-section of 15 agency-affiliated and 15 independent family day care providers in southern Ontario were interviewed over the course of a year and a half. They were recruited through family day care agencies, provider networks, resource centres and a provider registry; from newspaper ads, supermarket bulletin boards and by word of mouth from other providers. All but one had worked a minimum of two years as a provider.

Intensive semi-structured interviews, averaging two to three hours in length, were conducted in providers' homes. While all providers were asked basic questions about their care work, there was no set order to the questioning and each provider was encouraged to speak about her own ideas and experience in her own way. All the interviews were tape-recorded and fully transcribed. Coding categories were built up inductively from the data using Nud*ist software (Richards and Richards 1994), rather than fitting the responses into pre-determined categories. These categories were then analyzed to identify key themes and issues.

The providers

Providers ranged in age from 25 to 55 years, with half falling in the 30–39 age group. Their cultural backgrounds were diverse and included women of Greek, Italian, East Indian, West Indian, Spanish and Middle Eastern origins, as well as those of British and European descent. While providers reported an average total family income between $40,001 and $55,000 (1994), several married providers were the major income earners in their family. One family day care provider received social assistance.

Providers' caregiving and training experiences were varied. Seven had training in early childhood education at a community college; two had formerly worked as agency home visitors; a few others had worked as nannies or foster parents; one had been a youth worker and another, a primary school teacher. Twelve providers had high school training or less. Most providers saw themselves continuing to offer care for the next several years, although two of the providers with training in early childhood education saw themselves as moving to work in community programs in the near future.

Home and community settings

Most of the thirty providers interviewed lived in metropolitan Toronto. Six were from nearby, smaller, more rural communities in southwestern Ontario. The majority lived in houses rather than apartments, some of which had spaces (such as a playroom) set aside for childcare. In most homes there was comfortable evidence of children's presence, with various toys and equipment on display. Five providers lived in high-rise apartments in the more dense urban areas of Toronto. The standard of housekeeping in providers' homes was quite variable, from neat and tidy to extremely messy, with most homes being somewhere in between. Most providers talked about the challenge of keeping up their housework while doing care work, and a few regularly hired 'cleaning ladies'. In some locations, a variety of community resources such as parks and recreation centres were nearby. Many of the providers took part in local playgroups, drop-ins, resource centre programs and provider groups, but a small number were quite isolated. A few providers were involved in setting up support groups and in advocating for providers. Many others described being involved with members of their extended family, neighbours and other family day care providers.

Because so few representative studies of family day care providers have been carried out in Canada, there is no baseline against which to systematically evaluate the representativeness of the study sample. However, the diverse backgrounds and experiences of those who were interviewed suggest that, at least in southern Ontario, notions of what characterizes a 'typical' family day care provider may be far too narrow and stereotyped. The common assumption that supervised providers are different from independent providers and automatically offer a higher quality of care did not hold true for providers interviewed in this study, and appears too simplistic. Variations within and across both supervised and independent provider groups were much more complex. In her study of Vermont providers, Nelson (1990) also found more similarities than differences between registered and unregistered providers. 'Both...remain committed to providing homelike care, rely on the model of mothering and root their skills in their own experience' (p.177).

Family day care providers' perspectives on quality

In this study, Ontario providers' ideas about what is involved in offering quality care suggested a much more thoughtful and multi-layered understanding of care work than they are usually credited with. Their accounts not only challenge professional constructions that their care work is largely custodial, they also deepen our understanding of the nature of care work. Overall, providers' comments reflected the day-to-day work of living – the making of, and learning from, mistakes; the small triumphs and moments of satisfaction and shared meaning as well as the occasional misunderstandings and defeats. Quality care did not mean being perfect or never making mistakes, but rather that, as problems arose, providers thought about what they did and made efforts to change and find ways to overcome whatever difficulties had arisen. While aware of, and to various degrees experiencing the social devaluation of care work, many providers nevertheless created a sense of meaningfulness for themselves and a pride and satisfaction in their work that transcended, and to some extent, neutralized their experience of public devaluation. In a field noted for its lack of career opportunities, a number of providers found ways to enhance their work by seeking formal training, by connecting with other providers to develop provider networks and support groups, and by acting as an advocate for family day care.

Although providers in this study reported offering day care to contribute to the financial support of their families, many tended to see their care work as an extension of their mothering role. Often, it was described as a way to combine paid work with caring for their own children. They took pride in the 'home-like' nature of the care they offered, which they saw as differing from 'institutional' centre-based care by being more responsive and flexible, and allowing for more direct involvement with day care children and their parents. Many providers viewed their caring relationships with children as among the most satisfying aspects of their work.

In talking about their care work, providers made both explicit and implicit comments about what constituted good and poor quality care. Table 8.1 summarizes the six major inter-related factors providers identified as being important in offering quality care, and how they felt when these elements were missing.

Table 8.1: Factors identified by family day care providers that contribute to quality care

What quality is...a sense of:	When it's missing...a sense of:
1 **Intentionality, choice** Provider makes a conscious choice to care for children over other kinds of work. Supported by husband, other family members in care work	**Feeling trapped** Provider doesn't feel she has work or economic choices other than home childcare – she's in it 'for the money'. Lack of support by husband, other family members for care work
2 **Meaningfulness, satisfaction with their work** Provider has a sense that what she does matters; that she is contributing to children's learning and well-being, helping out parents and contributing to the community. Feeling of being respected. Sense of fascination with children; and pride in children's achievements	**Devaluation, dissatisfaction** Provider feels • that her skills, training and experience are not valued or recognized • she is being taken advantage of, or taken for granted by parents, agency staff • that her care work is not socially valued
3 **Caring relationships, interdependence and social support** Provider works to build enduring, caring relationships with day care children and families; to find ways to connect with other providers, and community programs to obtain and share support, relief	**Superficial relationships; isolation** Provider experiences high turnover of families and children involving short-term, transitory relationships Provider feels isolated; lacking social support and feedback from others
4 **Personal integrity and ethicality: trustworthiness, honesty, taking responsibility** • for her own learning, and development • for preparation and planning aspects of her work • for setting clear expectations, resolving problems Personal sense that she is respected and seen as a competent caregiver	**Provider feels she is not trusted** Her skills and experience are not respected **Diminished sense of responsibility** Passivity, doing things because she may be afraid of being caught, rather than because she personally believes doing them is important Provider avoids dealing with problems, differences of opinion with parents

5 Having control [power] over, organizing their own work	Feeling of powerlessness, being silenced
Characterized by flexibility, creative responsiveness; not 'rule' bound: • altruistic helping: extending themselves beyond 'business' obligations, agency requirements • speaking up for themselves [having a 'public' voice] advocacy re: home childcare	Lack of control over their work: • feeling that they have little or no say in determining the conditions of their work • no security that work (i.e. children, subsidies) will be available No public voice or visibility; self-deprecation Lack of language to articulate care work
6 Appropriate setting of boundaries • able to find a balance between work and family obligations • making time, and finding ways to meet own personal needs	Difficulty setting and keeping appropriate boundaries Sense of not being able to stop being exploited Erosion of personal time; lack of attention to own physical and mental health needs; to family needs

Although this table may appear at first glance to be dichotomous, each factor should be seen as a continuum. For example, the first factor – intentionality, or choosing to work as a caregiver – should be understood as incorporating a range of possibilities, from a sense of having made a real choice to do care work, to a sense of dissatisfaction and feeling trapped and unable to find other work. Providers' comments typically included several factors, for example, combining ideas of intentionality, an interest in children, the importance of obtaining social support, and of setting boundaries between their work and family life. Many providers were also very clear about the kinds of factors that made for poor care and about what kinds of things could cause problems if they were neglected.

Understanding this continuum between 'good' and unsatisfactory care is important because it changes the way provider comments are interpreted. Early on, in listening to providers, I found myself troubled by many of the negative, stressful aspects of care work they described. They talked about the long hours, the differences of opinion with parents, their trouble collecting fees and the lack of back-up when they were ill. It would have been possible to write a report detailing these issues and reinforcing the view of care work as difficult, exploitive and demeaning. While there are, indeed, serious issues of devaluation and inequity in the treatment of family day care providers, on the whole their comments made it clear they did not see themselves as passive victims, but rather saw their work as making an important contribution to society. Although they identified a number of problems, the providers' stories contained many examples of actions they had taken to address these concerns, what they had learned from their mistakes, and the pride they felt when children did well. This active taking responsibility for their care work is an indication of *personal* agency – a factor that has often been overlooked in most public constructions of quality. While the concept of personal agency includes the idea of conscious choice or intentionality, it also includes the making of moral choices (Giddens 1994), as well as a sense of self-efficacy or personal competence (Kyle 1999). There was also a strong resonance between providers' accounts of what constitutes quality and feminist discussions about an ethics of care. In both, moral development is seen as related to caring activities and manifested through the taking of responsibility for oneself and others, and through building meaningful relationships with others (e.g. Brabeck 1993; Tronto 1993).

The remainder of this chapter will explore these six quality dimensions in greater detail, making use of both positive and negative examples to illustrate the nature of the continuum.

'Raising the next Prime Minister': An ethical, agentic view of care work

Embedded in providers' comments about quality were many ethical or value statements that stemmed from a belief that they had an important role to play in how children are raised. One provider explained:

> ...I'd like to feel that the public knows that...those of us who have decided our choice in life is to be home day care providers, to look after these children and to help them with their foot to the future, is an important job. Because one of these children is going to be the next Prime Minister, and somebody else is going to be the next brain surgeon, and another one is going to be a teacher, and these are all very, very important people in our community, and they start off as being little toddlers.

Providers tended to see themselves as sharing parenting responsibilities with the children's own parents, often drawing on their maternal values to guide their work and basing their ideas of what was good for day care children on what they thought was good for their own children. In the following example, I have highlighted the ethical language used by a provider in talking about her work:

> First of all, let me say that I think of my job as caregiver as being, I'm helping raise the children. I'm not the primary parent, but I'm helping raise the children, so *I take that kind of responsibility seriously.* So I'm not just looking at amusing them during the day, or making sure that they learn their ABCs, but also *their moral development...*I know they're getting it at home, but that kind of thing carries over as *my responsibility* because they are spending five days a week here... So I consider myself to be like parent number two to them and their family here as well, and that *just takes on all the responsibility that parenting does.*

For the most part, providers expressed a mature understanding of the importance of rules and regulations. Their motivation for adopting good practices stemmed from a belief that regulations made sense and were beneficial to children, rather than a sense they must observe the rules because they had been told to follow them. The following comment is fairly typical of providers' views:

> I think actually they [regulations] are good. All the safety rules and what you shouldn't have, and what you should have. If you had small children you would be careful about that, too. Yes, and for other children you would be extra careful.

Another provider talked about the importance of personal integrity:

> I always think if you're sort of hiding something under the table... If you're feeding kids all the time spaghettios from the can, that's not quite right... In the bottom of your heart, you know it's not right. And that's when you have trouble with regulations, and that's when you have trouble complying with anything that's required. But if you set high standards for yourself, then you don't have problems. If they [home visitors] come to me and tell me...this could be dangerous, it can get burned, or whatever it is, then I'll improve it. I have no problem with that kind of thing...

Her comment was both ethical and agentic; she recognized the need to take responsibility for setting her own standards (to listen to her conscience about what's not right) and explained that if she did that, she would be unlikely to find it difficult to comply with regulations.

The role of social support: from family, other providers and community resources

Another provider discussed the importance of taking responsibility for her work, and linked her ability to do so with the availability of social support. Her comments were made in the context of a discussion about quality that she had had with other providers and agency workers:

> ...things that enhance quality are supports, be it an agency or resource centre... It came down to [it's] the caregiver who's responsible for the quality of care that's being provided...if the caregiver is strong then you have quality care; if the caregiver is weak, you have poor quality care.

Many other providers also talked about the importance of being connected with others and obtaining social support. This could be from their families, from the children's parents, from home visitors and from various provider groups and community programs. As the literature on social support suggests, it is the availability of a range of ongoing supports that helps to sustain providers' care work, by providing information, resources, empathy, and occasional relief (e.g. Larner and Chaudry 1993; Miller 1996).

Many providers also saw caregiving as a continuing and progressive learning experience, and talked about their ongoing interest in learning about children:

> ...There's still all kinds [of things] more that I need to learn...things change all the time from one technique to the next and I want to constantly be informed of what changes there are. These guys [her own and the day care children] are really important. They're going to grow up and be their own people, and I want to be part of that [and] make sure I'm planting all the right seeds if I can.

Having control over their care work

In general, one of the things providers liked about caring for children in their own homes was the freedom to control their own work, to set their own routines, and to be flexible and change them if they felt circumstances warranted this. Having such flexibility was important because it seemed to be the basis for being creative and offering children and families more individualized, responsive care. For example, a provider talked about how she took a flexible approach in her negotiations, making changes according to children's needs and their parents' circumstances, while still addressing her own need for financial security:

> I found the best thing for me is that we come to an agreement on how much they're going to pay, because it's different for everybody. I take their circumstances into consideration. [IK: Do you say this is what I charge, and then have them react, or how do you negotiate that?] Well, when they ask me how much I charge, I say it depends on the age of the child, the hours they're here, the situation with the parents... I give them, it's usually between this and this [amount], and how much were you looking to pay? And then we sort of negotiate from there. But what I usually like to do is establish a firm price per week and that's paid every week because as a single parent, that's my only income and I have to budget.

A number of providers talked about the importance of clearly negotiating the business details of the childcare arrangement with parents (agency providers have a somewhat different experience because the home visitor and agency policies mediate this process). One provider explained:

> If you've never done it before, I would say, start slowly. Don't take on five children at once, because you'll be overwhelmed. It takes a lot of planning and organizing and experience to deal with that many children competently... Make sure that you've got a good rapport with the parents and that you can work together as a team, because if you can't then you're just frustrated all the time.

Advocacy: speaking up for quality

For some family day care providers there was a collective aspect to taking control over their work that involved speaking up for themselves and making efforts to do things that could help to improve their own circumstances and the lot of other caregivers. Providers talked about getting together to share ideas, to organize support groups, to lobby on behalf of providers, and to form a union. One provider, involved in organizing a network in her neighbourhood, explained how working together helped improve the quality of care:

> One of the main reasons for getting this group together was to raise the general standard because I care about the other kids and the kind of care they're getting in the community. I don't want to look at a caregiver down the street and say, 'Oh, how can she do *that*! Just let them all run outside and

she's not even there to supervise them! … How come she has so many [kids]?' Do something about it. Get everybody together… I believe in people learning by example, so I think if there's a group of caregivers who, if they're setting an example, that it'll encourage the others…

Family day care providers took part in various activities to give themselves opportunities to be with and learn from other providers, but also saw these activities as supporting other, less experienced caregivers, and helping to improve public recognition for family day care in their community. In speaking up for themselves and their work, providers learn to articulate, integrate and internalize ideas about quality in a much more conscious way. This, in turn, can lead to a greater sense of professionalism. One provider talked about how being part of a network had helped:

> … We probably have about 20 members… I really, really enjoy it because I think it's something that helps the providers and we've needed it. Plus it makes us more visible and more – professional…that's not the word. I always wish there was another word…

While a number of studies have identified the link between providers' participation in family day care associations and higher quality care (e.g. Cohen 1992; Kontos *et al.* 1995; Pence and Goelman 1991) providers' accounts help to clarify how this process works.

Balancing work and family life

Another area family day care providers identified as essential for good caregiving was the importance of setting appropriate boundaries between their work and family life, and finding ways to meet their own personal needs. Providers suggested that this involved deciding on and communicating clear expectations to their own family, to day care parents and to agency workers, about how and when they wanted to work. Being able to set limits is an important element of personal agency. This is especially the case for home-based workers whose care work typically extends for nine or ten hours a day. Experienced providers described various strategies they had developed to manage this. They included making ground rules, formally contracting with parents, making a schedule, setting aside clear times and spaces to be with their own children and families, and making specific plans to take care of themselves.

Providers also gave a number of examples of getting help with this from others such as their children and husbands, their extended family, and sometimes the day care children's parents. One provider talked about her parents occasionally taking her own and the day care children for an outing to a nearby park. Several providers arranged for a cleaning lady to come weekly; others regularly enlisted the help of their husbands and older children in household tasks such as vacuuming, doing dishes and grocery shopping. One provider had parents bring their children's lunches, so she would only have to prepare snacks; another provider hired a teenager to come in after school to help when the older day care children returned from school.

Providers also made it clear that making time for themselves was something they had to work at. It did not occur automatically. One provider explained:

How do I make time for myself? My time, I guess is when all of them are sleeping… I'll have my cup of tea and maybe make myself something fancy for lunch… And I'll sit and knit, or crochet, or read, or something just for me. I might only get a half hour, I might get an hour… Now that (names her son) is older [he] has decided he'd like to work around the house so that he can earn an allowance… I couldn't believe the first week when he started doing them [the chores]. I thought, this is just too wonderful for words… I could *finish* my cup of tea at dinner. It was great.

Another provider talked about how she scheduled her care work to be able to spend time with her own children, by asking parents to have their children picked up by 2 p.m. on Friday afternoons. One independent provider talked about putting an ad in the local paper offering her services as a consultant to family day care providers who were just starting up, giving them advice about how to organize their care work. She also talked about the importance of providers getting exercise and making time for outside interests and activities.

During the interviewing process I became aware of how over the years some providers had neglected themselves. Some were overweight, and did not have the time nor the finances to attend to their teeth. Many others reported finding it hard to make time to have their hair done, or shop for clothes. Some providers even had difficulty taking time off when they were ill. It was clear from providers' comments how their difficulties in setting limits might lead to poor quality care. A failure in this area could result in a lack of attention to their own physical and mental health needs, an erosion of their own personal time, and insufficient attention to their family life. If care workers are not physically and mentally healthy, they will be hard put to find the energy, stamina and creativity that offering high quality childcare requires.

Providers' dimensions of quality and the research literature

A number of the factors that providers identified, such as intentionality, pride in their work, responsiveness, seeking learning opportunities and social support, have been noted in other research studies of family day care as key factors that contribute to the quality of care (e.g. Fischer and Eheart 1991; Kontos *et al.* 1995; Pence and Goelman 1991). Many of these factors have also been described in the social psychology literature as being related to concepts of self-efficacy (Bandura 1982), self-esteem, greater creativity, more trust, and better physical and mental health (Deci and Ryan 1987). In the social support literature they have been related to a sense of personal empowerment (Cochran 1989). There are also parallels between the various dimensions of personal agency and the experiences of powerfulness and powerlessness identified by caregivers who care for the elderly (Rutman 1996). The ethical aspects embedded in a number of quality factors strongly echo work on the ethics of care (Brabeck 1993; Tronto 1993) and Ruddick's (1989) work on maternal thinking.

Conclusions and implications for research

These provider perspectives on quality are important for a number of reasons. First, they extend our notions of quality beyond children's experiences, to consider what working conditions and supports carers need to be able to access in order to offer quality care.

Second, they recognize that quality is lived daily, and point to the dynamic, agentic nature of quality. Providers stressed the importance of taking initiative, of problem-solving and continuous learning. When need be, they were prepared to advocate on their own behalf and that of other providers for greater recognition of care work and their needs as workers. 'Good' care happens when a provider decides quality is something she considers important and wants to make happen.

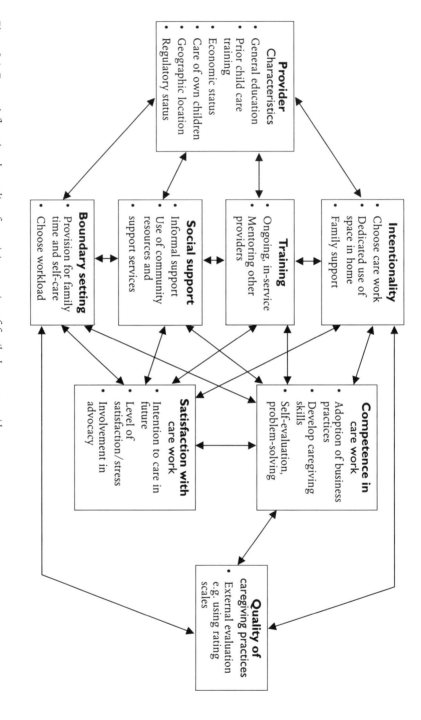

Figure 8.1: Factors influencing the quality of caregiving practices of family day care providers

Provider Characteristics
- General education
- Prior child care training
- Economic status
- Care of own children
- Geographic location
- Regulatory status

Boundary setting
- Provision for family time and self-care
- Choose workload

Social support
- Informal support
- Use of community resources and support services

Training
- Ongoing, in-service
- Mentoring other providers

Intentionality
- Choose care work
- Dedicated use of space in home
- Family support

Satisfaction with care work
- Intention to care in future
- Level of satisfaction/stress
- Involvement in advocacy

Competence in care work
- Adoption of business practices
- Develop caregiving skills
- Self-evaluation, problem-solving

Quality of caregiving practices
- External evaluation e.g. using rating scales

Third, the providers' perspectives are full of value or ethical statements about why the work they do is important for children and families, and of the need for integrity and honesty in carrying it out. Most were also quite clear about what is poor quality, or unacceptable care.

Fourth, their views recognize the important role of environmental factors such as support from their own and day care families and from various community services, and of adequate resources, in helping them to achieve and sustain quality.

The quality factors identified by family day care providers independently confirm a number of factors discussed by researchers in various studies and could be used to deepen and extend our current models of quality in family day care research. Figure 8.1 is a schematic model that suggests some of the possible inter-relationships between the variables that providers identified as being important, which could be tested in future research.

The model as portrayed is a 'systems' model, as opposed to a causal model. Although providers' accounts of their care work suggest that a number of these variables are inter-related, there is no direct causal path. Rather, these factors are dynamic. For example, training may lead to providers' greater participation in support networks, but such participation may also lead to providers' seeking additional training. Similarly, a provider's conscious choice to do care work may influence her decision to seek additional training, which in turn may reinforce her commitment to caregiving. There is also some conceptual overlap that needs to be sorted out, for example, regarding the relationship between general education, training in childcare, and on-going learning. More research needs to be carried out to help understand which of these factors are most critical for quality and how they inter-relate in everyday life.

In conclusion, providers' constructions of quality move our thinking to a more challenging and proactive notion of the factors that are necessary to promote quality. They help us to understand that quality is not just about child outcomes, but has to do with the complex daily interplay between a family day care provider, the children she cares for, her family and social network and the resources and supports that are available in her habitat. Providers in the study recognized that training and standards are elements which contribute to quality. However, they also suggested a number of additional ethical, agentic and contextual factors that make it possible to sustain quality on a daily basis, such as taking responsibility for their own learning, balancing their work and family obligations and seeking social support.

Perhaps most importantly, the wisdom and strong commitment to children and families reflected in many providers' comments suggests the presence of a valuable, and often untapped, resource that argues for greater recognition of the vital contribution providers make to family day care. It also argues for a greater respect of them by childcare professionals and for their greater involvement in the planning and development of family day care services and training programs, as colleagues and co-workers.

References

Bandura, A. (1982) 'Self-efficacy mechanism in human agency.' *American Psychologist 37, 2,* 122–147.

Brabeck, M. (1993) 'Moral judgment: Theory and research on differences between males and females.' In M.J. Larrabee (ed) *An Ethic of Care: Feminist and Interdisciplinary Perspectives,* 33–48. New York, NY: Routledge.

Childcare Resource and Research Unit (2000) *Canadian Early Childhood Care and Education in the 1990s.* Toronto, ON: Ministry of Community and Social Services, University of Toronto.

Cohen, N.E. (1992) 'Increasing the quality of family child care homes: Strategies for the 1990s.' *Child Care and Youth Forum 21,* 5, 347–359.

Cochran, M. and Cornell Empowerment Group (1989) 'Empowerment through family support.' *Networking Bulletin: Empowerment and Family Support 1,* 1, 2–12. Ithaca, NY: Cornell (University) Empowerment Project.

Dahlberg, G., Moss, P. and Pence, A. (1999) *Beyond Quality in Early Childhood Education and Care: Postmodern Perspectives.* London: Falmer Press.

Deci, E.L. and Ryan, R.M. (1987) 'The support of autonomy and the control of behaviour.' *Journal of Personality and Social Psychology 53,* 6, 1024–1037.

Ferri, E. (1992) *What Makes Childminding Work? A Study of Training for Childminders.* London: National Children's Bureau.

Fischer, J.L. and Eheart, B.K. (1991) 'Family day care: A theoretical basis for improving quality.' *Early Childhood Research Quarterly 6,* 549–563.

Giddens, A. (1994) *The Constitution of Society: Outline of the Theory of Structuration.* Berkeley, CA: University of California Press.

Kontos, S., Howes, C., Shinn, M. and Galinsky, E. (1995) *Quality in Family Child Care and Relative Care.* New York, NY: Teachers College Press.

Kyle, I. J. (1992) 'Models of family day care and support services in Canada.' In D.L. Peters and A.R. Pence (eds) *Family Day Care: Current Research for Informed Public Policy,* 209–228. New York, NY: Teachers College Press.

Kyle, I. J. (1999) 'Rethinking carework in home child care: Providers' perspectives in context.' Unpublished doctoral dissertation. Guelph, ON: University of Guelph.

Larner, M. and Chaudry, N. (1993) *Promoting Professionalism through Family Day Care Networks.* New York, NY: National Center for Children in Poverty, The Joseph L. Mailman School of Public Health, Columbia University.

Miller, S.H. (1996) 'Quality infrastructure for family child care.' In S.L. Kagan and N.E. Cohen (eds) *Reinventing Early Care and Education: A Vision for a Quality System,* 193–212. San Francisco, CA: Jossey-Bass Pubs.

Ministry of Community and Social Services, Ontario (no date, circa 1973) *Private home day care guidelines.* Toronto, ON: Ministry of Community and Social Services, Children's Services Bureau.

Ministry of Community and Social Services, Ontario (1975). *Progress report II. Advisory Council on Day Care.* Toronto, ON: Ministry of Community and Social Services.

Nelson, M. (1990) *Negotiated Care: The Experience of Family Day Care Providers.* Philadelphia, PA: Temple University Press.

Owen, S. (1989) 'The unobjectionable service: A legislative history of childminding.' *Children and Society 4,* 2, 367–386.

Pence, A.R. and Goelman, H. (1991) 'The relationship of regulation, training and motivation to quality of care in family day care.' *Child and Youth Care Forum 20,* 2, 83–101.

Pence, A. and McCallum, M. (1994) 'Developing cross-cultural partnerships: Implications for child care quality research and practice.' In P. Moss and A. Pence (eds) *Valuing Quality in Early Childhood Services: New Approaches to Defining Quality,* 108–122. New York, NY: Teachers College Press.

Richards, T.J. and Richards, L. (1994) 'Using computers in qualitative research.' In N.K. Denzin and Y.S. Lincoln (eds) *Handbook of Qualitative Research,* 445–462. Thousand Oaks, CA: Sage Publications.

Ruddick, S. (1989) *Maternal Thinking: Towards a Politics of Peace.* New York, NY: Ballentine Books.

Rutman, D. (1996) 'Caregiving as women's work: Women's experiences of powerfulness and powerlessness as caregivers.' *Qualitative Health Research 6,* 1, 90–111.

Tronto, J.C. (1993) 'Beyond gender difference to a theory of care.' In M.J. Larabee (ed) *An Ethic of Care: Feminist and Interdisciplinary Perspectives,* 240–257. New York, NY: Routledge.

Tuominen, M. (1994) 'The hidden organization of labor: Gender, race/ethnicity and child-care work in the formal and informal economy.' *Sociological Perspectives 37,* 2, 229–245.

Willner, M. (1967) 'Report on family day care of children: An essay review.' *Child Welfare 46,* 100–103.

CHAPTER NINE

The Everyday Life of Children in Family Day Care as seen by their Carers

Malene Karlsson

Sweden has a long tradition of publicly funded family day care, and almost all family day care providers are employed by the local authority. In recent years, numbers have fallen as centre-based care has expanded greatly. In this chapter Malene Karlsson describes the everyday life of children in family day care in Sweden, based on an analysis of log books kept by the caregivers. She discusses the children's experiences in relation to the Swedish National Guidance for Family Day Care, and considers whether family day care is particularly able to provide a setting that values children as 'beings' rather than as 'projects'. The need for external training and support is identified, but so is the importance of family day carers meeting together in self-help groups to support each other and to develop a professional pedagogy that does not just reflect the ideas and practice of centre-based care.

Introduction

Within the European Union, family day care is one of the most common kinds of non-parental care for children under the age of three. In 1996 around a million children across Europe were estimated to be in some kind of organized care (Karlsson 1995). It therefore seems important to find out more about the nature of the care that these children receive. Most research on children in family day care, however, has concentrated on trying to measure the outcome of the care, often compared with other kinds of care. One problem with this sort of outcome research is that it is not always clear whether the groups being compared are actually comparable. In several studies from the United States, for instance, the children in centre-based care were older than the children in family day care (Clarke-Stewart 1986; Phillips 1991). In a Swedish longitudinal study, the mothers of children in centre-based care were more highly educated (Andersson 1986). Few studies have asked family day carers themselves about their experiences and those of the children themselves.

This chapter describes the everyday life of children in family day care in Sweden, based on an analysis of log books kept by caregivers. After outlining the way in which family day care has developed and currently operates in Sweden, I present the findings from the study. The children's experiences are discussed in relation to the Swedish National Guidance for Family Day Care, and to different understandings of the nature of children and childhood. Based on the results from the study, I then suggest how family day care could be supported and developed.

Family day care in Sweden

Sweden has a long tradition of publicly supported childcare. In 1946 financial support from local authorities was introduced in some major cities for family day care. In 1968 the local authorities were granted state funding to employ family day carers provided that they were employed according to a national agreement made with a Trade Union, and that the local authorities inspected the caregivers' homes. Since then, there have been no further binding national regulations, and it is up to local authorities to decide for themselves what qualifications, training and support they want to offer.

According to Swedish Educational Law, family day care is part of the public childcare system for both pre-school and school-age children. All childcare services are the responsibility of the Ministry of Education and the National Agency for Education. In 1977, 47 per cent of all children in public childcare were in family day care. The number of children in this form of care peaked in 1988 but, since then, both the percentage and the actual number of children in family day care have decreased due to a massive expansion of centre-based care. By 1999 only 10 per cent of all children in public childcare were in family day care. There are large regional differences, however, with the percentage of children in family day care tending to be higher in rural districts. Almost all carers are employed by their local authorities, although in areas such as Stockholm some carers are self-employed but approved and subsidized by the authority. There might also be a number of unregulated carers who work without being approved or subsidized.

Despite the fact that family day care is part of the public pre-school services, the pre-school curriculum does not apply. Instead, family day care is expected to conform to National Guidance (Skolverket 2000), which builds on the Childcare Act and the pre-school curriculum. The National Guidance places fewer demands on the carers than the curriculum places on the staff of centre-based care. However, it does include a common value-system, which applies to all childcare workers. The National Guidance highlights a number of areas of particular importance for family day care. It describes the functions of family day care as being responsive to the needs of every child and focusing on the care, development and learning of children. Much emphasis is put on the influence and responsibility of the children, in accordance with the UN Convention on the Rights of the Child.

It is very much up to local authorities to decide how to operate family day care. Some have tended to view family day care as a temporary kind of service, necessary only as long as centre-based care has insufficient places. In recent years the falling birth rate in Sweden and a considerable increase in the children/staff ratio in the centres, have caused the provision of family day care to decline in many of these authorities, despite protests from parents. In other local authorities, family day care is seen as an important alternative to other kinds of care, and parents are guaranteed several options for care of their children.

There is also variation in the training that the carers are required to undertake. In some places, they are expected to do the same amount of in-service training as other childcare workers; in others, they get very little. All carers have a supervisor, but the workload of the supervisors also varies. Some may be responsible for supervising hundreds of carers; others only a few, but then they will have other duties as well. During the 1970s it became common for family day carers to set up self-help groups, meeting together and planning different activities for the children in their care. These groups have now become common all over Sweden and local authorities generally help to find suitable premises. Often, the carers will meet at a kind of drop-in centre, called an open pre-school.

Until recently, the national agreement between the trade union and the association of local authorities ensured a similar level of working conditions for all family day carers. Now, each local authority negotiates its own agreement with the local branch of the trade union, and this has led to a great diversity of agreements. Most restrict the carers' weekly working hours to between 40 and 50 a week. Since parents who work full-time may need longer hours of childcare than this, or mothers who work part-time may need childcare at different hours, this has created a situation where many children need to have two alternating carers. Alternatively, part of their care is provided in a group setting such as an open pre-school. There have been few attempts to study how this affects children.

The log book study

The study focused on the everyday life of children in family day care. I used logbooks or diaries (completed by carers) as the main method of collecting information. This choice of method was inspired by applied, participatory-orientated research, as described by Maguire (1987) and Starrin (1993). In this approach, research is carried out in co-operation with the participants, and aims to record issues of importance to them. Family day carers in a local authority near Stockholm were contacted, and seven volunteered to assist in the design of the study, including piloting the research tools.

Twenty-one carers in twenty family day care homes participated in the study by completing log books (two carers worked together alternately in each other's homes). They lived in five different authorities in Sweden, both north and south, and were recruited through their family day care co-ordinator or, in one case, the local union. All were sent instructions for completing the log books followed by a telephone call to discuss any queries.

In the instructions, the carers were asked to choose one child of about three years of age. With the consent of the children and parents involved, the carers wrote down all the child did during a two-week period while in their care. They were asked to note what time the child arrived in the morning, what other children and grown-ups they met, what kind of activities they were involved in and with whom, and how the child reacted to different activities. The approximate time spent on different activities was also noted, and carers were asked to provide information on their own background, training and family situation. Full anonymity was guaranteed.

The completed log books varied greatly in length, from 3 to 30 pages. Some carers described the selected child's activities in detail, while others had merely made short notes. The log books were transcribed and analyzed. The analyses were then sent to the carers for their comments, which were incorporated into the subsequent analysis.

The carers

The carers represented a broad sample of Swedish family day carers. They varied in terms of experience, training, education and working conditions. They had different working hours, varying numbers of children in their care, and differing access to supervision. In this respect they were quite representative of Swedish carers, although their willingness to be part of the study could well be a sign of high confidence in their work, which may not be shared by all carers.

The experience of the carers ranged from three-and-a-half years to thirty years of work in family day care. All had experience of other jobs, mostly low-paid care work. Five of the carers in the study had experience of working in centre-based care. One was a trained pre-school teacher, and ten were trained nursery nurses. The other carers had all attended various courses for working in family day care.

All of the carers were living with a partner and had children of their own, most of whom were grown up or teenagers. Eight cared for children of their own as part of the group. They looked after between three to nine children, although not all attended full-time. In one case, two carers worked together. Half of the carers looked after groups of children aged from one year to five years, and the other half cared for school-age children as well.

The children

The twelve girls and eight boys whose daily experiences were recorded in the log books were aged from nineteen months to four years. Seven of the target children had a sibling in the same family day care setting. Half attended full-time, while the others had one or more days off a week.

The everyday life of children

A number of themes emerged from analysis of the everyday life of these children in family day care. They included the children's activities both indoors and out; their involvement in housework tasks; care situations such as mealtimes; children's interactions with each other and group activities when family day carers met together with the children they cared for. In all of these areas, I was interested in how far children were able to influence and take responsibility for their activities.

The activities

The log books revealed that children in Swedish family day care play a lot. All family day carers gave examples of different kinds of play: with dolls, cars, trains and building bricks. The children often dressed up and engaged in role-play. They built dens out of cushions, rugs, chairs and blankets. Research on children's play (Knutsdotter Olofsson 1991) has shown the importance of continuous time for play. Although all the carers participated in planned activities with other carers, children still seemed to have enough time for continuous play. Many carers described how children hurried to the playroom as soon as they arrived in the morning, in order to have time for such free play.

All the family day carers described some kinds of creative activities. Some simply mentioned that the children had done some drawing, while others wrote about a variety of creative activities: play-dough and clay, painting with different kinds of paint, using scissors and glue to create all kinds of toys. The children played with water, sand or mud. They built huts of branches and twigs, and they played in the snow.

Some kind of singing and music activity was found in all the log books, but again in varying amounts. Some carers mentioned that the children listened to music or that they sang while playing. For others, singing was on the agenda every day. In family day care homes attended by somewhat older children, drama was also mentioned. For example, one log book described an afternoon when an older child who used to be looked after by the day carer came to visit:

> Ellie (3 years 3 months) is making a puzzle. Andy (5 years 6 months) and Greta (8 years) have made tickets for a circus. Ellie is very excited and sits down on her chair to watch. The parents of Ellie, Andy and Greta arrive during the performance. No one wants to leave, so the parents are invited to sit down and watch. Ellie sits next to her dad and watches with great interest while Andy and Greta perform their tricks. She applauds when we do.

In some homes, reading aloud to children happened every day. Other carers mentioned reading to a child if they were tired or unhappy and in need of comfort. Paula, for example, described making a fire and sitting with the children by the fire, reading aloud. Not all log books indicated that children were read to or had access to books. However, in their response to the analysis of the log books, several carers explained that books were so natural in their family day care homes that they had not thought to mention them.

The children in family day care appeared to participate in outdoor activities every day. Most log books reported that children went outdoors at least once, and often twice a day. As well as spending time in the garden (if they had one), carers described going to different parks or playgrounds. Walks in the woods were very popular, often with a picnic brought along to share. Elisabeth describes one such outing:

> We walk towards a hill, and up that. We find a tree the children can climb, large stones and stumps. Tom (2 years 6 months) joins the big, five-year-old boys. Works hard to climb and jump like they do. We go on towards a big birch that has fallen down. The children climb it and crawl under it. The tree becomes a car, a train and an aeroplane.

The log books showed how children benefited from the learning opportunities these expeditions offered. They were able to study insects and traces of animals, find a cone half eaten by a squirrel, look at birds and feed them.

Children's involvement in household tasks

A characteristic of family day care is that the carer is responsible not only for the care of the children, but also for all practical work involved in running a home, such as shopping, cooking meals, cleaning and gardening. All these activities contain rich learning opportunities for children, if creatively used. So I looked for notes on this.

In six of the log books there were no signs of children being actively involved in household tasks, although they might play in the kitchen while the carer cooked. However, in many family day care settings the children did help with cooking sometimes, and many carers seemed to plan food, such as pizzas or hamburgers, in order to give the children a chance to participate in the preparation. Baking bread or cakes with the children was also a common activity in many family day care homes.

Fewer children were actively engaged in cleaning, although some log books described how children used the vacuum cleaner in their playroom, or took all the blankets used in their play outside to air. Shopping could also provide pedagogical possibilities. Brigit describes a trip to the supermarket with Luke (2 years 3 months) and Charlie (4 years):

> Charlie and Luke sing on the way to the supermarket. They take the small shopping-trolleys and I tell them what to fetch: biscuits, bread, milk, cheese. Then we take some grapes to eat on our way back. At the cash desk we help each other to pick up and pay for the goods. We eat the grapes as we walk back home.

The log books gave many examples of everyday situations in which children were involved, and illustrated how many carers made use of these opportunities to interact with the children. 'We go by bus to the centre, go shopping, to the post office, and the library, learn about the traffic.'

The care

The log books differed in the extent to which they described the physical care that children received. Some carers hardly mentioned this, others described such care at great length, especially when the target child was in the younger age range. Providing food figured prominently in most log books. There appeared to be a good deal of eating in family day care. Children who arrived early were served breakfast. Later, there was often some kind of fruit or snack, followed by a cooked lunch. Around 2.30 to 3 p.m. most children had an afternoon snack, often sandwiches and milk. Many carers seemed to be very good cooks, and almost all children were described as healthy eaters. Sometimes an older child would help a younger one at the table, and the young children apparently copied the older ones where eating was concerned.

Peer interaction

Most parents who choose family day care for their children mention the small, mixed-age group of children as a reason (Karlsson 1994). All the children in this study were cared for in a group containing a similar-age child. Many carers described how a child had a special friend among the other children, although this was not always a child of their own age. The log books gave many examples of children playing with older or younger friends. When school-age children arrived in the afternoon they would start projects of their own, often involving the younger ones.

Group activities

All the carers in this study were part of a local group of carers, meeting at least once a week at premises such as an open pre-school together with the children they cared for. In the groups, there was always some kind of planned activity, such as singing and dancing, creative activities (in one group, the children tried body-painting), or quieter activities like colouring ready-made pictures. Often, the carers divided the children. For example, some carers would take the older children for excursions while the others stayed behind with the younger ones. Most of the carers met with colleagues on other days as well as at the open pre-school, often at some park or wood where the children could play or build huts.

The close co-operation among the carers gave children many chances to make friends. One log book described how Tom, aged two and a half, played with a child brought by another carer to the open pre-school:

> Tom is jumping in the cushion-room. Right now, jumping is his great joy. He stands on the sofa and jumps right down into a heap of pillows. There are only two children in the room, Tom and his 'girlfriend' Matilda, one and a half years old. He worships her and helps her all the time, he gives her a push when she wants to get up on the sofa and tries to catch her when she jumps down.

The log books in relation to the National Guidance for Family Day Care

The log books give a picture of family day care as a childcare service where children play a good deal and have access to other children, both of their own age and of other ages. They are outdoors a lot and enjoy many different experiences, both in the family day care homes and in group settings.

All the log books illustrated this variety of opportunities. However, there were also differences in the experiences of children in family day care. One key source of difference was how the carer arranged her weekly working hours. Local agreements stipulated the maximum hours a family day carer could work each week. Some children could be cared for by the same carer, but others needed more hours of care than the local agreements allowed their family day carer to provide. In response, some local authorities had employed a substitute carer to look after children in a group while their carers had a day off, which seemed to provide more stability. In other cases, children regularly had to go to other carers, or other children temporarily joined their group. In both cases, children had to adapt to new situations all the time.

Discussion

Children's everyday life in family day care contained many planned activities, but also freedom to influence how they wanted to spend part of their time. In this respect, the log books showed that the family day carers' practice was in tune with the intentions of the National Guidance (Skolverket 2000). The mixture of care and pedagogy, the consideration of children's individual needs and the many different experiences, especially outdoors, combined to create a stimulating environment that could provide many possibilities for development and learning.

Does this suggest that family day care offers a service as good as other kinds of childcare services? The answer to that depends on what is seen as important for children, and how children and their childhood are viewed. The perception of childhood and of children has varied throughout time and between cultures. The Swedish ethnographer Gudrun Dahl (1992) points out that the care of children has generally been the responsibility of women, while pedagogical theories have generally been constructed by men. Dahl finds that there is often a discrepancy between the perception of parents and that of professionals, who see it as their task to develop other people's understanding of children. Relatively little attention is paid to how parents, especially in working-class families, view their children.

An exception is a study carried out by another Swedish researcher, Gunilla Halldén, who interviewed parents and suggests that there are two diverging ways of perceiving children: the 'child as project' and the 'child as being' (Halldén 1992). In the first, the child is viewed in terms of the future, as someone to be moulded by parents and society. Parents set goals for their child, and have a firm belief in expert knowledge. The 'child as being' implies that the child develops autonomously. The child is an individual with their own driving force to develop and learn, needing adults as support only. Parents who take this view feel less need of professional advice. Halldén found that parents with a perception of children as 'beings' were more likely to live in smaller towns or villages, and to have had less education than parents who saw children as 'projects'.

In an earlier study, I found that parents who wanted family day care for their children mostly had a clear perception of their children as beings (Karlsson 1994). What they wanted for their children was respect for them as individuals, giving them a chance to develop at their own pace without too many activities being forced on them. In our western society much emphasis in the training and early education of children is placed on their intellectual development. The pedagogics of family day care may not be capable of moulding children into some set form. Rather, family day care may provide a setting where children are respected as individuals and as 'beings', and where they can develop in their own right and at their own pace and thus meet the wishes of parents using family day care.

The log books point to the existence of an overall similarity in the everyday lives of children in family day care, independent of the background and working conditions of the carers. There were some differences in focus, although of course the fact that an activity is not mentioned does not necessarily imply that it does not take place. Rather, it may be that it is something the carer finds so obvious – or of so little interest – that it is not necessary to mention it. In their accounts, some carers focused particularly on care situations, whereas others hardly mentioned them. Some described the relationship between the children, their conflicts and friendship, whereas others mostly wrote about the activities and learning situations of the children.

These differences in focus of the carers cannot be related to qualifications and training, to experience, or to supervision of the carers. For instance, one of the carers who wrote at length about the learning situations of the children had no formal childcare training, although she had undertaken short courses. It appeared that an important impact on the focus of the carers was their participation in the groups. Some of the carers in the study belonged to the same group and their log books showed similarities, both in their way of organizing the work, and in their focus when describing the life of the children in their care. This would suggest that carers in the group are influencing one another in terms of practice. I will return to this below when discussing how to enhance the quality of family day care provision.

Do the similarities in the log books of the carers suggest that there is a family day care pedagogy and a professional approach? Researchers in

Scandinavia have reached different conclusions about this. In Denmark, Lis Nielsen (1997) has studied family day care from different perspectives, but primarily through observation. She concludes that family day care has no professional tradition, but is a mixture of what is supposed to be the competence of the traditional mother/housewife and the traditions of centre-care pedagogy. Nielsen can find no explicit family day care pedagogy or vision. Nielsen's conclusions are partly supported by the Norwegian researchers Abrahamsen and Mörkeseth (1998), who have been conducting observations in a number of family day care homes. They concluded that family day carers tend to reflect centre-based practice and that it is important for family day care to develop an approach and an ethos of its own.

In contrast, the Swedish researcher Annerblom (1991) suggests that family day care does have its own pedagogy. She followed ten family day carers during one year and observed their work in detail. She concluded that the carers did share common values in their attitudes towards children. They gave priority to the emotional development of the children. In particular, they emphasized the children's need for security, to be accepted as a person in their own right, and to their right to their own individual personality. Annerblom states that the carers expressed a holistic view of children that was firmly based on experience and reality.

The differences in the conclusions of the Swedish compared to the Danish and Norwegian researchers are interesting. It may be that the differences can be explained by different research methodologies. However, although family day care in the Scandinavian countries has much in common, there are also big differences. The services have a longer history in Sweden, and there is a tradition of providing for children up to ten years of age. Family day care in Norway and Denmark, on the other hand, almost entirely provides for children up to the age of three. A particularly interesting difference is the fact that Norway and Denmark have always had more regulations and much more supervision of family day care than Sweden. In Norway and Denmark, family day carers are visited regularly by supervisors, whereas, in general, the Swedish carers meet their supervisor only occasionally. Most supervisors in the Scandinavian countries have training and experience from centre-based services, and there are no requirements for them to have experience or knowledge of family day care. Thus, they may have a tendency to emphasize the philosophy and pedagogy of institutional childcare.

In the 1970s, the lack of supervision and support of Swedish family day carers led to a rapid increase in co-operation between groups of carers. The idea of co-operation was supported by an official report (SOU 1981) and by a privately edited magazine for family day care, first published in 1981. Through the magazine, family day carers and their supervisors had a chance to learn about new projects in Sweden, as well as good practice in other countries. During the 1990s, it became even more important for family day carers to co-operate in groups, because of the new local agreements which reduced their working hours. The groups allow carers to organize cover for when they are not working, and to arrange activities that might be difficult to carry through alone and individually. Crucially, they also enable family day carers to share ideas and to inspire each other.

Dahlberg, Moss and Pence (1999) argue that discussion among peers is very important for developing a childcare service of high quality. It may seem ironic that the lack of supervision has forced the Swedish family day carers to work closely together, and thereby to be able to develop a culture of their own. Because of the necessity of creating fora for mutual help and exchange of experience, the carers have often become more active in developing their work practice and reflecting on the quality of their work than if they had had more formal support and supervision. This is because supervisors with experience of centre-based care rather than family day care may not always be able to help family day carers to develop their own pedagogy. Working together, however, encourages them to find ways of explaining what they do, how they do it and why, which are important steps towards creating a professional attitude and pedagogy. This is not to suggest that training and formal support are not important for family day carers. However, it seems that a very important predictor of high quality family day care is the development of co-operation between carers through meeting in groups, combined with support and in-service training. Several other researchers, like Fischer and Eheart (1991); Larner and Chaundrey (2002); Musick (1996) and Wetherington (1996), support this view.

My log book study is only able to give a glimpse of the kind of service that family day care offers to children. Many questions are still unanswered and more research is needed to fully understand the nature of family day care. It would be interesting to carry out log book studies in other countries, where the carers have different working conditions, in order to shed light on the influence of different kinds of support and training, and to gain more information about how knowledge is shared among carers.

References

Abrahamsen, G. and Mörkeseth, E.I. (1998) *Roller och relasjoner i familjebarnehagen. En studie av kvalitet i familjebarnehagen for barn under tre år.* [Roles and relations in family day care. A study of quality in family day care for children beyond the age of three]. Tidvise Skrifter. Samfunn og helse. Stavanger: Høgskolen i Stavanger.

Andersson, B-E. (1986) *Hemma eller på dagis?* [At home or in centre care?] Fast Projektet 45, Barn og Ungdoms-psykologiska forskningsgruppen, Stockholm: Högskolan för lärarutbildning i Stockholm.

Annerblom, M-L. (1991) *Kvinnotradition i focus* [Focus on the traditions of women]. Pedagogisk-psykologiska problem 556, Institutionen för pedagogik och specialmetodik, Malmo: Lærarhøgskolan i Malmö.

Clarke-Stewart, A. (1986) 'Family day care home: A home away from home?' *Children's Environments Quarterly 3*, 1.

Dahl, G. (1992) 'Idéer om barndom och barnets nature' ['Ideas on childhood and the nature of children']. In K. Aronsson, M. Cederblad, G. Dahl, L. Olsson and B. Sandin (eds) *Barn i tid och rum* [Children in time and space]. Malnœ: Gleerup.

Dahlberg, G., Moss, P. and Pence, A. (1999) *Beyond Quality in Early Childhood Education and Care. Postmodern Perspectives.* London: Falmer Press.

Fischer, J.L. and Eheart, B.K. (1991) 'Family day care: A theoretical basis for improving quality.' *Early Childhood Quarterly 6*, 549–563.

Halldén, G. (1992) *Föräldrars tankar om barn* [Parents' thoughts about children]. Stockholm: Carlssons Bokförlag.

Karlsson, M. (1994) *Varför föräldrar väljer familjedaghem* [Why parents choose family day care]. FoU-Rapport 1994:9, Stockholm: FoU-byrån.

Karlsson, M. (1995) *Family Day Care in Europe: A report for the EC Childcare Network.* Brussels: European Commission (Equal Opportunities Unit).

Knutsdotter Olofsson, B. (1991) *Varför leker inte barnen? En rapport från ett daghem* [Why don't children play? A report from a childcare centre]. Stockholm: HLS Fœrlag.

Larner, M. and Chaundry, N. (2002) *Promoting Professionalism through Family Day Care Networks.* Columbia University. Internet article, http://cpmcnet.columbia.edu/dept/nccp/publications/fdcn.html.

Maguire, P. (1987) *Doing Participatory Research: A Feminist Approach.* The Center for International Education. School of Education. University of Massachusetts.

Musick, J.S. (1996) *Uncovering the Many Sides of Family Child Care: A Study of the Family Child Care Connection.* Chicago: Family Child Care Connection Funding Collaboration.

Nielsen, L. (1997) *Dagplejen i dag og i morgen* [Family day care today and tomorrow]. Vejle: Kroghs Forlag A/S.

Phillips, D.A. (ed) (1991) *Quality in Child Care: What Does Research Tell Us?* Washington, DC: National Association for the Education of Young Children.

Skolverket (2000) *Allmänna råd med kommentarer för familjedaghem* [General guidance with comments]. Stockholm: Skolverket.

SOU (1981) 25 *Bra daghem för små barn* [Good centre-care for young children]. Stockholm: Statens offentliga utredningar.

Starrin, B. (1993) 'Tillämpad social forskning' ['Applied social research'] In Holmer and Starrin (eds) *Deltagarorienterad forskning [Participant-oriented research].* Lund: Studentlitteratur.

Wetherington, P.R. (1996) *Reducing Isolation of Family Child Care Providers by Participation in a Provider-Initiated Support Network.* Thesis: Nova Southeastern University.

CHAPTER TEN

Family Day Care in France

Liane Mozère

A common theme in many of the chapters of this book is the low status accorded to family day care work and the lack of training and qualifications among family day care providers. Are women attracted to this work because they have few opportunities for alternative employment? Through an in-depth study of a group of registered childminders in a deprived area near Paris, many of them unable to find children to care for, Liane Mozère raises important issues about the nature of 'work' and 'care'. She argues that further research and debate about an 'ethics of care' is needed in order to move away from a situation where unqualified women remain confined to what she describes as 'an archipelago of small, ill-paid feminine jobs'.

Introduction

As in other European countries, female employment rates have been rising in France, particularly since the late 1960s (Maruani 1996), although French women have always had a significant role within the labour market (Schweitzer 2002). In the last 40 years not only have more women participated in the labour market, but their presence in the labour market has continued even when unemployment rates have risen. The pattern of maternal employment has changed too. Women used to withdraw from the labour market on the birth of a child, returning to employment later. This 'discontinuous pattern' of employment (Labourie-Racappée, Letablier and Vasseur 1977) is less obvious today. Continuity of employment is now the dominant pattern for women in France, at least those with one or two children (Maruani 1996). Nor do parental leave policies appear to have significantly affected levels of employment amongst women with young children, despite shortages of childcare provision. In France, parents are entitled to take parental leave until children are three years old, but the flat-rate payment is pitched at a relatively low level.

This chapter describes the general features of childcare in France and traces the historical development of family day care from its origins in the eighteenth century practice of wet nursing (*nourrices*) to the present day system of *assistantes maternelles*, or mother's assistants. The chapter then draws on the author's socio-anthropological research with a group of registered childminders in an underprivileged area near Paris to understand why they did this type of work. The study explored the skills and competencies required to obtain work as a childminder, and the chapter concludes by considering how far this perpetuates the oppression of women by restricting them to ill-paid, so-called 'feminine', jobs.

Childcare in France

Childcare, always an important issue, has a long history in France. It was common practice, as far back as the Middle Ages, for childminders or 'wet nurses' in the country to care for city children (Garden 1975; Tilly and Scott 1987). A 'wet-nurse industry' developed in Paris, organized by agencies which recruited wet nurses in provincial, rural areas, and set up arrangements for them with urban customers (Faÿ-Sallois 1980). Once an agreement had been reached, the wet nurse would return with the baby to their home in the countryside, though many infants died in transit. Not only was wet-nursing costly to parents, but it resulted in high infant mortality, due to the way the system operated without adequate control and the poor living conditions of many wet nurses.

In the nineteenth century, industrialization and concern about the population led to the development of philanthropic (or charitable) systems for the care of young children. The first *salle d'asile* (now called *école maternelle* or nursery school) was opened in 1826 by a charitable organization, though expansion of the system was slow. The growth in children attending nursery schools (écoles maternelles) really took place after World War II. Crèches or nurseries first appeared in 1844 and catered for children from birth to three whose mothers worked and were of good behaviour. They were intended for the children of working class families and had wealthy patrons. The crèches developed alongside pre-schools (salle d'asile) and sewing schools for young girls (*ouvroir*) as part of a philanthropic system to moralize and discipline the emerging working class (Foucault 1975). However, until Pasteur and Lister identified sources of contagion, death rates were high. Subsequently, crèches were developed along a medical model and became part of the health system. These crèches were only a small part of the wider informal system of day care where unregulated care was the norm. Child protection legislation was first set up in 1874 (loi Roussel) and tried to prevent the fatalities arising from the chaotic wet-nursing system. This policy of assuming responsibility for the health and safety of children was pursued during the twentieth century. Regulations now specify that every person (except parents) who cares for a child under the age of six (compulsory school age), either in an institution (nursery) or in a private home (family day care), must be legally registered.

Today the main services are day nurseries (*crèche collectives*)[1], nursery schools (écoles maternelles) for children from two or three to six years, and family day care. Responsibility for these services is divided between welfare and education. Crèches and family day care are under the jurisdiction of the Ministry of Health. Regulation and inspection is undertaken by the Infant and Maternal Protection Agency (*Protection Maternelle et Infantile*). Nursery schools (écoles maternelles) are under the responsibility of the Ministry of Education. This pre-school system is state-funded and therefore free of charge for parents, whereas parents have to contribute towards the cost of nurseries (crèches) and family day care.

This welfare/education split in services can be explained by their separate development. France has a long history of nursery education, which has developed within the national education system and has always been held in high esteem. The childcare system developed from a welfare model in which health improvement and protection from infant mortality and risk were paramount. Theories of maternal deprivation, expounded by psychologists, psychoanalysts and physicians, led to the belief that mothers should remain at home when their children are young. Mothers who worked were thought to be endangering the psychological development of their young children. This had the effect of stifling any political will to develop childcare services. Consequently, there was little public childcare and an unprecedented growth in informal family day care because women continued to work outside the home (Schweitzer 2002). This form of childcare was viewed as preferable since, although not as acceptable as 'mother care', family day care providers were considered 'mother substitutes'.

All children aged three to six have a full-time place at the école maternelle, although attendance is not compulsory. The écoles maternelles are usually open from 8.30 a.m. to 4.30 p.m. every day except Wednesday and Saturday afternoon and Sundays. However, écoles maternelles in urban areas usually provide childcare outside these hours, opening from 7 a.m. to 6 p.m., five days a week, the same as crèches. All children aged three to six attend école maternelle whether their mother works or not. An estimated one third of two- to three-year-olds also attend école maternelle. The Ministry of Education would like to extend this provision to all children aged between two and three, but this proposal has not been welcomed by nursery school teachers, who do not want to see such young children in their classes where teacher:child ratios average 2:25.4.

Although there is universal, publicly provided, provision for children over the age of three, this is not the case for children aged under three. Precise figures are unavailable, because of the difficulties of comparing statistics across systems. Some estimates[2] suggest that a quarter of children under the age of three are in some form of non-parental care. However, the data is not reliable, not least because some children are in the care of illegal (unregistered) childminders, which parents will be reluctant to reveal for fear of reprisals.

The family day care system in France

Until 1976 childminders were called nourrices, which means wet-nurses. The name provides evidence of the roots from which family day care grew. Childminders had to be legally registered by the Infant and Maternal Protection Agency. This involved an inspection, which focused on health and safety. Providers did not have to be trained or qualified to provide childcare. The suitability of the applicant to childmind was based on the inspector's judgement that the applicant was a 'good' mother and therefore capable of looking after other people's children. Although providers and parents entered in to a private arrangement unsupervised by the Agency, providers were inspected every two years. These inspections were undertaken by a social worker, specialized nurse (puéricultrices) or, occasionally, medical doctors, sent by the Agency. No official training was required although some local authorities did occasionally provide training sessions on a voluntary basis. These sessions, generally led by a psychologist, offered the opportunity to change unsatisfactory childcare practices among providers. For example, it was not uncommon for providers to be potty-training children at six months (Mozère 1978).

In 1976 new regulations came into force, which gave childminders greater professional status than they previously had. They became known as *assistantes maternelles* (mother's assistants). Professionalization of the service included their pay being considered a salary, entitlement to social security (their contributions paid by the National Family Allowance Agency), entitlement to a retirement pension and agreed working hours and holidays, in consultation with parents. Training was still, at this time, not stipulated. The Infant and Maternal Protection Agency's aim was to improve the service and reduce the number of illegal childminders (still referred to as nourrices), who, it was thought, offered a poorer service.

Further regulations were introduced in 1992 providing training for *assistantes maternelles*. It is now compulsory for childminders to do a minimum of sixty hours approved training during the first five years (registration is effective for five years). It is recommended that training is provided over one year rather than over five. Training focuses on hygiene, nutrition, nursing, psychology and education. It aims to help childminders meet children's educational needs, deal with relationships with parents, and adapt to new demands. However, some authorities choose to delay training until after the first year. For example, the local authorities in the département of Seine Saint Denis, which includes La Courneuve where my research took place, have taken this decision because they have observed a high turnover among childminders in their first year of childminding. Those that stay longer than one year tend to be more committed, and more likely to remain in the job. The investment in training is therefore less likely to be wasted.

Childminders (assistantes maternelles) are allowed to care for no more than three children including their own. This compares with carer:child ratios of 1:5 (non-walkers) and 1:8 (walking) in crèches, and one teacher and one assistant to a class of between 15 and 25 in the écoles maternelles. Childminders often care for older children outside the opening hours of écoles maternelles or primary schools and/or during school holidays. When younger these children may have been looked after by the same childminder or have younger siblings who are cared for by the childminder during the day.

Family day care in France includes childminders in an organized scheme (*assistante maternelle agréée de crèche familiale*) and employed by a local authority; private registered childminders employed by parents (assistante maternelle agréée); and those illegal childminders who are not registered and are outside the system altogether (nourrices).

Crèche familiale

Childminders in organized schemes (crèche familiale) are employed and paid by the local authority or through grants to a Non-Government Organization (NGO) operating the scheme. A crèche familiale brings together 30 childminders on average under the supervision of a specialized nurse (puéricultrice) or a social worker. Supervisors are responsible for administering the budget, employing childminders, placing children, collecting parents' fees, and supporting childminders and parents. They must visit childminders regularly and provide a training programme. They also organize activities for the childminded children several times a week, which provides an opportunity for the children to interact with their peers in larger groups. This helps to prepare them for the école maternelle. In 2000, there were 258,000 assistantes maternelles working in crèches familiales.[3]

Assistante maternelle agréée

Private registered childminders (assistante maternelle agréée) are employed by parents and enter into a private contract. In 2000, there were 376,000 assistantes maternelles registered (agréée).[4] Private childminders are supported by services paid for by the regional family allowance funds *(Caisses d'allocation Familiales* – CAFs). The support services (*les relais assistantes maternelles*) are organized differently across regions. They can offer advice, guidance and information, training sessions, opportunities for childminders to meet and for children to socialize and play. Today there are 928 relais assistantes maternelles in France.

For parents with a child under six using private, but registered childminders (assistante maternelle agréée) the regional département family allowance funds (CAFs) make two payments. A payment is made to social security funds to cover parents' social security contributions as employers, and a payment to parents to cover childcare costs, 'Allocation aux Families qui emploient une assistante maternelle agréée (AFEAMA). The AFEAMA is only available to parents using registered provision. It is also intended to provide an incentive to unregistered minders, but since there are compelling reasons to remain unregistered, it is unlikely to have this effect.

The payment for both childminders in organized schemes and those working privately is market regulated. All have the right to social security and are entitled to five weeks holiday. If they work more than ten hours a day, they get an additional payment.

Research study

These developments in family day care have tended to 'professionalize' childminders and should lead them to see themselves as more than 'just mothers'. But what competencies are actually required to be a childminder? To address this question, I undertook a two-year socio-anthropological research study in La Courneuve, an underprivileged area near Paris where unemployment is high.

Of the 102 registered childminders in the area, 37 took part in the study. The sample was located through the Infant and Maternal Protection Agency and childminders were selected from different neighbourhoods and to represent different nationalities, ages and length of registration. Although there is one *crèche familiale* in La Courneuve,[5] none of the study participants were working in this organized scheme. In part, the study aimed to explore the reasons why private childminders were working in this way. Of the 37 childminders in the study, more than half were from ethnic minorities (19 of North African origin, 1 Spanish and 2 Indian). This group was on average older, with older children. They were more likely not to have had any other employment experience.

I spent time with each childminder, talking to her and accompanying her in her daily activities both in her home and outside, for example on trips to the park. Using this method, which I call 'urban strollings', it was possible to observe how each childminder behaved and the way in which opportunities were utilized to find business. I wanted to understand how childminders saw their work, and to deconstruct the image of 'maternal care' which is seen as the norm. The aims of the research were to explore why women went into childminding, how this labour market operated and how much scope there was for them to move out of highly gendered, low-paid work such as childcare.

Reasons for becoming a childminder

The traditional route into childminding has been due to women wanting to remain at home to care for their own children while earning an income – what I refer to as the 'maternal care' pattern. Once children are three they attend écoles maternelles, (which often have extended opening hours), at which point women can choose to work outside the home. Only 20 per cent of the childminders in the study still had a child under three, so there were other reasons besides their own childcare responsibilities for their choice to stay at home and childmind. Although there is little research on family day care in France, information from the Infant and Maternal Protection Agency suggests that the reason women enter childminding is often because there are no other employment opportunities. Most of the 102 childminders in La Courneuve area had no qualification to enable them to enter the labour market easily. Most childminders in the study saw themselves as 'workers' but had found employment difficult to obtain, partly because of the labour market and their own low status as unqualified immigrants within it. The study found that many women turn to childminding when they cannot find alternative employment or when either their husband or older children are unemployed (Mozère 1999). Many then give up childminding when better paid, more interesting or more convenient employment becomes available, or when they discover that they do not enjoy working at home (Mozère 1999).

Maternal competencies or qualifications?

Childminders in the study said that as mothers they were 'naturally' qualified to care for young children. They talked about their love of children and how much they loved to care for them. Traditional home-making skills, such as home cooking, were valued. In emphasizing the importance of maternal competencies and not wanting someone else to care for their child, childminders are in effect presenting themselves as 'good' mothers. In so doing, they are devaluing mothers who work outside the home and use childcare. This means that childminders view their task as essentially care, thus legitimizing the importance they place on maternal competencies. Although earning an income was the raison d'être for childminding, in order to be consistent with the rhetoric they had adopted they had to downplay the financial side of childminding. Their commitment was explained in terms of 'caring', and consequently childminding was rarely described as work (Mozère 1978, 1995).

The view that motherhood equips women for childminding is reinforced by the regulatory agency since applicants for registration have only to meet hygiene and space standards. For registration purposes there is no requirement to be trained or qualified, although childminders must undertake 60 hours post-registration training. Parents also endorse the traditional maternal care model because they want to leave their child with childminders who will care about their children and act maternally. In order to get work, childminders conform to the model and overlook the contradictions that it is low paid and held in low esteem by others.

Inactive (unemployed) childminders

Over a third of childminders in the La Courneuve area (37%) were unable to find work. Such a childminder would be classified as unemployed and entitled to unemployment benefit if she had been previously registered as a childminder, and been in work looking after children. But if she had been registered but never had children to look after, as was the case for many of the sample, unemployment benefit was unavailable. In La Courneuve over the last ten years unemployment (i.e. not having children to care for) amongst registered childminders has risen from 20 per cent to 60 per cent. In the study, 17 of the 37 were unemployed. Amongst the 102 registered childminders, unemployment was highest among those who were more recently registered and therefore had less experience of childminding, and among childminders from ethnic minorities, half of whom were unemployed. The unemployed childminders were, however, well established in the neighbourhood and had raised their children there. So why was it difficult for them to find children to care for? Many lived in the most deprived areas of La Courneuve and it is likely that parents were reluctant to use a childminder living in such an area. Unemployment generally is high in La Courneuve and the supply of childminders exceeds the demand for childcare. However, the results from the study also point to other reasons influencing unemployment among childminders.

Parents in need of childcare can use a list of registered childminders. As one childminder explained: 'They telephone and ask what my fees are. They say they will visit me, but then never telephone again.' Another childminder said: 'she didn't even ask for the price, she asked me when she could come, but never turned up'. It would seem that one of the reasons why these childminders were not getting business was that they were not using the French language correctly. Training organized by the Maternal and Infant Protection Agency had highlighted in role play sessions that childminders were using the more intimate and familiar 'tu' instead of the more formal 'vous' used between people who do not know one another well. Making this mistake would leave parents with a poor impression of the childminder and they may be less likely to leave their child with a childminder who had an inadequate grasp of the language.

So why did these childminders remain registered if they could not find work? The main answer seemed to be that, whether in or out of work, these childminders had few employment opportunities open to them. Most had little education and training and their only skills were those conferred by motherhood. Furthermore, those childminders who were from ethnic minority groups and more likely to have no work were often in families where their husband or adult children were unemployed. They were attempting to use their maternal skills to earn an income, though often without success. Does this suggest that maternal competencies alone are insufficient to find work as a childminder?

Social competencies

There were some differences between the working and non-working childminders. The latter were less likely to take an active role in looking for work. They saw childminding as very much situated within the home. Their home environment was perceived as safe and secure. 'I love staying home, I love my home. That's why I like childminding', says Mrs Vatier who used to sew at home for a factory before losing her job. These childminders tend not to want to stay in public places any longer than they have to or to interact with people they do not know well. They wait for parents to come to them: 'I wait near my telephone, but it never rings.'

On the other hand, working childminders took advantages of opportunities arising outside the home. They were linked to social networks in the neighbourhood, illustrating that childminding is more than an activity grounded in the private sphere of the home. To be successful, childminders must be integrated within these networks. Most of the childminding arrangements were the result of every day encounters: 'The mother *saw* me in the garden with my child and asked me whether I could care for her new-born baby when she returns to work.' The expectation is that if one has a child, one can care for a baby. For these childminders, public spaces as defined by Habermas (1978) are familiar to the childminder and areas in which she feels at ease and able to interact effectively. In order to find work childminders must seize opportunities offered by unexpected situations. This requires the skill to interpret and understand interpersonal signals in social situations, but there is also a serendipity element. Active childminders appeared to have developed these social skills and were therefore able to overcome the disadvantage of living in a poor neighbourhood or not speaking French fluently.

Childminders need to present themselves to parents as competent, credible and showing empathy and sensitivity to their situation. Some childminders would seem better able to develop these skills than others. Moreover, operating within a private market, they also need to understand how the market works. Although speaking very poor French and living in a particularly deprived area of the city, Mrs Tizi always had children to care for. As she explained: 'When a mother who earns 450 euros wants me to care for her child, I can't ask the "normal" price, which is 19 euros, so I say 12 euros.' This salary is close to that earned by an unregistered childminder (nourrice). What she is doing, however, is being flexible and adjusting her fees to accommodate parents' financial situation and what they can afford to pay.

Thus, childminders have to manage social situations as well as having to cope with the conditions of the market place, the needs of parents and the needs of their own family. This requires a wide range of skills if childminders are to remain active. It needs more than maternal competencies. Despite unfavourable circumstances, such as living in a deprived neighbourhood or having poor language skills, some childminders have been successful because they have employed particular social skills, and have 'social capital' through their existing networks. The more isolated the childminder, the more difficult it is to engage with others. Those from ethnic minorities, and/or who face language barriers, may need support in engaging in local networks. It is important to bear in mind that this research was undertaken in a very deprived area. The situation may be quite different in other neighbourhoods.

Social mobility

If they do acquire 'social capital', would childminders have social mobility? Could they move on to other jobs? It would seem unlikely that childminders can move easily into other occupations given their lack of qualifications. Some childminders do train to become crèche assistants (*auxiliaires de puériculture*), but most of the child minders in La Courneuve have been childminding for many years. Moreover, those who had tried to change jobs had been unsuccessful. For example, some had tried to sell jewellery from a market stall, or build up a small business with their partners. In areas that are more affluent, social workers have reported women who have turned to childminding despite being trained secretaries or accountants because they cannot find work in their field. This suggests that childminding might be work that women take up when there is little alternative employment.

Nevertheless, childminders could in theory transfer the skills acquired through childminding, such as flexible working and sensitivity, to other jobs requiring similar skills. The jobs available to many childminders in the study were in many ways similar to childminding. They were jobs such as caring for the elderly or helping in households, which tend to rely on so called 'feminine' competencies (Causse, Fournier and Labruyère 1998; Mozère 1999). The working conditions of such jobs are often poor with little chance of promotion. Many researchers have shown how this sector of work, the care and service industry, is growing in advanced economies. Such work relies on women and the caring skills they are perceived to 'naturally' possess. For example, Soares (1996) has reported that feminine skills, such as diplomacy and a caring attitude, are selection criteria in the recruitment of female cashiers in supermarkets. In these occupations, the most conservative social norms apply in terms of gender relations and women are condemned to conform to them in order to keep their jobs. They would appear to have no choice other than to perpetuate these norms, as demonstrated by many of the childminders in this study. Women in this situation are often exploited and confined to remaining in these low-paid female-gendered jobs.

Is there no way out then? Is it inevitable that these untrained women will be confined to these 'little feminine jobs'? As long as it is thought that innate, feminine competencies are sufficient to be efficient in an occupation, whatever that is, there will be subjection and conservative gender relations. Only with the development of professional training can women escape this socially constructed trap. Only a policy which develops equality of opportunity for men and women, for example having men care for children, could bring a change to this situation and turn childminding into a 'real' job, just like any other one.

Conclusion

The study has shown that there is still widespread belief that maternal competencies are enough to become a childminder. However, maternal competencies are not sufficient to find work as a childminder. Social competencies are important too, and help to overcome barriers to finding work such as a poor neighbourhood or poor language skills. Nevertheless, these additional skills are not able to lift such women out of the poorly paid, female-gendered care and service sector of the labour market.

Care work, such as nursing and social care work, and one can add childminding, is devalued within society (Sevenhuijsen 1998). In France, in particular, where work and working hours are generally well regulated, such caring work is referred to disparagingly as 'small jobs'. Yet such caring work underpins all other work. One could say that the women who undertake such caring work are themselves mis-cared for. They are ineligible for the benefits, conditions and unionization that shape the public understanding of what work is, at least in a French context.

It is important therefore to engage in both theoretical discussion and empirical research about what 'work' is, and what 'care' is, and in what ways they are similar and in what ways they differ, and challenge the preoccupation with 'maternal competencies'. Such an exploration might indicate how the situation could be improved or changed (Tronto 1993). Unless the discourses are challenged in this way, unqualified women will stay confined and condemned to this archipelago of 'small, ill-paid feminine jobs'. How can they be enabled to change the situation for themselves and become empowered?

References

Causse, L., Fournier, C. and Labruyère, C. (1998) *Les aides à domicile. Des emplois en plein remue-ménage*. Paris: Syros.

Faÿ-Sallois, F. (1980) *Les nourrices à Paris au XIXè siècle*. Paris: Payot.

Foucault, M. (1975) *Surveiller et punir*. Paris: Gallimard.

Garden, M. (1975) *Lyon et les lyonnais au XVIIIè siècle*. Paris: Science Flammarion.

Habermas, J. (1978) *L'espace public*. Paris: Payot.

Labourie-Racapée, A., Letablier, M-T. and Vasseur, C. (1917) *L'Activité Feminine.* Paris: Presses Universitaires de France.

Martin-Fugier, A. (1978) 'La fin des nourrices.' *Mouvement Social 105,* 14–26.

Maruani M. (1996) 'L'emploi à l'ombre du chômage.' *Actes de la recherche en Sciences sociales 115,* 48–57.

Mozère, L. (1978) *Analyse des expériences d'ouverture et de décloisonnement dans le secteur de l'enfance.* Paris: CERFI-EXEE.

Mozère, L. (1995) 'Agrément ou désagrément. Le staut des assistantes maternelles: ambiguitiés et réticences.' *Ethnologie française 25,* 4, 640–648.

Mozère, L. (1999) *Petits métiers urbains 'au féminin' ou comment échapper à la précarité? Les assistantes maternelles et les nourrices.* Paris: GRIS et CERFI-EXEE.

Sevenhuisen, S. (1998) *Citizenship and the Ethics of Care. Feminist Considerations on Justice, Morality and Politics.* London: Routledge.

Soares, A. (1996) 'Le Non-choix d'être caissière.' In L. Mercier and R. Bourbonnais (eds) *Le travail et l'emploi en mutation.* Montreal: AFCAS.

Schweitzer, S. (2002) *Les femmes ont toujours travaillé.* Paris: Odile Jacob.

Tilly, L.A. and Scott, J.W. (1987) *Les femmes, le travail et la famille.* Paris: Rivages Histoire.

Tronto, J.C. (1993) *Moral Boundaries.* New York: Routledge.

Notes

1   A small number of children attend *crèches parentales,* which are run by parents. In 2000 there were 8,700 places, compared with 319,000 places in *crèches collectives* (Ministère des Affaires sociales, du Travail et de la Solidarité, 2002).

2   Most of these estimates are extrapolated from qualitative studies and have no statistical significance.

3   The French Health Ministry prefers to count the assistantes maternelle, since it is impossible to estimate the number of children they care for. (Service d'Études et de Systèmes Informatiques (SESI), Ministère des Affaires sociales, du Travail et de la Solidarité, 2002).

4   SESI, Ministère des Affaires sociales du Travail et de la Solidarité, 2002.

5   In the département of Seine Saint Denis in which La Courneuve is located there are 639 assistantes maternelles agréées in crèches familiales and 4,575 private assistantes maternelles agréées.

Part III

Carers' and Parents' Perspectives

CHAPTER ELEVEN

Provider and Parent Perspectives on Family Day Care for 'Children in Need'

A Third Party In-between

June Statham

Early childhood services fulfil many different functions: care, education, family support, social cohesion, a source of employment. But in many countries different services focus on particular aspects of the needs of children and their families, rather than taking an integrated, holistic approach. In this chapter June Statham illustrates this fragmentation using the example of 'sponsored' family day care in the UK. This is an arrangement whereby local authorities purchase family day care from independent providers for children in need, as a way of supporting families at a time of crisis. She analyzes the operation of this service from a variety of perspectives – the family day care providers who receive sponsored children, the parents who use it and the officers who make the arrangements – and considers how well this form of provision meets the needs of vulnerable children and their families.

Introduction

Family day care is the most common form of formal childcare service in the UK. In 2001, over 70,000 registered family day carers provided places for more than 300,000 children in England alone (Department for Education and Skills 2001). In the great majority of cases, such care involves a private arrangement between parents and provider, with little involvement of the public authorities beyond a duty to maintain standards through a system of initial registration and annual monitoring. The introduction of the National Childcare Strategy in 1998 has resulted in more government support for childcare services. Childcare Information Services have been established to help parents to find suitable provision, and childminding networks are being developed to bring together individual family day care providers and help parents access good quality care (see Chapter Five). Some parents are eligible for help with childcare fees, for example through tax credits if they are on a low income, or through the nursery education grant scheme if their child is aged three or four and is cared for by a family day care provider who is also approved as a provider of nursery education (see Chapter Seven for further details). Despite these developments, however, the responsibility for arranging and paying for childcare usually remains with families themselves (Organisation for Economic Cooperation and Development 2001).

This chapter is concerned with an exception to this general rule, where the local authority intervenes in the relationship between parent and childcare provider. For a small group of children, mostly those who are judged to be 'in need' under the terms of the Children Act 1989, a place in family day care is arranged by welfare professionals such as social workers and health visitors and paid for by the local authority. This service is often referred to as sponsored or community childminding,[1] or children who are 'placed and paid for'. Sponsored places are typically used to support families when they are struggling to cope for a variety of reasons, or when the child is judged to be at risk of harm. In these circumstances, the local authority becomes what one family day care provider in my study described as 'a third party in-between', intervening in the usually private arrangement between parent and provider. The carers with whom such children are placed may be chosen from a pre-selected group of day care providers, but sometimes any registered provider who lives near the family may be used (Dillon, Statham and Moss 2001).

This chapter draws on information from a four-year research project that examined the role of voluntary and private day care services, including family day care, in supporting children who are placed and paid for by the local authority. The full findings are reported in Statham, Dillon and Moss (2001). After a brief description of the research study, I outline the circumstances in which children are placed or sponsored, and the nature and extent of the service they receive. The factors that lead family day care providers to undertake this work are examined, along with the training and support they receive and their perceptions of the advantages and disadvantages of providing such care. The views of parents whose children have been offered a place in family day care by the local authority are also explored. The chapter concludes by discussing how well the UK model of community childminding is able to meet the needs of vulnerable children and their families, and considers alternative models for supporting children and families through the provision of childcare.

The research study

The sponsored day care study was undertaken by the Thomas Coram Research Unit at London University between 1996 and 2000.[2] It was conducted in three stages, first, a postal survey of all English local authorities and an analysis of local authority documents such as childcare plans, which provided a national overview of the use of sponsored day care. The second stage comprised a more detailed study in twelve authorities, both urban and rural, selected because they demonstrated some elements of good practice in the use of day care services in the private and voluntary sectors for children in need (Dillon and Statham 1998). Finally, an in-depth study was carried out in two authorities, which included tracking the progress of individual children referred for a place in family day care, and in-depth interviews with 17 providers and 23 parents of children who had been offered a sponsored place in family day care. Local authority day care officers with responsibility for arranging the placements were also interviewed, and the quality of care provided in the family day care homes in the study was rated using the Family Day Care Rating Scale (Harms and Clifford 1989). Although the study covered centre-based care as well as home-based care, this chapter focuses on the latter.

The nature and extent of sponsored family day care in England

The Children Act 1989 gave local authorities in England and Wales a new duty to provide services for 'children in need', defined as those who need such support to 'achieve or maintain a reasonable standard of health or development', to 'prevent significant or further impairment of their health or development', or who are disabled (Department of Health 1991). The concept of 'in need' is a crucial one, because it effectively became the gateway to accessing publicly-funded day care services (Statham 1997).

The intention of the Children Act was to widen the support given to families who were having difficulties at an early stage, before their problems got too severe. However, we found that the focus on children in need had resulted in sponsored day care becoming more closely targeted on families with a high level of need. Subsidized places used to be offered by some local authorities to single parents or low-income families in order to enable women to work or study. However, in the last ten years or so, such support has increasingly become restricted to children whose families are in contact with welfare agencies because of some kind of family crisis (Novak *et al.* 1997). Almost two thirds of English local authorities responding to our survey at the end of 1996 reported that the criteria for access to sponsored day care had recently been tightened (Dillon and Statham 1998).

Nationally, only a very small proportion of children (less than 2% of children under five) are 'placed and paid for' in either a home-based or centre-based independent day care service. Not only are places available for very few children, but the amount of care offered is frequently limited. Funding usually covers only part-time attendance (generally two or three half days per week) for a short period of time, until the particular difficulty is resolved. Places are reviewed on a regular basis, and if the child is deemed to be no longer in need, funding is stopped. The sponsored day care service is seen as a short-term, crisis intervention to meet a particular need, rather than to provide ongoing day care. The kind of situations where local authorities in the study had supported families through purchasing family day care are:

- mother needs to attend a two-month drug and alcohol programme
- severely depressed mother coping with domestic violence
- young isolated mother, poor housing, finding it hard to cope
- grandmother in poor health caring for a disabled child, needs a break
- father caring for several young children, mother in hospital with mental health problems

In each case, the authority had assessed the child as being 'in need' and paid for a family day care place to prevent the family from breaking down. Most of these places were part-time. Full-time care was rarely offered, because the main aim in most cases was to rectify family functioning so that full parental responsibility – perceived normality – could be resumed. As one local authority officer explained:

> Sponsored day care is part-time and short-term to help families cope with specific family crises…if it's longer parents get used to it and expect it to continue…if we offer more than two days a week, it takes the problem away from the parent.

From the point of view of the local authority officers, family day care offered a valuable addition to their range of family support services. There was a lack of centre-based provision for children under two, and in any case many of these professionals thought that a home-based service was preferable for very young children. By placing children with self-employed family day care providers, the local authority could offer flexible support to families within the child's local community. But why would family day care providers want to undertake this work?

The providers' perspective

Motivation

Many of the children who are placed by welfare agencies come from vulnerable or challenging families and, as the criteria for the provision of such support are tightened, the needs which family day care providers are expected to meet become correspondingly greater. The emphasis in the Children Act on providing family support services means that sponsored day care providers are increasingly expected to support parents as well as to care for their children. More than a third of the family day care providers in our survey said that they had been asked to work with parents as well as children in sponsored placements. For example, they had provided advice on parenting skills; reminded parents about appointments; accompanied them to the doctor, therapy group or parent-and-toddler session and helped them to complete forms. Given the additional demands, what motivates providers to undertake this work?

We found that financial considerations appeared to play a relatively small part. Most family day care providers were paid no more by the authority to care for a sponsored child than they would have received from parents making a private arrangement, although sometimes there was a small supplement. A few were actually paid less than the 'going rate' charged by family day care providers in their area. Others were paid a higher rate only if the child had special needs or needed a lot of one-to-one attention, and this had to be negotiated on an individual basis. Even so, pay and employment conditions were poor for what could clearly be very demanding work. Only a quarter of authorities gave holiday pay (three or four weeks a year) and a half did not pay if the sponsored child failed to turn up. The additional work and expense of sponsored placements was not always recognized, as one family day care provider described:

> Some children and their siblings are pretty destructive. I incur more expense than other childminders. The house takes a beating. Bathing, washing clothes, extra heating for the special needs child. Parents using my telephone, providing them with cups of coffee and so on.

The most frequently mentioned reason for accepting children placed by welfare agencies was the sense of satisfaction and achievement that family day care providers obtained from seeing children improve, and being able to help families who were having difficulties. Their comments reflected their pleasure in children's progress while in their care. One described how 'Joe didn't interact with me at all when he first came. Now he does it's so satisfying, it's lovely.' Another explained that 'it's a very fulfilling job. To see a child come on and progress well is the best part of my job.'

Another common motivation was that family day care providers felt more 'professional' and less isolated. Working with the authority was perceived as giving them more status and useful contacts, as well as better support and recognition. When their relationship with the authority was good, they described feeling valued and taken seriously, working as part of a team and feeling supported by local authority staff. However this sense of partnership clearly had its limits. One family day care provider noted how working with the authority helped her to 'feel like a semi-professional', but then added that 'we are at the bottom of the hierarchy in social services'.

A third reason for undertaking sponsored work was that the hours and working conditions suited providers, and it helped them to obtain a regular supply of children to care for. The children placed by the local authority usually had parents who were not working, so children were often collected when schools finished rather than at the end of the working day, and the family day carer could often negotiate the hours she was prepared to work so that it fitted around other activities, such as another part-time job. Although the pay was poor and often late, local authorities did at least pay regularly.

Other reasons for undertaking sponsored day care were seeking a challenge, the opportunity to learn new skills, and wanting to provide an inclusive community service where children from advantaged and disadvantaged backgrounds could mix and learn from each other.

The family day care providers who said it helped them to fill places were a cause for some concern. When we visited and observed a sample of providers in the final part of the study, it seemed that the ones who gave this as their main reason for accepting children referred by the authority were mostly the ones who had difficulty finding children to care for privately. This was sometimes because they had only recently begun providing a service and were not yet known, but in other cases it could be because they were not able to attract fee-paying parents. For example, one carer explained that by accepting children placed by the local authority, 'it has meant I am more certain of getting work as I live in a high-rise council maisonette'. Others had advertised for children but had little response. 'We have tried to advertise for children locally but we often have to wait a long time. It's a good way of getting children rather than having to advertise.'

It was frequently pointed out that the family day care providers with a good reputation were usually full from word-of-mouth, and did not have any vacancies when the authority wanted to place a child with them. Local authorities often tried to keep a list of family day carers whom they considered would be particularly suitable for sponsored placements. However, the reality of trying to find a family day carer with a vacancy at very short notice, living near to the child's home and prepared to offer very part-time hours, meant that in practice welfare officers often had little choice over whom they could use. In a number of the cases that we tracked over a three-month period, thirty or forty providers had to be approached before one was found who was able and willing to take on the child for the hours required.

Difficulties with sponsored placements

From the providers' perspective, caring for a child placed by the local authority could have a number of disadvantages, although overall most judged that these were outweighed by the advantages. Problems included difficulties with parents, who could be unreliable or demanding; the low pay and lack of recompense for the additional workload and expense; insufficient information from the authority about the needs of children placed with them and requests for short-term, part-time care that made it difficult to balance local authority with private work. Many providers felt that such short-term care was not in children's best interests, because 'they just get used to you and start to make progress and then are taken away'.

These short-term placements also made it difficult for providers to plan and manage their workload, especially as the great majority received no subsidy from the authority except when they had a child placed with them. As one said:

> I cannot rely on the local authority to keep me in work. I need to be in regular employment, so I don't always have a vacancy for the local authority when I would like to.

Another described how she lost money because of wanting to be available to accept referred children:

> I want to do sponsored placements but sometimes there is no work. Sometimes I refuse private work in the hope that I will get sponsored work so I go without money while I wait for work to be offered me.

Sponsored placements were usually just agreed for a few months and then reviewed. At the review, the social worker might decide to carry on paying for the child, but by then the family day care provider could have arranged another private placement to make sure she had an income. One family day care provider described the potential impact of this on continuity for children. She had been caring for twin babies who were placed with her for an initial period of three months, but at the review it was decided to extend their sponsored placement:

> I have taken on a baby in November and it turns out the twins will be long-term. So their time with me will have to be cut down or they'll go to someone else. If I'd known, I wouldn't have taken the other baby on.

Training, experience and qualifications

It could be expected that family day care providers who are asked to care for children 'in need' would have more experience and a higher level of training and qualifications than average. To some extent, this was true. Providers of sponsored family day care in our survey had been caring for children for an average of nine years, compared to six years in a recent survey of family day care providers in general (Mooney *et al.* 2001). Twenty-nine per cent of those with experience of taking sponsored children had a childcare qualification, compared to 21 per cent in Mooney's study.

However, that still means that over two thirds of family day care providers who were caring for some of the most needy children had no formal childcare qualification. Nearly half (41%) of them had undertaken some special training for working with referred children, usually covering topics like child protection procedures, HIV/AIDS or working with parents. But this often involved no more than two or three sessions, and over half had not done even this. In common with other studies (Mooney *et al.* 2001; Nelson 1994; Ferri 1992) we found family day care providers had mixed feelings about the relevance and need for formal qualifications, although most were keen to obtain further training. Many felt strongly that it was being a parent and bringing up their own children that made them able to care for other people's children. When asked if they had any experience that particularly helped them to meet the needs of children placed by the local authority, family day care providers tended to mention working in another childcare setting and being a parent or foster parent, unlike centre-based childcare workers who were more likely to describe courses they had taken. Typical responses were 'four children of my own, fostering, helping at Sunday school and playgroup', or 'just my experience of many children including my own five'.

Support

Less than 40 per cent of sponsored family day care providers judged the level of support and training offered by the local authority to be good. Nearly half thought it was only 'adequate', and one in eight said it was 'insufficient'. What providers had appreciated most was support and advice, and having someone they could call on if they felt they needed help. This did not always happen. In some cases, providers felt that once a child had been placed with them, the authority 'just leaves us to get on with it'. Local authority staff often noted that, although they would like to have had the time to visit regularly, in practice it was left to providers to get in touch if there were any problems. Where authorities had allocated staff specifically to support and work with sponsored day care providers, there was a much higher level of satisfaction with the support and training they received. Childminding networks also offer the potential to improve support and training for providers who undertake this kind of work.

Many family day care providers thought it would help to know more about the particular difficulties faced by the families whose children they cared for. One said that 'looking after referred children is completely different to private customers. The family as a whole are usually very poor and have many learning difficulties. So far, I have just had to use my intuition as to how to deal with them.' They also wanted to know more about the circumstances in which children had been offered a sponsored place, although recognizing that this could raise issues of confidentiality. A common complaint was that welfare officers did not tell them enough about the family and the reasons the child was in need, and that they could help better if they had more information. As one provider explained, 'if we are good enough to take the child, then we are good enough to be told what the problem is'.

Perceptions of care

When we explored how family day care providers thought about their work with children who were sponsored by the local authority, we found, as with other studies reported in this book, that they stressed the importance of being able to offer children a homely environment and individual attention. However, providers with sponsored children also sometimes talked about compensating for a perceived lack of 'normality' in the child's home environment. For example, one family day care provider whose husband was at home for part of the day, noted that 'the children I look after come 80 per cent from single parent families, so we provide a lovely caring family atmosphere'. Another said 'I feel we are the only normality in his life', and a third that 'I'm there for [the child] in a way her mum can't always be at the moment.'

Many local authority staff thought that purchasing places in independent day care services, which were open to all families in the local community, could be a less stigmatizing form of support for families at a time of crisis than state-run nurseries which, if they existed at all, catered predominantly for children in need. However, this perception of sponsored family day care as a service to compensate for deficits in the child's home, rather than a childcare service for working parents, could create a stigma of its own.

Parents' views

How did the parents who had been offered a free place in family day care feel about this form of support? We were initially surprised to find in our study that a half of those who had been offered such support had not accepted the place, sometimes because the crisis had passed and it was no longer needed, but also for reasons discussed further below. Those who took up the family day care place all judged it to have been helpful, and for some it had been a lifeline. One admitted that 'I don't know what I would have done without it – thrown myself into the lake I expect.' Some mothers, especially young single mothers, particularly appreciated the fact that they were 'mothered' as well as their child:

> She was sort of like a grandmother really. You could sit down and have a cup of tea with her if you're really down.

> I could still go round there if I wanted support. I haven't spoken to her for about six months, but if I was to phone her and say, Sue I'm having troubles, she would be there. She showed me how to be a mum, I've got a lot to thank her for.

However, accepting a sponsored place in family day care could create feelings of ambivalence and inadequacy, especially for older mothers. The common fears that their child might become too attached to the carer, and guilt at leaving them in someone else's care, were made worse for some mothers of sponsored children by the fact that family day care is generally perceived as a service for working parents. Needing care for reasons other than to enter employment was therefore felt to reflect badly on their own parenting abilities. Typical was the single mother, depressed and unable to cope, who had recognized that she needed help to care for her children but would have preferred not to be in this position; 'I hated it. I still do. I never had help with the other children. I felt really bad not being able to cope.' It was not only mothers who expressed this point of view. One father was happy to accept a sponsored place in family day care while his wife was hospitalized, but asked for it to end as soon as she returned home, even though her circumstances still required a great deal of support. A grandfather was similarly unwilling to agree to social services providing family day care to support his wife, who was struggling to care for their grandchild, because he did not think it appropriate for someone outside the family to look after the child. This perceived 'normality' of maternal care for young children was underlined by the allocation of a sponsored family day care place to a father so that he could continue in employment when his wife was in hospital with severe depression, despite the fact that the eligibility criteria for sponsored day care excluded parental employment.

The circumstances in which family day care was offered appeared to make a difference to how it was perceived. It was easier for a mother to accept when it was seen as supporting rather than challenging her ability to care for her own children. For example, one local authority paid for a one-year-old child to attend family day care several half-days a week so that his mother could spend time with her older child who was terminally ill and take him to hospital appointments. This mother was happy with the arrangement and felt in control:

> I liked the way she looked after him. We discussed his needs. I could say he doesn't need that, or would you not do that. After a couple of weeks we were on the same wavelength.

Another mother, a single parent with triplets aged eleven and a one-year-old, was suffering from depression and was offered a place so that she could attend a mental health support group. However, she found it hard to leave her child and to accept help, saying that she felt she had 'given up on him' and 'felt bad because I wasn't coping'.

Almost all parents with experience of sponsored family day care were positive about the person caring for their child. They described her in terms that suggested they particularly valued the qualities of emotional involvement, flexibility and a non-judgemental approach. It was important to them that their child liked the carer, was made to feel special and was treated like the carer's own children. Yet there was also a perception that by operating as 'substitute mothers', family day care providers were less able than other types of day care service to meet children's educational needs. As two mothers explained:

> I still feel I would rather have had a nursery. If you leave a child at home with a childminder she has activities: cooking, cleaning, ironing. She does not have time to teach the children.

> I liked the way she [family day care provider] looked after him. But you could see the changes in him when he went to the [local authority] nursery. No way a childminder could be able to make those changes. It's the other children too, and the back-up of other staff. And the training.

Some parents had refused the offer of a family day care place because they would have preferred a nursery or playgroup. These group services were viewed as offering a more 'professional' service focused on the needs of the child, for example for learning opportunities and contact with peers, rather than as a replacement for something that mothers should be able to provide themselves. This view was articulated most clearly by the mother who rejected sponsored family day care on the grounds that 'I felt that whatever she could do, I could do'. Others had accepted the place, but still had conflicting views about whether such care had been the best choice for their child.

Sponsored day care: meeting children's needs?

Although this chapter has focused on some of the difficulties and tensions around sponsored family day care, it should be emphasized that the service was valued highly by local authority officers, and often by the parents themselves. It had given them a break and often helped them to cope at a particularly difficult time in their lives. This will obviously help children, because when their parents are less stressed or depressed, they can look after them better. However, the UK system of sponsored day care does raise a number of issues that need to be considered. These concern the nature of public support for day care services, the lack of a coherent framework for bringing together the different functions of early childhood services, and the quality of care that some of the most vulnerable children receive.

Administratively, the process of deciding whether a family was eligible for a sponsored place, then finding and arranging the care, was time-consuming and not always productive. As explained earlier, a large number of family day care providers often had to be approached by the local authority before a placement was set up, and then it was not always accepted by parents. The difficulty in finding places partly reflects the tensions created by basing a short-term crisis intervention for children in need on a general service designed to meet the needs of working parents. The requirements of many sponsored day care placements – short hours, taking and collecting children from home or school, accepting sibling groups – simply did not make economic sense for many family day care providers. As fewer women enter and remain in family day care work in the UK (see Chapter Seven), this situation is likely to worsen, unless more support and incentives can be provided. The consequence was that, compared to the amount of work put into setting up the sponsored placements, the amount of service children actually received appeared rather limited.

The study also raised questions about the quality of the care that children then received. Looked at from the child's point of view, it is hard to avoid the conclusion that the system of sponsored day care as it currently operates in the UK may not be the best way of meeting their needs. First, the family day care environment was not of a particularly high quality, when measured using a standardized observation scale for such settings, the Family Day Care Rating Scale (FDCRS). In the two authorities where we observed family day care providers with sponsored children, the average scores on this scale ranged from 'adequate' to just below 'good', but in neither authority did they reach 'excellent'. This was not the fault of the family day care providers; they were generally very committed and doing a difficult job for very little money, and many gave a lot of support to parents as well as children. But these were children who were particularly vulnerable or challenging and particularly needed a high quality environment. The problem was compounded by the lack of training and support available in most cases for those who were caring for children placed by the authority.

Second, there was often a lack of continuity for children, who commonly received only short periods of part-time care until their parents were able to cope again. There was rarely sufficient time to prepare or settle a child into the new environment, because places were offered at a time of crisis, and if care was needed again, the original carer could have taken on other children and be no longer available. Once a child was judged as no longer being 'in need', funding was withdrawn, even if the child was enjoying and benefiting from the family day care experience. Our research showed that most of the families receiving sponsored day care were poor, many were single parents, and most had no income earner in the family. They would fall through the net of the tax benefits and other welfare-to-work initiatives, which the government has introduced to make childcare more accessible and affordable (Daycare Trust 2001). Few could afford to continue paying for childcare once the local authority funding ended.

Could such support be provided differently? One alternative would be to provide a much higher level of publicly funded day care for all children, with extra support for those caring for children with additional needs. This is the case in a number of other countries, such as Sweden, France and Denmark, which accept greater collective responsibility for the well-being and upbringing of children (Moss 2001). In Sweden, for example, all parents have a right to publicly funded childcare if they work or study or their child has special needs, with fees dependent on their incomes.

There are a number of specific measures that could be taken to improve the ability of family day care providers in the UK to provide effective support for children in need and their families. These include improved training and support for carers, perhaps through the childminding networks discussed in Chapter Five; enhanced payment which reflects the demands, importance and value of the work and a questioning of the assumption that 'children in need' should only receive short hours of care for a limited period of time. Ultimately, however, we need to move away from a model of early childhood services that compartmentalizes the needs of children and families into 'childcare for working parents', 'education for pre-school children' and 'support for families experiencing difficulties', to one which recognizes the multiple roles of day care services in the lives of all children.

References

Daycare Trust (2001) *The Price Parents Pay: Sharing the Costs of Childcare.* London: Daycare Trust.

Department for Education and Skills (2001) *Statistics of Education: Children's Day Care Facilities at 31 March 2001, England.* London: Department for Education and Skills, UK.

Department of Health (1991) *The Children Act 1989 Guidance and Regulations Vol. 2: Family support, daycare and education provision for young children.* London: HMSO.

Dillon, J. and Statham, J. (1998) 'Placed and paid for: a national overview of the use of private and voluntary day care facilities for children in need.' *Child and Family Social Work 3*, 113–123.

Dillon, J., Statham, J. and Moss, P. (2001) 'The role of the private market in day care provision for children in need.' *Social Policy and Administration 35*, 2, 127–144.

Ferri, E. (1992) *What Makes Childminding Work.* London: National Children's Bureau.

Harms, T. and Clifford, R. (1989) *The Family Day Care Rating Scale.* New York: Teachers' College Press.

Mooney, A., Knight, A., Moss, P. and Owen, C. (2001) *Who Cares? Childminding in the 1990s.* Bristol: Policy Press.

Moss, P. (2001) *The UK at the Crossroads.* London: Daycare Trust.

Nelson, M.K. (1994) 'Family Day Care Providers: Dilemmas of daily practice.' In E. Nakano (ed) *Mothering: Ideology, Experience, Agency.* New York, NY: Routledge.

Novak. T., Owen, S., Petrie, S. and Sennett, H. (1997) *Children's Day Care and Welfare Markets.* Kingston upon Hull: School of Policy Studies, University of Lincolnshire and Humberside.

Organisation for Economic Cooperation and Development (2001) *Starting Strong: Early Childhood Education and Care*. Paris: Organisation for Economic Cooperation and Development.

Statham, J. (1997) 'Day care for children in need: Universal provision or a targeted service?' *Early Child Development and Care 136*, 1–15.

Statham, J., Dillon, J. and Moss, P. (2001) *Placed and Paid For: Supporting Families through Sponsored Day Care*. London: The Stationery Office.

Notes

1   The term 'childminding' is still commonly used for family day care in the UK, but I have chosen to use 'family day care' in this chapter.

2   The study was commissioned and funded by the Department of Health, but the views expressed in this chapter are those of the author and do not necessarily represent the views of the Department, the Thomas Coram Research Unit or the Institute of Education, University of London.

CHAPTER TWELVE

Partnerships with Providers?
Why Parents from Diverse Cultural Backgrounds Choose Family Day Care
Sarah Wise and Ann Sanson

This chapter by Sarah Wise and Ann Sanson of the Australian Institute of Family Studies draws on early findings from a study called 'Childcare in Cultural Context', which is exploring why parents from diverse cultural backgrounds choose particular forms of care. The chapter considers how far parents look for childcare that reflects their own values and practices, how far they are able to find this, and whether such a 'match' is linked to high quality care.

Introduction

The qualities that parents consider in their choice of childcare (for example, the type and quality of the childcare, when a child starts using a childcare service and the time they spend in care settings) ultimately shape the nature and impact of the child's experience of childcare. Parents also have many different requirements and priorities in the childcare they choose, including allowing them to engage in paid employment and enhancing their children's social and educational development. Knowing whether the childcare available suits parental requirements and ideas about quality is important in this regard.

A large body of research has shown that the factors involved in the decision-making process are quite complex. Characteristics of childcare that support a child's learning and development (such as the responsiveness and emotional quality of carer-child interactions) as well as those aspects that meet parents' own needs (for example, cost and convenience) are important factors in the decision-making process (Ispa, Thornburg and Vender-Barkley 1998). Research has also shown that child factors (a child's age, gender and special needs), and family characteristics such as income and parental education play a role in determining the childcare options that parents consider acceptable (Lee Van Horn, Mulvihill and Newell 2001). It is also suggested that cultural ideology, such as the value placed on the parenting role and attitudes toward maternal employment, could influence childcare decisions (Lamb and Sternberg 1992). Of course, overlaying all of these issues is the accessibility and availability of practical childcare options.

Our aim for this chapter is to explore the reasons for choosing family day care among a diverse group of parents in Melbourne, Australia. The limited information available as to why parents choose one type of childcare option over another suggest the emphasis that parents place on nurturing compared with educational aspects of childcare (such as intellectual stimulation and teaching styles) could be important. It has also been suggested that parents shift in the relative weight they place on care and education as children get older, with increasing emphasis on education (Long *et al.* 1996, p.52).

Harkness and Super (1992) introduced the concept of 'ethnotheories' to describe the culturally based beliefs that parents hold about childhood, children and child raising, and our chapter focuses on the role played by parents' ethnotheories in determining selection of a family day care arrangement. The extent to which parents value a childcare setting that matches the practices, values and orientations of the home gets particular attention. An ecological perspective on development (Bronfenbrenner 1979), which emphasizes interrelationships among different social settings, suggests that children may benefit if parents and carers have similar views about the ways in which children should be nurtured and socialized. Home-childcare continuity could therefore constitute an important dimension of childcare quality (van Ijzendoorn *et al.* 1998). As childcare services often reflect the child-rearing ideology of the dominant culture, issues of home-childcare continuity have particular relevance for children from minority cultures. This is pertinent in Australia, where approximately one-quarter of the population is born overseas (Australian Bureau of Statistics 2001).

It is expected that parents choosing family day care prefer childcare that resembles, rather than conflicts with, the child-rearing beliefs and practices adopted at home, because family day care is home-based and families can choose a particular care provider. The informal nature and the small scale of family day care may also encourage more extensive communication and closer relationships between parents and carers, all of which encourage a match between children's home and care settings (van Ijzendoorn *et al.* 1998). Some research has also concluded that parents from ethnic minority groups prefer to use childcare in situations where carers share the parents' beliefs about childcare issues (Morelli and Verhoef 1999).

We begin the chapter by providing some general information about family day care in Australia. This material is meant to help frame the issues that are raised in the next section that present preliminary trends from the Australian Institute of Family Studies new childcare study, called *Childcare in Cultural Context*. The extent to which parents emphasize childcare that reflects the caregiving values and orientations of the home is discussed first. Agreement between carers and parents on child rearing philosophies is then explored, including the importance placed on children becoming independent, obedient and/or conforming. Finally, carer attitudes toward parental involvement in the childcare program and carer-parent communication are presented, because they constitute important connections between childcare and home settings.

Background to family day care in Australia
Provision

Family day care services are a network of approved carers who provide care and developmental activities in their own homes for other people's children. Family day care is primarily for children who have not yet started school full-time (five days per week, approximately six hours per day),[1] but can also provide care for school children up to twelve years of age. Care is flexible and can be tailored to suit each family's needs, including full-time, part-time, casual, relief, vacation care and care outside normal working hours and, if needed, overnight care (National Family Day Care Council of Australia 2001).

In Australia, family day care places are administered through a 'co-ordinating team' or 'co-ordinating unit', which is sponsored by an 'operator' or organization that takes out a funding agreement with the Commonwealth Government. A family day care 'scheme' includes the carers, co-ordination staff and management involved in delivering family day care services within a particular area or program. Co-ordination units support and administer the network of carers in their area and are responsible for the effective operation of all components of family day care, including recruiting, training and supporting carers, monitoring care and providing advice, support and information to parents. They also assist parents to select an appropriate carer for their child. Historically, local government bodies, non-profit community groups and religious and charitable organizations have been involved in family day care co-ordination. Since 1 January 2001, other operators, including private for-profit providers, have been able to apply to the Commonwealth to provide family day care services. An exception to this pattern of family day care being operated at a local level is the State of South Australia, where the State Government operates family day care services.

Family day care has been operating in Australia since the 1970s, initially through a range of experimental non-Governmental schemes. Schemes were officially made eligible for funding in 1973. In 1976–77, 114 family day care schemes were being supported under the Children's Services Program (National Family Day Care Association of Australia 2001). By June 1999, 360 family day care schemes were operational, catering for some 87,000 children, approximately 12 per cent of all Australian children who use formal childcare (Australian Bureau of Statistics 1999).[2] In the 1980s, some ten years after its beginnings, there were a similar number of places in family day care as in centre care. This proportion decreased dramatically in the 1990s, however, when for the first time the Commonwealth Government introduced subsidized childcare places for commercial childcare centres.

Childcare support

The Commonwealth Department of Family and Community Services (FaCS) has major responsibility for family programs and early childhood education and care policies, excluding schools and pre-schools. It is responsible for the administration of the Family Assistance Act 1999 and for policy relating to income support for families. Through its Childcare Program, FaCS is concerned with policy and funding in relation to long day care services, including family day care. The Commonwealth Government assists families with the cost of childcare through Childcare Benefit funding for parents. To be eligible, family day care services must participate in the

Family Day Care Quality Assurance system (FDCQA) (see below) and comply with State and Territory regulations.

Cost of family day care

Family day care fees are not regulated by Government, so they vary from scheme to scheme, and loadings apply for part-time (less than 30 hours) and outside usual hours care (8 a.m. and 6 p.m. weekdays). A survey conducted by the National Family Day Care Council of Australia in 1999 suggested that family day care fees ranged between A$127.00 and A$178.00 for 50 hours of family day care (National Family Day Care Council of Australia 2001), which is very similar to fees in childcare centres. The average Australian gross weekly income was A$658.00 per week in 1997–98, and the current minimum wage is A$382.00 per week (Press and Hayes 2000, p.33). Childcare Benefit is paid up to a specified amount, not the actual fee charged. At July 2001 the maximum rate of Childcare Benefit was A$129.00 per week for one child in childcare, and the minimum rate of payment for one child was A$21.70. As a result there is a 'gap fee' which must be bridged by almost all parents regardless of their income.

Quality assurance

The Family Day Care Quality Assurance (FDCQA) system, administered by the National Childcare Accreditation Council, was launched in July 2001 as part of the Commonwealth Government's commitment to ensuring that children in childcare services have stimulating, positive experiences and interactions that foster all aspects of their development. As mentioned previously, family day care schemes are only eligible for Commonwealth funding on behalf of parents if they participate in the FDCQA. The FDCQA is also linked to the Operational Assistance approval for family day care schemes. The Australian quality systems are the first quality systems in the world to be linked to childcare funding through legislation and to be funded and supported by a Federal Government.

FDCQA is structured in terms of six Quality Elements, or areas of family day care:

- carer-child interactions
- physical environment
- children's experiences, learning and development

- health, hygiene, nutrition, safety and well-being
- carers and co-ordination unit staff
- management and administration.

Each Quality Element has a number of supporting Principles that summarize and define quality in family day care. These elements and principles guide the schemes in maintaining and improving the quality of their childcare practices. They also provide the framework by which quality is measured as the scheme passes through the five steps of FDCQA. The five steps to accreditation are: registration; self-study and continuing improvement (involving a self-assessment of quality of care using the six Quality Elements and Principles); validation of quality practices (involving observations and discussions with co-ordination unit staff and carers); moderation; and the accreditation decision. Although it is the family day care schemes that are ultimately accredited, the accreditation process involves the individual carers, the co-ordination unit staff and management as well as families. Quality practices are validated on a representative sample of care providers in each scheme.

With regard to staff training and qualifications, family day care providers are not required to have a qualification other than a First Aid Diploma. Information on 'relevant qualifications' held by childcare workers was collected in the Commonwealth Child Care Census for every service type.[3] In 1999, 21 per cent of family day care providers and 70 per cent of co-ordination unit staff had at least one relevant qualification, and an additional 5 per cent of providers and 6 per cent of co-ordination staff did not have relevant qualifications but were studying for them. Further, 18 per cent of co-ordination unit staff and 44 per cent of family day care providers have three or more years experience. The majority of providers and co-ordination staff had undertaken in-service training in the 12 months prior to the survey (77% and 88% respectively) (Australian Institute of Health and Welfare 2001).

Operators of family day care schemes are not licensed in all Australian States and Territories, but family day care providers must be 'registered', or 'approved' by a scheme. Although registration or approval processes will differ according to the different scheme or licensing body procedures, they generally include an inspection and assessment of the prospective provider's home, a criminal record check of the prospective provider and other household members and completion of a medical examination. Prospective providers must also be seen as responsive to children, able to meet the physical and emotional needs of children and be able to respond to a medical or other emergency (Moyle *et al.* 1996).

Cultural differences in parents' childcare decisions

Parent satisfaction with childcare is a function of whether parents can arrange care to suit their individual requirements. It is increasingly recognized that definitions and measures of quality in childcare should reflect particular social and cultural contexts, and may not be universally applicable (Dahlberg, Moss and Pence 1999). What might be high quality for one social or cultural group may not necessarily be so for another. It has also been suggested that parents may look for characteristics in childcare that are qualitatively different from the criteria of 'experts'. There is a growing consensus that the characteristics of childcare should be congruent with those valued by the families they serve (Long et al. 1996, p.53).

Although the decision process is complex, and many questions remain unanswered, some studies suggest that childcare that matches culturally based beliefs about early child rearing may be key to parents' childcare decisions (Rosenthal 2000; Wise and Sanson 2000). In most countries, provision of childcare is largely defined and shaped by the dominant culture. Existing research indicates that differences between parents and carers about childcare issues appear to be greatest for children whose parents are from ethnic minority and low-income populations. Disagreements between carers and parents over practices regarding instruction, physical discipline, encouragement of play that breaks gender stereotypes, and over basic care routines such as changing nappies, feeding, comforting and toilet training are well documented (Gonzalez-Mena 1993). The extent to which parents from diverse cultural backgrounds use formal childcare services may depend to some extent on the availability of childcare that reflects parental values (see Fuller, Holloway and Liang 1996; Holloway *et al.* 1995).

There are also strong theoretical grounds for fostering continuity between home and childcare settings. Bronfenbrenner's ecological model (1979) discussed interrelations among children's various social settings. According to Bronfenbrenner, positive child development is supported when the demands of different environments are compatible, and when there are productive connections across these settings, such as parent-carer communication. Research has also demonstrated that children develop security and trust when there is continuity in the care they receive between home and childcare (Harrison and Ungerer 1997). They do less well along academic, emotional and social dimensions when family and early childhood settings are incompatible. For example, a recent study conduced by van Ijzendoorn and his colleagues from the Centre for Child and Family Studies in the Netherlands (van Ijzendoorn *et al.* 1998) concluded that 'it seems in the child's best interests if parents and non-parental carers are attuned with each others' child-rearing styles' (p.779).

Overseas studies support the expectation that cultural ideology influences choices among various childcare options, and that families of differing ethnic backgrounds make different childcare choices (Blair, Legazpi and Sampson 1995; Fuller *et al.* 1996). Of course these differences may be the product not only of differing cultural preferences, but also of the differential cost of childcare options (Uttal 1999).

Research studies also show that parents from different cultures approach the parenting task differently and choose childcare that best matches their particular values and practices. For example, Fuller *et al.* (1996) showed that when selecting childcare Latino mothers in the United States take into account childcare providers' views about how children should behave (for example, showing respect for adult authority and contributing to the welfare of others). Parents' childcare decisions may also relate to culturally preferred teaching styles. Some research suggests that mothers from some ethnic minorities believe that formal teacher-directed instruction is the best method for encouraging learning (Rosier and Corsaro 1993), whereas many early childhood specialists tend to favour child-centred processes that include child-initiated, exploratory activities.

Cultural attitudes to maternal employment and the mothers' role also influence childcare decisions (Lamb and Sternberg 1992). For example, parents with traditional views about maternal employment (i.e. believing work outside the home is inappropriate), but where a mother's paid work is nevertheless perceived to be an economic necessity, may be more likely to use home-based arrangements in preference to centres. In contrast, parents in cultures that approve of mothers working outside the home may be more likely to use centre-based care.

Parents' expectations of childcare are also determined by cultural beliefs about where the responsibility for young children's care and education lies (Dahlberg *et al.* 1999). For example, Uttal (1996) found that some employed women in a United States West Coast community saw themselves as primarily responsible for the socialization of their children. Even though their children spent long hours in non-maternal care, childcare was perceived as custodial in nature, providing for their children's health and safety, but not much more.

Carer–parent partnerships

Continuity between home and childcare may be linked to the level of communication that takes place across settings and the amount of information and/or experience that exists in one setting about the other (van Ijzendoorn *et al.* 1998). Early childhood programs that build on parents' cultural knowledge and traditions and promote strong parent–carer relations and effective communication between parents and carers are thought to enrich both carer and parent capacities to provide sensitive and supportive care to the child (Owen, Ware and Barfoot 2000, p.413). Carers therefore need to work in partnership with parents, and to encourage a two-way process of information flow to increase knowledge and understanding of children's experiences in other childcare settings (Organisation for Economic Co-operation and Development 2001, p.117).

In many countries, the approach of professionals is to share responsibility for young children with parents, and to learn from the unique knowledge that parents from diverse backgrounds can contribute (Organisation for Economic Co-operation and Development 2001, p.117). In Australia, for example, carer–parent communication is a component of accreditation in the Quality Improvement and Accreditation System for long day care centres (QIAS) and the FDCQA. The QIAS expects frequent interactions between parents and centre staff in high quality programs. Similarly, the FDCQA includes effective communication with families about children and the family day care service as one of its key quality principles.

Historically, family day care providers have been considered to have better relationships and stronger interpersonal ties with parents than have providers in centres. This is possibly because the informal nature and the small scale of family day care is conducive to more extensive communication between parents and carers, and because the same carer is always present at drop-off and pick-up times. However, there is evidence that parent–carer relations can be less than optimal in family day care, particularly when parents and carers disagree about the role of women in the workforce, or when carers see parents as deficient in some way. Studies conducted outside

Australia suggest that, although parents' and carers' intentions to communicate appear to be good, these intentions are often not acted upon (Leavitt 1987), and communication may be a problem approximately one-third of the time (Bryant, Harris and Newton 1980). Overall, a summary of considerable research on this topic conducted in countries outside Australia has 'painted a somewhat dismal picture of the relations between the adults in the settings, and especially the communication between parent and caregiver' (Feagans and Manlove 1994, p.588).

The Childcare in Cultural Context study

The Australian Institute of Family Studies study, called *Childcare in Cultural Context*, is looking at the effects on children of differences between home and childcare settings (Wise and Sanson 2000). Data are currently being collected, via parent and carer questionnaires and through direct observation, on the development of one- to three-year-old children from Somali, Vietnamese and Anglo-Australian backgrounds attending either family day care or centre care within Melbourne. Information about various characteristics of the home and childcare settings believed to influence child development is also being collected. At the time of writing, data collection is still underway, but initial findings are beginning to emerge.

Findings: preliminary analyses

The current data set comprises information on a total of 197 children, of whom 73 were using family day care. Of those children using family day care there were 46 matched parent–carer pairs (where information was available from both carer and parent). The data set also includes information on 114 children using centre care (including 90 matched parent–carer pairs). Some of these data are used for comparison with the family day care data in the analysis. There were ten children in the data set using informal care.

The proportions of children in the Somali, Vietnamese and Anglo groups in family day care and centre care are presented in Table 12.1. The proportions of children in the Somali, Vietnamese and Anglo groups in the two settings were slightly different. This is important to note, as findings may simply reflect differences in the proportions of Somali, Anglo and Vietnamese parents in the family day care and centre care samples. It is also relevant that a higher proportion of children in family day care were looked after by a carer from the same cultural background compared with children in centre care.

Table 12.1 Proportion of children from Anglo, Vietnamese and Somali backgrounds using family day care and centre care				
	Family day care		Centre care	
	number	%	number	%
Anglo	13	28	40	45
Somali	21	46	12	13
Vietnamese	12	26	25	28
Other/unknown	0	0	13	14
Total	46	100	90	100

Families using childcare centres were also more affluent than the family day care group. Approximately 78 per cent of families using family day care had incomes under A$20,000 compared with only 22 per cent of families using childcare centres. More than a third (39%) of parents using childcare centres had incomes over A$60,000 compared with very few parents using family day care. A far greater proportion of parents using family day care were not in paid work (64% of mothers and 22% of fathers in family day care compared with 28% of mothers and 4% of fathers in childcare centres). Further, 11 per cent of children in family day care were in a lone-parent household compared to 4 per cent of children in the centre care sample.

Choosing childcare that reflects the culture and values of the home

The parent questionnaire contains a series of 21 items related to the importance of various qualities of childcare. These include factors that reflect parents' needs (such as service cost, convenience and flexibility), factors that meet a child's interests (such as the sensitive responsiveness of carers) as well as features of childcare that affect continuity in the child's socialization (such as the language used in childcare). Parents rated how important each characteristic was to them on a three-point scale.

Previous studies have shown that when presented with a checklist of items most parents affirm that nearly everything is important (Lee Van Horn *et al.* 2001). Generally speaking, parents in our study placed a high priority on carer characteristics, structural characteristics of the care (such as staff training, group size, child-staff ratios) and health and safety issues. When we factor-analyzed the remaining items, we were able to group three items under the general heading 'parent-related reasons' for childcare selection (alpha =.75) and eight items under the heading 'culture-related reasons' (alpha =.46). The latter included items such as carers talking to the child in his/her own language, the child being given food that he/she is used to at home, and carers taking time to understand parents' ideas and practices about bringing up children.

We compared parents using family day care to parents using centre care on these parent- and culture-related factors. The findings indicated an overall tendency for parents using family day care to value childcare that reflects the culture and values of the home slightly more than families using centre care. However, differences between the total family day care and centre care groups were non-significant. A significant difference was only detected when Vietnamese parents using family day care were compared with Vietnamese parents using centre care (p=.04).

Parent-carer attunement

The child-rearing attitudes of carers and parents were surveyed to determine how children's day care experiences fitted with their experiences at home. The extent to which parents and carers placed importance on initiative, self-direction and independence as goals of child socialization in comparison to obedience and conformity goals was examined.

Parent and carer questionnaires contained a series of 20 statements about child rearing concerned with self-directing, conforming and social behaviours. The scale was based on the Index of Parental Values, as modified by Schaefer and Edgerton (1985), and included 11 of the original items. Respondents indicated how important it was that a child learns obedience, independence and social behaviours. An orientation toward obedience prioritized values such as neatness, compliance and good manners; an orientation toward independence in children prioritized values such as personal responsibility, self-direction and curiosity; and an orientation toward social behaviours prioritized children's empathy and consideration toward others. Factor analysis of the 20 items showed 'obedience' and 'social/independence' factors clustered together as separate scales (alphas =.73 and .81 for carers and parents on the obedience scale and .51 and .67 for carers and parents on the social/independence scale).

The relationship between parent and carer attitudes toward children's socialization was examined using correlation analysis. Parents and carers in the family day care group were in greater agreement on both 'obedience' and 'social/independence' measures than parents and carers in the centre care group. A correlation of .25 ($p<.05$) showed parents and family day care providers tended to share the same views about the importance of child obedience, whereas parents and centre carers did not significantly agree ($r=.16$, $p=.06$). Similarly, parents and family day care providers agreed to a moderate extent on the importance of social/independence goals for children ($r=.411$, $p<.01$), whereas parents and centre carers did not significantly agree ($r=-.084$, $p=.22$). In general, obedience was seen as a more important goal for children in family day care than centre care (as reported by both parents and carers), although this difference was non-significant.

Correlates of parent-carer attunement in family day care

As cultural factors were a priority for some parents, and those using family day care in particular, it is important to understand whether close correspondence between carers and parents in their values was related to Anglo-Australian concepts of 'quality care'. The issue here is whether qualities of childcare services that parents value, and which are likely to determine their selection of childcare (i.e. co-ordination between children's home and childcare experiences) go together with expert definitions of high quality care. This relationship was explored by correlating the differences, or discrepancies, between parent and carer child-rearing attitudes with a 'quality' score derived from a standardized observation scale for family day care (Harms and Clifford 1989). Correlation analysis showed no relationship between total quality scores and the level of agreement between parents and carers about children's socialization.

Carer-parent communication

Carer-parent partnerships are important in facilitating continuity between home and childcare settings. The extent to which linkages between home and childcare settings are formed through parent-carer communication and negotiation was analyzed using carers' responses to 22 statements. Carers reported how much they agreed or disagreed with statements about parent-carer communication and other family-centred practices, such as valuing parents' child-rearing goals and cultural sensitivity.

Factor analysis showed that seven items could be grouped on a scale called 'assimilation' (alpha =.75), reflecting carers' beliefs that children should fit in with mainstream cultural values and basic care routines in childcare. Five items could also be grouped on a scale 'sensitivity to diversity' (alpha =.55), reflecting carers' beliefs that care should reflect parents' cultural values. 'Assimilation' and 'sensitivity to diversity' are also likely indicators of the characteristics of partnerships between carers and parents, with 'sensitivity to diversity' reflecting relationships that are underpinned by open, two-way communication and recognition and valuing of the parent as a partner in decision-making. These two scales were used in an analysis comparing family day care providers and centre staff. Comparisons showed that family day care providers were slightly more in favour of 'assimilation' and less in favour of 'sensitivity to diversity' than centre carers, although these differences were non-significant.

Discussion

Cultural reasons for childcare selection

The data presented here do not pretend to provide a complete picture of what parents from different cultural backgrounds value in a childcare service, and how this may influence their childcare decisions. As Early and Birchinal note:

> A complete model of childcare selection would include not only demographic characteristics and preferred childcare characteristics, but also information on availability (for example, options within the family's price range, options that meet the parents' scheduling needs) and data on parents' information (for example, information on the extent to which the care they select indeed has the characteristic they believe it has). (Early and Birchinal 2001, p.494)

From a cultural perspective, valuing childcare that reflects the values and practices of the family may also be influenced by the parents' length of time in the host country as well as their attitudes toward assimilation. For example, it has been suggested that Vietnamese parents sometimes use childcare centres as an acculturation experience, to introduce children to Australian ways so they can do well at school, or more generally because they wish to be seen to be fitting in with cultural mores. Indeed, data collected as part of the Institute's Parenting-21 project showed Vietnamese-Australian parents generally felt comfortable adapting their child-rearing practices to reflect those of the mainstream Australian culture (Kolar and Soriano 2000). Formal schooling is also highly valued in both the Vietnamese and the Somali communities. It is quite possible that parents from these cultures choose centre care for older children because they feel it will help prepare them for entry to formal schooling.

Although parents using family day care valued a childcare service that was sensitive to the child's cultural background slightly more than parents using centre care, these differences were only significant for the Vietnamese sample and the numbers in this group are small. Although cultural factors may come into play, our findings suggest that parents' reasons for choosing family day care over centre care are likely to be complex and multi-faceted. Issues such as cost, location, convenience and other aspects of the care received (such as carer characteristics) that have not been taken into account in the current analysis are likely to have a bearing on childcare selection.

However, as Early and Birchinal (2001) point out, parents make decisions about their children's childcare based on the options available to them. The fact that Somali parents using family day care did not differ from Somali parents using centre care in the importance they placed on cultural sensitivity may well be the product of childcare supply. Anecdotal information collected during the course of the study suggests that more Somali families would be using family day care if it was readily accessible. There are currently long waiting lists among Somali families for family day care places in some schemes that were involved in the study. Initiatives are also currently underway to recruit and train Somali family day care providers in local areas where such families have settled, to meet the demand.

It is equally possible, however, that those Somali parents who value cultural sensitivity in a childcare service feel that there is little advantage to using family day care over centre care. In Australia, regulations ensure more uniform and better quality centre care than is typically found in the UK and United States (Organisation for Economic Co-operation and Development 2001), where studies have shown ethnic membership to be related to the type of childcare used. Indeed, accommodating children's individual needs and respecting diversity of background is a key principle of the QIAS. Many of the centres involved in the current study had high proportions of children from non-English speaking backgrounds, and many aspects of the childcare curriculum were observed to reflect the language, values and customs of the different backgrounds of the children. Further, childcare fees are relatively similar in family day care and centre care, so the economic circumstances of ethnic minority families may not be a particularly discriminating factor in parents' choice of one type of care over another.

Parent-carer attunement

Although correlations were not very strong, the data revealed a significant level of attunement among family day care providers and parents on measures of parenting values. Although parents were not asked specifically about their reasons for choosing their current childcare arrangement, this may suggest that parents seek family day care providers at least in part based on their views about how children should behave. This appears to occur more in family day care compared to centre care, where parent and carer values were entirely unrelated.

Parent-carer attunement was not correlated with quality as measured by the widely used Family Day Care Rating Scale. This suggests, on the one hand, that the extent of agreement between parents and carers on core values may not go together with aspects of childcare thought to support children's positive development. However, it is difficult to know whether elements of high quality childcare are actually incompatible with certain core values that parents and family day care providers tend to agree upon.

Parent-carer communication

Despite some signs that choice of family day care is based on parents' child-rearing values, the assumption that family day care providers have better relationships with parents than centre care staff, and are more likely to promote cultural inclusion, was not supported. Although differences were non-significant, family day care providers were less willing to adapt routines in childcare around individual requirements, and had generally less favourable attitudes to parent-carer communication and negotiation than centre-based staff.

On first impressions these findings appear inconsistent with the idea that parents using family day care prefer to match children's childcare experience with the home. However, within the family day care sample the majority of carers and parents were from the same cultural background. Given parents' preferences for a family day care provider from their own cultural background, an attitude among carers that children should 'fit in' with group norms and practices may actually reflect parents' preference for childcare in which carers teach their children their own cultural and religious values. It is also possible that parents seek compatibility with carers in terms of religious beliefs and specific cultural practices of a broader nature than the parenting values reported here.

Conclusion

There is a literature suggesting that parents' choice of family day care reflects a preference among ethnic minority families in particular for their children to be cared for in a household where the values and beliefs reflect the family culture. Some research also suggests that parents and family day care providers are likely to agree on important values concerning a child's caregiving, and that extensive communication and close relationships between parents and carers maintains this 'attunement'. In contrast, another body of research suggests that parent-carer relations are less than optimal in family day care, especially when carers perceive parents as poor parents (Kontos and Wells 1986). Research has also demonstrated relationships between childcare selection and a whole raft of other factors such as personal qualities of the carer, health and safety issues, educational components of the program, cost and convenience.

Findings from the current study are only preliminary, yet a pattern is emerging to suggest that the level of agreement between parents and carers on childcare issues is greater in family day care than centre care. Our findings are also beginning to suggest that parents using family day care value childcare that is like the child's experience in the home. However, the strength of these relationships is not especially strong, and the data showed that carers' attitudes toward communicating with parents and cultural sensitivity in group care settings may not necessarily support continuity between home and childcare. These findings will need to be confirmed when all the data are collected.

In all likelihood family day care is important for families from particular cultural backgrounds who want childcare to reflect their cultural values. However, it is over simplistic to suggest that interactions between home and day care characteristics can explain parents' choice of family day care, particularly in the Australian context where high quality centre care is relatively accessible for families living in urban areas. Furthermore, cultural considerations may not be as important for some families as other features of childcare, such as cost, location, personal characteristics of the carer and a curriculum that promotes school readiness.

What parents from different cultures value in childcare has implications for the development of programmatic structures, standards and criteria for good quality that are consistent with developmental goals valued by different cultural groups. This study demonstrates a need for further developing the evidence base on the qualities parents value in the childcare they select for their children and, more critically, how this relates to children's developmental outcomes, an issue to be addressed in further analyses in this study. However, we suggest that cultural child rearing and linguistic considerations will continue the demand for family day care services in Australia, especially if parents' ideas are not consistent with the dominant cultural ideology. The challenge for the future is to meet this demand and to ensure that both parents' requirements and children's needs are related in appropriate ways.

References

Australian Bureau of Statistics (1999) *Childcare Australia*, cat. no. 4402.0. Canberra: Australian Bureau of Statistics.

Australian Bureau of Statistics (2001) *Migration, Australia*, cat. no. 3412.0. Canberra: Australian Bureau of Statistics.

Australian Institute of Health and Welfare (2001) *Australia's Welfare 2001*. Canberra, Australian Institute of Health and Welfare.

Blair, M., Legazpi, B. and Sampson, L. (1995) 'Choice of child care and mother-child interaction: Racial/ethnic distinctions in the maternal experience.' In C. Jacobson (ed) *American Families: Issues in Race and Ethnicity*. New York, NY: Garland Publishing Inc.

Bronfenbrenner, U. (1979) *The Ecology of Human Development Experiments by Nature and Design*. Cambridge, MA: Harvard University Press.

Bryant, B., Harris, M. and Newton, D. (1980) *Children and Minders*. London: Grant McIntyre.

Dahlberg. G., Moss, P. and Pence, A. (1999) *Beyond Quality in Early Childhood Education and Care: Postmodern Perspectives*. London: Falmer Press.

Early, D. and Birchinal, M. (2001) 'Early child care: Relations with family characteristics and preferred care characteristics.' *Early Childhood Research Quarterly 16*, 475–497.

Feagans, L., and Manlove, E. (1994) 'Parents, infants and day care teachers: Interrelations and implications for better child care.' *Journal of Applied Developmental Psychology 15*, 585–602.

Fuller, B., Holloway, S. and Liang, X. (1996) 'Family selection of child-care centers: The influence of household support, ethnicity, and parental practices.' *Child-Development 67*, 6, 3320–3337.

Gonzalez-Mena, J. (1993) *The Child in the Family and Community.* New York, NY: Merrill.

Harkness, S. and Super, C. (1992) 'Shared child care in East Africa.' In M. Lamb, K. Sternberg, C. Hwang and A. Broberg (eds) *Child Care in Context*, pp. 441–462. Hillsdale, NJ: Lawrence Erlbaum.

Harrison, L. and Ungerer, J. (1997). 'Child care predictors of infant mother attachment security at age 12 months.' *Early Child Development and Care 137*, 31–46.

Harms, T. and Clifford, R. (1989) *Family Day Care Rating Scale.* New York, NY: Teachers College Press.

Holloway, S., Rambaund, M., Fuller, B. and Eggers-Pierola, C. (1995) 'What is "appropriate practice" at home and on childcare?: Low-income mothers' views on preparing their children for school.' *Early Childhood Research Quarterly 10*, 451–473.

Ispa, J., Thornburg, K. and Vender-Barkley, J. (1998) 'Parental child care selection and program quality in metropolitan and non-metropolitan communities.' *Journal of Research in Rural Education 14*, 3–14.

Kolar, V. and Soriano, G. (2000) *Parenting in Australian Families: A Comparative Study of Anglo, Torres Strait Islander, and Vietnamese Communities.* Melbourne: Australian Institute of Family Studies.

Kontos, S. and Wells, W. (1986) 'Attitudes of caregivers and the day care experiences of families.' *Early Childhood Research Quarterly 1*, 47–67.

Lamb, M. and Sternberg, K. (1992) 'Sociocultural perspectives on nonparental child care.' In M. Lamb, K. Sternberg, C. Hwang and A. Broberg (eds) *Child Care in Context.* Hillsdale, NJ: Lawrence Erlbaum.

Leavitt, R. (1987) *Invisible Boundaries: An Interpretative Study of Parent-Provider Relationships.* Campaign-Urbana, IL: University of Illinois.

Lee Van Horn, M., Mulvihill, B., and Newell, W. (2001) 'Reasons for childcare choice and appraisal among low-income mothers.' *Child and Youth Care Forum 30*, 4, 231–249.

Long, P., Wilson, P., Kutnick, P. and Telford. L. (1996) 'Choice and childcare: A survey of parental perceptions and views.' *Early Childhood Development and Care 119*, 51–63.

Morelli, G. and Verhoef, H. (1999) 'Who should help me raise my child? A cultural approach to understanding non-maternal child care decisions.' In L. Balter and C. Tamis-LeMonda (eds) *Child Psychology: A Handbook of Contemporary Issues*, pp. 491–509. Philadelphia, PA: Psychology Press/Taylor and Francis.

Moyle, H., Meyer, P., Golley, L. and Evans, A. (1996) *Children's Services in Australia 1996: Services for Children Under School Age.* Children's Services Series Number 2. Canberra: Australian Institute of Health and Welfare.

National Family Day Care Council of Australia (2001) *Information Kit.* New South Wales, National Family Day Care Council of Australia.

Organisation for Economic Co-operation and Development (2001) *Starting Strong: Early Childhood Education and Care.* Paris: Organisation for Economic Co-operation and Development Publications.

Owen, M., Ware, A. and Barfoot, B. (2000) 'Caregiver-Mother Partnership Behavior and the Quality of Caregiver-Child and Mother-Child Interactions.' *Early Childhood Research Quarterly 15*, 3, 413–28.

Press, F. and Hayes, A. (2000) *OECD Thematic Review of Early Childhood Education and Care Policy: Australian Background Report.* Canberra: Commonwealth of Australia.

Rosenthal, M. (2000) 'Home to early childhood service: An ecological perspective.' *Childrenz Issues 4*, 1, 7–15.

Rosier, K. and Corsaro, W. (1993) 'Competent parents, complex lives.' *Journal of Comtemporary Ethnography 22*, 171–204.

Schaefer, E. and Edgerton, M. (1985) 'Parent and child correlates of parental modernity.' In I.E. Sigel (ed) *Parental belief systems: The psychological consequences for children.* 287–318. Hillsdale, NJ: Erlbaum.

Uttal, L. (1996) 'Racial safety and cultural maintenance: The child care concerns of employed mothers of colour.' *Ethnic Studies Review 19*, 43–59.

Uttal, L. (1999) 'Using kin for child care: Embedment in the socioeconomic network of extended families.' *Journal of Marriage and the Family 61*, 845–857.

van Ijzendoorn, M., Tavecchio, L., Stams, G., Verhoeven, M. and Reiling, E. (1998) 'Attunement between parents and professional caregivers: A comparison of child rearing attitudes in different child care settings.' *Journal of Marriage and the Family 60*, 771–781.

Wise, S. and Sanson, A. (2000) *Childcare in Cultural Context: Issues for New Research.* Research Paper no. 22. Melbourne: Australian Institute of Family Studies.

Notes

1   Six States and Territories offer a full-time pre-Year 1 'preparatory' program within their education system for children aged five years. The remaining two States, Queensland and Western Australia, offer sessional pre-Year 1 programs for five-year-old children. Funded pre-school and kindergarten programs also operate in all States and Territories for children in the year prior to pre-Year 1 for children aged four.

2   Includes children in before and after school care and pre-school.

3   Relevant qualifications generally include qualifications in early childhood and primary teaching, child care, nursing and other relevant areas such as business management and social work.

CHAPTER THIRTEEN

'Who Says What is Quality?'

Setting Childcare Standards with Respect for Cultural Differences

Kathy Modigliani

There is no national framework for early childhood services in the United States. Regulation requirements vary, but these are often very minimal and the standard of care in both centre-based and home-based services can be poor. In such circumstances, voluntary accreditation schemes, especially if they are linked to eligibility for government subsidies, can offer a way of raising standards. In this chapter, Kathy Modigliani outlines the process of developing a new national accreditation system for family day care in the United States in the late 1990s, and describes the efforts that were made to ensure that the standards took account of cultural differences in perceptions of what counts as good quality care.

Introduction

'Who says what is quality?' This important question was asked by a provider of family childcare at the beginning of a project to develop a new national accreditation system for such services in the United States.[1] This chapter describes the process of developing the accreditation system, and the efforts that were made to ensure that the standards took account of possible cultural differences in perceptions of what counts as good quality care.

There are a number of reasons why developing a widely accepted framework for standards in family childcare is important. In the first place, large numbers of children use this form of provision. It has been estimated that approximately a million family childcare providers in the United States care for and educate about four million children (National Association for Family Child Care 2002). Second, in the United States there is no national co-ordinated policy framework for early childhood education services (Organisation for Economic Co-operation and Development 2000). Individual state requirements for the licensing of family childcare homes vary considerably in relation to the standards of quality expected. In some cases, this is limited to very basic hygiene and safety requirements, and some states exempt family childcare homes that care for a small number of children from any form of licensing. Regulations differ from one state to another but, typically, one provider can care for up to six or eight children in a small family childcare home. About two thirds of the states also allow a provider with an assistant to care for approximately twice this number of children. Most states also have some limit on how many very young children are permitted (The Children's Foundation 2002).

Parents shoulder the main costs of childcare, although childcare services are subsidized for some low income families (earning less than 85% of the median state wage) through a federal Child Care Development Fund. Families who are eligible for a subsidy can use any provider who meets the basic health and safety requirements, but many states have long waiting lists for this programme. The effect of minimal regulation and limited public funding is that standards can sometimes be poor, in both centre-based and home-based care (e.g. Galinsky *et al.* 1994; Costs, Quality and Child Outcomes Study Team 1995).

Standards of quality are also important because accreditation is increasingly becoming a means to encourage providers to raise their quality above the often minimal requirement set by state regulations. Accreditation, which is voluntary, is a process whereby providers evaluate their service against a set of standards set by professional organizations. These standards are higher than state requirements and in some states, higher subsidies are paid to high quality programmes as measured by accreditation. The National Association for the Education of Young Children (NAEYC) has for seventeen years operated an accreditation system for centre-based childcare. Approximately half of the 50 states pay a higher rate for accredited programmes than for programmes that have only met basic licensing standards. This trend is driven by the desire to offer a policy-incentive 'carrot' for quality improvement, while licensing tends to be the 'stick' used to ensure a basic standard of health and safety protection.

It is not only policy makers who need to know how to assess quality. It is important for other groups of stakeholders too, such as private funders who want to support quality improvement initiatives and college faculty and community trainers who design curricula. The standards of quality are important for providers themselves, the professional associations and groups who support them, and parents who entrust their children to the care of others. Finally, researchers, who depend on specific, non-judgmental descriptions to measure programme quality and evaluate the success of quality-improvement initiatives, need a clear definition of quality.

Who should define quality and write the standards? Twenty years ago, the answer would no doubt have been 'the experts', implying recognized academic researchers and perhaps some early childhood professional leaders. But most of the recognized experts in the United States and other English-speaking countries are White and middle-class. Their perspectives are likely to be limited by a lack of diversity in experience, and they may find it difficult to see that other ways of being with children may be just as effective in achieving desired outcomes as their own, perhaps even more so. The recognized experts in most countries belong to a somewhat elite mainstream that does not represent most of those who use childcare services. In the United States there is increasing diversity among children and families, reflecting the changing demographics of our nation. The Hispanic population, for example, grew by 58 per cent between 1990 and 2000. People from Hispanic and Black ethnic groups now account for a quarter of the population (United States Bureau of the Census 2002). It is crucial that childcare services are able to respond to this diversity in ways that are equitable to people from all participating cultures, and that draw on the wisdom they bring.

This chapter describes the four-year consensus building process used to design the family childcare accreditation standards and procedures sponsored by the national provider association, the National Association for Family Child Care (NAFCC). It addresses the philosophical question of who should be empowered to define childcare quality. It describes the resolution of conflicts that arose between the values of providers and parents and research findings. It presents some specific differences that emerged among the three largest race/ethnicity groups – White, Black and Hispanic – and how the project chose to reconcile these differences. Finally, it describes practical activities to use with providers and others to explore cultural differences in child-rearing values, to reflect on implications for the daily work of family childcare and to build cultural competency with children and families.

The Family Childcare Accreditation Project

In 1995 the Family Childcare Project at Wheelock College in Boston, Massachusetts, was funded to work with the National Association for Family Childcare to develop a new accreditation system for home-based childcare.[2] Rather than modifying existing quality assessments that were designed for childcare centres, we decided to undertake research to find out what providers and parents, as well as researchers and other experts, defined as quality in a home-based setting. The goals of this project were to:

- design standards of quality for family childcare
- help parents and policy makers recognize high quality family childcare
- promote providers' self-assessment and professional development
- motivate providers to put training into practice
- serve as a cornerstone in state professional development systems.

The accreditation project was guided by a steering committee of key leaders from research and practice in the field of early care and education as well as an advisory committee of diverse family childcare providers, agency staff members, and other community supporters of the quality of family childcare.

Gathering information and building consensus

The Family Childcare Accreditation Project collected information from a variety of sources. Project staff reviewed research in related fields such as child development, early childhood education, family support, small business administration and cultural differences in child-rearing values (see the references in Modigliani and Bromer 2002, pp. 69–72). However, we also needed to gather original data from providers, parents, and other community experts concerning their definitions of childcare quality for babies, toddlers, pre-schoolers and school-age children in a home setting. This information was not currently available, but was essential to the task of developing culturally appropriate standards for family childcare.

A request for proposals was widely circulated, seeking groups of 8–12 people who would commit to four meetings over two years, to help define quality and develop procedures for the new accreditation system. The request stated that preference would be given to 'diverse groups that can speak for under-represented voices in family childcare' – without specifying what was meant by these terms. Fifty-two groups were assembled, involving nearly five hundred people. Participants included family childcare providers, parent consumers and support agency staff members. The groups were variously all White, all Black, all Spanish-speaking, or mixed. They lived in urban, suburban and rural communities across the country. They slightly over-represented Spanish speakers and African-Americans, the two largest 'minority' groups in the United States.

Each group had a facilitator who was paid a small sum to document their group's responses each time they met to undertake one of the four tasks: a focus group to define quality and another to design procedures, plus commenting on two successive drafts of the standards. Despite this minimal funding, most groups were enthusiastic and welcomed the opportunity to contribute to the project. Gradual attrition led to decreasing participation in some groups, but 48 of the 52 groups made a significant contribution to the new accreditation system.

Simple instructions about how to conduct focus groups were distributed to the facilitators with suggestions for questions to help their groups define quality and suggest provider-friendly assessment strategies. For example, the pilot research showed that most people have trouble answering an abstract question such as 'How would you define good quality in childcare?' However, they can answer more specific questions like 'If a friend or family member asked you what to look for in childcare for their baby, what would you say?'

Analysis of responses

A thematic analysis of the focus group responses to the definition of quality found that most placed 'a warm, loving, nurturing provider' at the top of their list. The thematic analysis yielded the basic structural outline of the final accreditation standards. The analysis also contributed numerous phrases that helped us begin to write standards in language that is commonly understood, rather than in academic jargon.

The groups' emphasis on the quality of the provider's relationship with the children posed a potential problem for designing an instrument to assess childcare quality, because measuring traits such as 'warm, loving, nurturing' could be deemed too subjective to be measured with reliability. However, recent research findings on early brain development, resiliency and the prevention of violence stress the importance of warm, secure relationships for children's well-being as well as their learning (see National Research Council 2000 for a review of this literature). We decided to write the most objective measures we could for this dimension and see how they fared. Examples are given in Table 13.1, which lists some of the indicators included in the standards to help observers assess quality under the two dimensions 'The provider with the children' and 'The children with each other'. These are part of the relationships section of the observer workbook, which has subsequently been used by a research firm (Abt Associates in Cambridge, Massachusetts) with good inter-rater reliability (Creps 2001).

Table 13.1: Selected indicators from the observer standards

The provider with the children

- The provider shows interest in what children say and do, and listens attentively to them most of the time.
- The provider shows affection to each child in some way.
- The provider acknowledges specific aspects of each child's efforts and accomplishments.
- The provider recognizes signs of distress in children and responds and comforts them with stress reducing activities.
- The provider helps children to notice each other's needs and feelings.

The children with each other

- The children listen to and respond to each other.
- Older and more competent children show some evidence that they are learning to help and take care of others.
- Younger children interact with older children as well as watch them.
- If there is any teasing, bullying or hurtful behaviour, the provider helps children notice it and stand up for each other and themselves, and assures that the outcome is fair and considerate of all.

© The Family Child Care Project

The first draft of the new accreditation standards was composed by integrating the themes from the focus group analysis with key findings identified in the review of relevant research. This first draft of the quality standards was much too long. To help us decide what should be eliminated, we again turned to diverse sources for advice. The first draft of the standards was reformatted into a survey and sent to approximately 400 members of the community workgroups and other experts in related fields, including researchers and teacher educators. The steering and advisory committees also contributed valuable advice.

The survey respondents were asked to rate the importance of each statement by deciding if it was 'required', 'very important', 'somewhat important', or 'not important' for accredited providers to meet this condition. They were also asked to re-word each statement 'the way they would say it', which resulted in around 16,000 suggestions. These suggestions were sorted by computer and were extremely helpful in editing the standards to reflect the nuances of meaning, using language that is commonly understood.

Cultural differences in values

The race/ethnicity distribution of the survey respondents was very close to that of the United States population, with substantial numbers of Hispanic and African-American as well as White respondents. Given the lower response rates expected from minority groups, over-sampling of these groups was needed to produce a representative sample. Analysis of the results suggested that the first draft had too much detail in the areas of curriculum and materials. There was clear agreement on this from the respondents. However, the survey also highlighted some cultural differences in values. For example, both African-Americans and Hispanics thought the first draft placed too much emphasis on each individual child. On the other hand, they placed more value than did White respondents on statements pertaining to the group of children and their relationships with each other, and to those pertaining to involvement with neighbourhood and community. Midway through the study, project staff constructed a typology of child-rearing values (Table 13.2), which could be used as a starting point for group discussions about culturally sensitive childcare. There were clear examples of differences in our survey sample on the dimension of independence versus interdependence shown in this table.

Table 13.2 Dimensions of child-rearing values

Following are some differences in child-rearing values that have emerged from our reading, observations, and discussions with caregivers and parents. People differ in the emphasis they give to any particular value and some people may equally value both sides of one of these dimensions. This chart is presented as a starting point for discussion about culturally sensitive childcare.

Independence	Interdependence
Individual achievement and self-sufficiency is valued.	Co-operation and meeting each other's needs are valued. Children are encouraged to help each other accomplish a task.
Competition is commonly used as an incentive.	
Children are encouraged to do things for themselves, self-help skills are emphasized.	Sharing, taking turns, empathy, and mutual support are encouraged and modelled by adults.
Materials are selected that children can use successfully by themselves.	Older children take care of younger children.

Children's activities are materials-centred	Children's activities are people-centred
Objects and toys are given to babies to play with on the floor or in a chair of some kind.	Babies are held most of the time. Eye contact is an important form of communication.
Pre-schoolers learn from numerous toys and materials.	Pre-schoolers learn by watching and doing things with others.

Children have their own special places	Children are included in the world of adults
Separate child-centred spaces and activities are provided for children most of the time.	Children are included in all activities of the family and community.
Children are encouraged to make choices about the activities they want to do.	If children are not welcome at a place or event, no one goes. (No babysitters.)

Verbal communication is emphasized	Multiple modes of communication are emphasized
Adults talk a lot to babies.	Children model the behaviour of adults and older children. They learn from body language and other unspoken cues as well as the context of a situation.
Direct instructions and explanations are the main ways of teaching young children.	
Information is given through books and verbal explanations.	Adults use storytelling and metaphors to help children learn about the world, moral values, and traditions.

The goal of discipline is for children to learn self control	The goal of discipline is to teach children to respect authority
Adults help children identify their feelings and learn socially acceptable ways of getting what they want or need. Children may be taught skills to resolve their own conflicts. Too many 'Nos' and 'Don'ts' are seen as limiting children's autonomy. Adults try to explain directions in a polite and positive way with an explanation the child can understand, e.g. 'Please walk when you're inside, so you don't bump into anything.' Punishment is considered ineffective as well as damaging to self-esteem.	Extended family members and other adults exert authority over children, assuring appropriate behaviour and obedience. Conflicts are usually resolved by adults. Adults use a direct style, and firm language if needed, to tell children what to do, e.g., 'Stop running.' 'Come put your coat on now.' Sometimes a look of authority is all that is needed. Punishment is likely to be used when a child does not obey the authority.
Open expression of emotions is encouraged	**Control of emotions is encouraged**
Children are encouraged to talk to adults about their feelings. Childcare activities include naming and understanding emotions. Individual expression of feelings such as excitement, anger, sorrow, joy, and frustration are encouraged and seen as healthy emotional development.	Children are expected to subordinate their individual feelings to the harmony of the group (family, class, or community). Children are encouraged to take on and share the affect, or mood, of the group.
Child-centred learning is valued	**Academic preparedness is valued**
Adults believe that young children learn most through play. Activities that build directly on their own interests serve as motivation and scaffolding for further learning. Reading, writing, and arithmetic are taught in the context of children's play, or not taught at all. Formal instruction is delayed at least until elementary school.	Adults believe that young children should be taught academic skills and the value of work. Emphasis is given to academic readiness activities such as learning the alphabet and phonics as well as numbers and completing math worksheets. Play is seen as a way of letting off steam and getting ready to get back to work.

© The Family Child Care Project

These findings persisted across educational levels, although they were less pronounced for respondents with relatively higher levels of education.

Reconciling differences in values

The next stage in the process of developing culturally sensitive standards was to conduct sessions at national early childhood conferences on cultural differences in child rearing values, to refine our early insights through discussions with participants. These sessions began by reviewing the dimensions of child-rearing values (Table 13.2). Although these examples of value differences reflect patterns of variation across cultural groups, it is also important to recognize that there may also be significant value differences within one subgroup and even within one family. An individual may also value both sides of a dimension – for example, a provider may support children in becoming independent through self-help skills while also building interdependence in teaching the children to empathize with and take care of each other.

Next, we asked participants to list differences in values that they themselves had encountered in their own work with children and families. Table 13.3 presents some of the examples identified by these groups. Participants sometimes felt that cultural differences were not important and did not apply to their situations, but often changed their minds by the end of the exercise. These discussions led project staff to amend some of the standards. For example, we agreed that in the United States too much emphasis is placed on autonomy, individualism and independence while not enough consideration is given to co-operation, mutual support and inter-dependence. We therefore eliminated about half the numerous references to 'each individual child', and expanded the standards pertaining to supporting children's empathy and taking care of each other. We retained a small section on neighbourhood and community, although most White respondents thought this was not very important. We also came to consensus, after some discussion with the community and advisory groups, that the first draft was overly materialistic, emphasizing things more than people. We therefore reduced the number of standards referring to the amount of materials and equipment.

In other cases the project intentionally chose to keep standards derived from the research findings even though a majority of respondents thought they were relatively unimportant. For example, providers are required for accreditation to read to babies and toddlers and to use positive guidance rather than punishment, shame or humiliation. They are encouraged to observe children and gather information from parents to guide their programme planning and spontaneous interactions with children. We believe that research clearly supports these practices for positive child outcomes, including lifelong well-being as well as school success.

Table 13.3: Examples of differences in cultural values

Culture may be defined broadly as the values, beliefs, behavioural patterns, and traditions of any group. Culture evolves constantly. It is usually invisible – 'as invisible to people as water is to a fish' – according to an unknown sage. Following are some examples of characteristics that vary by culture, identified in discussions with providers:

- Academic teaching (ABCs, numbers) vs. play, social skills
- Breast vs. bottle-feeding
- Caregiver's name – Ms, Mrs, first name, Auntie
- Child's role in the family
- Cleanliness and hygiene
- Clothes – dress-up vs. play clothes
- Communication – e.g. yes means that you agree or that you heard
- Competition vs. co-operation
- Discipline – strict or permissive, authoritarian vs. self-control, physical punishment
- Eye contact
- Feelings about photographs
- Food – what is appropriate for children, religious restrictions, meaning of offering food, using food as a reward, natural food vs. 'junk' food
- Gender issues – dress-ups, role-playing, nail polish
- Holding and carrying baby vs. putting unrestricted on the floor vs. cradle board
- Holidays – what and how to celebrate or not
- Lifestyle, family composition
- Manners
- Messy activities
- Nicknames
- Privacy around toileting
- Religion – prayer at the table, religious teachings
- Schedule – predetermined vs. flexible
- Showing affection towards children – amount and style
- Sleeping – how much, how and when, together in one bed or separate bedrooms
- Story telling, the role of stories in teaching
- Talking about sex, human bodies
- Toilet training timing and techniques
- Tone of voice – loud or quiet talking
- Use of pacifiers, age of weaning
- Wearing shoes indoors

© The Family Child Care Project

Reaching consensus

The second draft of the new quality standards was sent to the advisory committees and community workgroups. This time there was significant agreement on the standards and much support for some of the difficult decisions that had to be made as described above. The 301 standards cover the following six areas: relationships, environment, activities, developmental learning goals, safety and health, and professional and business practice. The standards can be found on the NAFCC website (National Association for Family Child Care 2002). As people from diverse cultures participate in accreditation, it will be important to continue to evaluate the cultural appropriateness of these standards and procedures for different groups and learn from any disagreements that emerge.

Generally, there has been widespread appreciation of the concrete, detailed description of best practice described by the quality standards, although some disagreements remain. Many providers to this day do not like some of the standards, especially those requiring frequent hand washing, limiting television to one hour per day, and minimizing the use of 'time out'. Some parents and providers do not agree with the standard 'Boys and girls have equal opportunity to participate in all activities.' However, some degree of flexibility is built into the accreditation system, to allow for and respect cultural differences in child-rearing values and to minimize the need for appeals. The scoring procedure requires that certain standards in each of the six areas are met, but the provider then has to meet only 90 per cent of the remaining standards. This means that some individual differences are respected, while requirements agreed upon are not compromised. For example, one family day care provider can choose to be weak in her music programme, another can choose to forgo gender equity and a third may have poor outdoor space in her urban apartment. However, all of them can be accredited if enough of the remaining standards are met. They meet the NAFCC's definition of high quality in their particular situation.

There is also some flexibility if providers can present a strong case for waiving a particular required standard, for example if a family feels strongly that their child should wear an amulet on a necklace even though this could be a strangulation hazard. During the interview which forms part of the accreditation process (see below), the observer asks the provider to comment on any standard that the observer scored as partially met or not met. Sometimes, a provider has a well reasoned argument, consistent with research and best practice. In such cases, NAFCC may grant exemption from the relevant standard.

The process of accreditation

In 1999, after pilot studies in five communities, NAFCC's new accreditation system was made available to family childcare providers across the country. To be eligible they must have graduated from high school or its equivalent, care for at least three children and have been licensed for at least 18 months (if eligible for licensing in their state). In reality, few providers pursue accreditation on their own – most are part of a training and support group that pays most or all of the fee. State or federal quality enhancement programmes, philanthropic foundations or community charities fund these support groups.

Upon application and payment of half the fee ($247.50), accreditation candidates receive the *Quality Standards Self-Study Workbook* (Modigliani and Bromer 2002) to keep track of their improvement plans and accomplishments. Once they have completed the self-study programme, with or without training and support, the provider requests a visit from an observer acting on behalf of the NAFCC and pays the second half of the fee. These observers are required to be familiar with family childcare as well as child development and early education. NAFCC sponsors two-day training courses for observers, focused on how to write clear, specific, non-judgmental observations that will document the standards. The observers are asked to give examples of evidence they might use to score a standard as fully met, partially met, or not met. They are taught how to be provider friendly and respectful of different ways of meeting the standards, using materials such as those in Tables 13.2, 13.3 and 13.4.

Table 13.4 Self-assessment for culturally competent care and education

These are cultural competencies that providers can implement in their work with children and families. Rate yourself on each one, thinking about how you are helping children learn to thrive in the multicultural environment of the twenty-first century.

- I have thought about and clarified my own values about caring for and educating children and I can explain them to prospective families.
- I learn about the values and practices of the families in my program through ongoing conversations and observations. I try not to make assumptions or stereotyped judgements, but to learn about the unique values of each new family.
- I try to recognize the strengths of each family and understand the positive reasons why parents act the way they do and hold particular values that are different from my own.
- I use the information I gain about each family's traditions to plan activities and respond in ways that are comfortable for the children and their families.
- I support children in forming positive attitudes about their own cultural/ racial/ethnic identities, while also helping them to be fair to and respectful of others. Children can learn about themselves and others through photographs, books, pictures, music and (if possible) people in the community.
- For babies and toddlers, I adapt my caregiving style to be consistent with the families' styles (except when this is dangerous – such as babies sleeping on their stomachs – when I encourage the parents to adopt the healthier way).
- I help pre-schoolers become bi-cultural, supporting their family values as well as preparing them to succeed in the mainstream world of school.
- If I cannot speak a child's home language, I learn key words and phrases to use with the child and play tapes in that language. If the parents do not speak my language, we try to find a translator to help us communicate.

© The Family Child Care Project

On the day of accreditation, the observer spends four or five hours documenting the family childcare provider's home, conducting the interview and completing the *Observer Workbook* (Modigliani and Bromer 2001). They also conduct an interview, during which the provider is asked to explain any quality standard that is scored less than fully met and their answer recorded in writing. Additional information is gained from self-observation by the provider, using the same observation instrument, and from a questionnaire completed by one parent from each family. The materials are scored and sent to a Commission, composed of one NAFCC staff member and three independent experts, for final review and the accreditation decision.[3] Accreditation is awarded for three years or deferred, requiring the provider to continue self-study for at least one year before re-applying. The entire process may take a year or more, depending on how much the provider needs to change and how much time can be devoted to this work. Due to cost constraints, no system has yet been put in place to monitor the homes during the three years between accreditation renewals, although if the provider moves the new home environment must be checked before the accreditation can continue. Neither has it been possible to undertake a formal evaluation of the accreditation system, although providers report that their programmes are improved through the accreditation self-study process.

Discussion

The United States is becoming culturally more diverse each year. Statistics show that White children are, or will soon become, a minority in many urban and suburban schools. The diversity of family childcare is one of its great strengths. While children in the United States benefit from learning English before they enter public school around age five, research has shown that linguistic continuity between a child's home and childcare is critical for the healthy development of babies and toddlers (e.g. Chang, Muckleroy and Pulido-Tobiassen 1996). Parents need to be able to choose a type of childcare that is comfortable for their family as well as offering quality high enough to support each child's development. This depends upon having a choice among different kinds of homes and centres, with caregivers who can adapt their practice to a family's cultural styles while offering a level of basic quality that supports each child. Of course, choice of childcare also depends on affordability, which is not explored here. As the OECD report on childcare in the United States acknowledged, 'selecting and using high quality programmes is a question of affordability. Only wealthy families seem to have full access to programmes of their choice' (Organisation for Economic Co-operation and Development 2000, p.10).

Another important issue is ensuring that the accreditation materials are accessible to providers who speak languages other than English. Spanish is the largest minority language in the United States, and all the provider materials are available in Spanish. This has enabled large numbers of Spanish speakers in several communities to pursue accreditation. In some communities, providers from other language groups are also seeking accreditation – including Hmong speakers from Laos, Mandarin and Cantonese speakers from China and Hong Kong and Creole speakers from Haiti. NAFCC is seeking funding to translate provider materials into languages in addition to English and Spanish, and perhaps to tape record the standards in Hmong, since this is usually a spoken language. The Association also aims to recruit bilingual observers to carry out authentic observations that avoid the threat to reliability of having a third party translator. However, this has proved difficult since no national funders have been identified. Recruiting observers as well as providers is therefore dependent upon community initiatives.

Culturally sensitive practice requires that people of all groups, including the dominant culture, are prepared to learn from each other. The accreditation project helped many of us adapt our ways of being with children as we learned from others. It was particularly important for White family childcare providers to be assisted to see the strengths of other communities. An example of this occurred in one community where English and Spanish-speakers were preparing for accreditation. There was little contact between the two groups although they lived within easy driving distance of each other. Midway through the accreditation class, a tour of homes was arranged, which involved visiting several model family childcare homes in both neighbourhoods. Afterwards, the Spanish participants acknowledged with appreciation some of the examples of good practice they saw in the English-speakers' homes, but not one provider from the English-speaking group mentioned something she appreciated in the Spanish-speakers' homes, beyond surprise that the homes were rather spacious and well furnished. This reflects a tendency for the dominant culture to be oblivious to the values of people who are different from themselves (McIntosh 1988).

Yet the Hispanic providers had much to offer. Most evident was the care that the children showed for each other, how well they all got along together and the lack of discipline problems. In one home after another, the children harmoniously moved together from one activity to another, helping each other without direction from the provider. The co-operation and lack of aggression among the mixed-age groups was particularly noticeable. Most providers require training to be able to help children learn how to appreciate differences in each other, resolve conflicts and avoid discrimination to prepare them to thrive in our increasingly diverse society.

Conclusion

In many ways, the project to develop a new culturally sensitive accreditation system for family childcare has been a success. By involving large numbers of diverse providers, parents and agency personnel as well as traditionally recognized experts in a process of consensus building, the accreditation system was able to reflect their perspectives and values and allow for diversity in the way standards are met. The assessment places great importance on the quality of relationships between provider and children, provider and parents, and among the children themselves. Providers from diverse cultural groups are seeking accreditation and appear to support the standards. By 2002, over 3000 providers were accredited or participating in self-study, and numbers are increasing as some states and communities begin to offer the training, mentoring and financial assistance needed for providers to succeed. There has been a gratifying amount of recognition and support from national, state and community leaders and policy makers. Several states are funding or proposing to fund accreditation projects. Most notably, the largest state, California, has funded 900 family childcare providers to become accredited in the next two years. A number of states pay higher purchase-of-care rates to family childcare providers that are accredited, and this can provide a particular incentive for providers serving low-income families who are eligible for such subsidies. Some parents who are aware of the importance of accreditation in communities where centre-based accreditation has become popular are seeking accredited family childcare providers.

On the other hand, if there are approximately one million family childcare providers in the United States, less than 1 per cent of them are expected to go through the accreditation process in the next few years. Raising standards through a voluntary accreditation system will take time, and requires support – financial and otherwise – if it is to reach providers in all communities. However, we believe that the project has shown that when accreditation is developed with input from diverse groups and consensus building among the communities it serves, it can indeed motivate and guide improvements in the quality of family childcare. At the same time, accreditation can respect the different views on quality and the different ways in which quality can be achieved.

References

Chang, H.N., Muckelroy, A. and Pulido-Tobiassen, D. (1996) *Looking in, Looking Out: Redefining Childcare and Early Education in a Diverse Society.* San Francisco, CA: California Tomorrow.

The Children's Foundation (2002) *2001 Licensing study.* Washington, DC: The Children's Foundation.

Cost, Quality and Child Outcomes Study Team (1995) 'Cost, Quality and Child Outcomes in childcare centers: Key findings and recommendations.' *Young Children 50,* 4, 40–50.

Creps, C. (2001) personal communication, May.

Galinsky, E., Howes, C., Kontos, S. and Shinn, M. (1994) *The Study of Family Child Care and Relative Care.* New York, NY: Families and Work Institute.

McIntosh, P. (1988) *White Privilege and Male Privilege: A Personal Account of Coming to See Correspondences Through Work in Women's Studies.* Wellesley, MA: Center for Research on Women.

Modigliani, K. and Bromer, J. (eds) (2001) *Observer Workbook for NAFCC Accreditation.* Second edition. Salt Lake City, UT: The National Association for Family Child Care.

Modigliani, K. and Bromer, J. (eds) (2002) *Quality standards for NAFCC Accreditation: Provider Self-study Workbook.* Third edition. Salt Lake City, UT: The National Association for Family Child Care.

National Association for Family Child Care (2002) (United States) website: www.nafcc.org/accred

National Research Council (2000) *From Neurons to Neighborhoods. The Science of Early Childhood Development.* Washington, DC: National Academy Press.

Organisation for Economic Co-operation and Development (2000) *Early Childhood Education and Care Policy in the United States of America.* Paris: Organisation for Economic Co-operation and Development.

United States Bureau of the Census (2002) www.census.gov/population/www/cen2000/tablist.html, Table 1 'Total population by age, race, and Hispanic or Latino origin for the United States: 2000.'

Notes

1   In the United States, we use the term 'family child care' to designate child care that occurs in the provider's home (although some still refer to 'family day care'). Parents and journalists often use the term 'babysitter' for those who provide such care, but this is felt to minimize and demean the education, loving nurturing, and all the other critical functions delivered by these teachers/service workers/small business entrepreneurs. We have rejected 'caregiver' as demeaning to the educational/developmental function. The term 'educarer' never received popular support. So we remain with the term 'providers' for those who provide family child care, although it is not wholly satisfactory.

2 It was funded by the Ford Foundation, the David and Lucille Packard Foundation, the A.L. Mailman Family Foundation, the American Business Collaboration through W/FD, Levi Strauss & Co, and additional pilot-community funders. The research was conducted by project director Kathy Modigliani and associate Juliet Bromer.

3 In all, the accreditation decision is based on 174 observation standards scored and documented with the observer's notes, 23 interview questions, 25 questions on the parent survey, 73 self-certificated standards and 12 records reviewed by the administrative office. The broad definition of quality described in the quality standards and used for provider self-study is assessed by one of these more objective means.

CHAPTER FOURTEEN

Conclusion
Whither Family Day Care?
Peter Moss

In this concluding chapter, Peter Moss reflects on the challenges faced by family day care, locating them within the wider context of a 'crisis in care' which is threatening the supply of workers for many services, not only for children and young people but also for elderly people. Drawing on current developments reported in this book, the chapter considers two of the possible scenarios for the future development of family day care: as an increasingly professionalized service with its own pedagogy, or as an increasingly marginalized service offering a precarious source of income for poorly educated or otherwise disadvantaged women who are unable to obtain other work. The chapter holds out the tantalizing prospect of family day care providers working together to develop new thinking and practice that would allow family day care to take its place within a widening global network of practitioners from all types of early childhood services.

The chapters in this book, with contributions from ten countries, reveal family day care in all its diversity. That diversity is partly organizational. Family day care is taking an increasing number of forms, and family day carers have a variety of relationships to the labour market. Family day care is also shown to be faring differently in different countries. In parts of the former Communist bloc in Central Europe (as described in the chapters by Marta Korintus and Ulrike Gelder), it is struggling to get established, having been introduced in part as a response to the dismantling of centre-based services for children under three years that formed the backbone of provision under the former regimes. In some other countries (for example, Sweden and the UK), family day care has been contracting in recent years, either in the face of policy preference for group care or as a result of recruitment and retention problems. While elsewhere, for example Australia and New Zealand, family day care has been growing and seems to be in rude health.

However, whatever its current state, the future direction of family day care is connected to one of the most important questions facing the so-called developed world[1] – who will do the caring in the future? The growing demand for care, not only for children but also for frail elderly people, and the diminishing supply, as societies move from a male-breadwinner household model to a two-earner household model, is producing what has been called a 'crisis in care' (Hochschild 1995; Lewis 2001). The crisis manifests itself in unpaid, informal care, but also in paid formal care.

The forces driving this crisis are in part economic. Not only are there more jobs for women, but there are better jobs, and a wider range of less skilled jobs is becoming available to women with lower education. It has been observed that the opening of a supermarket can lead to an exodus of care staff from old people's homes in the locality (Social Services Inspectorate, 2000). But there are other related forces at work too, in particular demographics and education. Coomans (2002) describes these forces and their likely consequence as follows:

> Our economic system [in Europe] was based over the last two centuries on an abundant labour supply, [but] the era that is opening implies moving rapidly to scarcity of human resources. This will change thoroughly the behaviour of the labour market and force us to unheard of organizational innovation... The number of young people aged 15–24 [in the EU] will be below the number aged 55–64 by 2007, meaning no possible overall replacement of the older working generations by young incomers – with a similar picture for candidate states [i.e. countries which have applied to join the European Union, mostly from Central and Eastern Europe]...

> Considering the 25–64 age group, and given the replacement of generations with lower educational levels by younger generations with higher levels...it can be taken for granted that the shortages for low level qualifications will become a large concern... [With falling numbers of people with low qualifications] all investments and work organizations based on low skill/low wage strategies will face ever increasing difficulties in terms of labour supply...

welfare state. Although part of the welfare system, family day care in Denmark plays a substantial role in the publicly funded system of early childhood services, and family day carers are public employees with relatively good levels of pay and support.[4] (Although the decline of family day care in Sweden, described in Malene Karlsson's chapter, shows how a generous welfare state is not a sufficient condition for family day care to thrive.)

What is less clear is whether this direction for family day care is possible elsewhere – either in countries where family day care has not been wholeheartedly incorporated into a system of early years education or in countries with other forms of welfare regime. Esping-Anderson's schema for welfare regimes includes two other main types: the conservative and the liberal. Countries with conservative regimes are most varied with respect to the development of care services, including family day care. The southern European countries are generally held up as having the lowest level of service development and, with the notable exception of Portugal, family day care has not yet taken off in these countries (Italy, Greece, Spain).

Among other countries with what Esping-Anderson describes as conservative welfare regimes there is considerable variation in levels of childcare, though all such countries have a family day care sector which is located within the welfare rather than the education system. Family day care varies in the way it is organized. In the Netherlands family day carers are mainly self-employed but work in collaboration with an agency (gastouderbureau) which helps to match parents with family day carers and offers support, training and other services – but no payment. In Germany, family day carers are self-employed and mostly do not work with an agency. In Belgium and France, some family day carers are employed in and paid through organized schemes, while others work alone, often as Liane Mozère describes, in the most precarious of conditions.

Liberal welfare states, such as the UK and the United States, emphasize private responsibility for care with the state's role targeted on those most 'in need' (as described by June Statham in her chapter), reliance on markets and the development of private businesses to operate in those markets. The question posed here is whether a professionalized workforce can develop where demand and payment for services depends so much on the ability and willingness of parents to foot the bill. For many parents in this situation, there is a difficult trade off between what they may feel is ideal and how much of their income they are prepared or able to pay for the ideal; while for some parents, the issue of a professionalized workforce may be irrelevant, if what they seek for their child is some sort of domestic carer. Family day carers can also find themselves in an ambivalent and confused situation, caught between care as commodity and care as ethic – theoretically running small businesses selling a commodity (childcare) to parents, and therefore expected to charge what the market will bear; yet feeling strong emotional ties to children and parents, both caring 'for' and caring 'about'.

Even with professionalization, the future direction of family day care is uncertain. The conditions which have traditionally brought many women into family day care – wanting to earn while at the same time caring for their own children, limited alternative employment opportunities, relatively low education – are changing. Can better conditions and training, a more distinct pedagogical identity, possibilities for career progression, new forms of collaborative work compensate? Certainly without the attempt to professionalize being made, it is difficult to see anything but a steady decline for family day care (alongside some other forms of care such as relatives), leaving a diminishing pool of poorly educated or otherwise disadvantaged women hoping to make a precarious living in a shrinking market. The pace with which this will happen may vary in different countries. But the end result will be the same: a return to a nineteenth century model, in which one group of marginalized women workers provide a service for other groups.

So far, I have tacitly implied that the future direction for family day care will be followed by women only. What is interesting for me, as the only male contributor to this volume, is the recurrent attention paid to diversity in its chapters – but (with a few exceptions) the neglect of gender as a dimension of diversity. Is it because ethnic, cultural and linguistic diversity is in some respects a safer issue to address? Or are these dimensions of diversity in some ways more readily amenable to action? Or does it reflect where the demands for action are most vocal and pressing?

Yet gender goes to the heart of the current situation and future possibilities for family day care. The work is almost entirely gendered: more family day carers are from ethnic minorities than are men. Public understandings and valuations of the work are inextricably linked to an idea of family day care as substitute mothering and work that women are essentially suited to do. Many family day carers take up the work because, as women, they have the main responsibility for the care of their own children and also believe that good mothering requires that they care for their own children at least until those children reach a certain age. The poor conditions of many family day carers are typical of many women workers in the care workforce and many other gendered service occupations. Family day care may, in fact, be needed because *parents* are employed, but it is commonly perceived to be a service for employed *mothers* – and it is mothers who mostly make and maintain arrangements with family day carers.

So one question about the future of family day care is whether it should or will remain women's work – or whether it should or can become work in which increasing numbers of men participate. Is Liane Mozère right when she argues that 'having men care for children could bring a change…and turn childminding into a "real" job just like any other one'? Of course this raises many contentious issues, which have been explored elsewhere in the early childhood field with respect to nurseries (Cameron, Moss and Owen 1999), but not, as far as I know, in family day care. Might an influx of men be in some ways at the expense of women? How should the recruitment of men address child protection concerns? And is it in practice feasible to recruit more men – a difficult task at the best of times in most services involving work with younger children and, arguably, an even harder one for family day care than for centre-based services such as nurseries or kindergartens?

A recurring theme of chapters in this book is the issue of diversity – though with a focus, as I have just suggested, on some dimensions rather than others. But introducing the question of gender also raises questions about our understanding of diversity in post-industrial or post-modern societies. It is now common to recognize multiple and diverse gender identities – not just 'feminine' and 'masculine' but 'femininities' and 'masculinities' (Connell 1987). More generally, identity is increasingly understood to be not only multiple but fluid, contextual and dynamic (Dahlberg, Moss and Pence 1999), making glib concepts such as 'male role model' problematic on the grounds that there is no such single essential condition as 'maleness' (Cameron *et al.* 1999). While structural concepts such as class, gender, ethnicity, religion and language remain of central importance in understanding inequality, discrimination and social exclusion, a full response to diversity requires recognition of the complexity of identities. Viewed in this light, family day care (and other services for children) are places where children and adults do not simply reproduce identity but increasingly engage in the co-construction of new identities. This appreciation will have major implications for the future direction of practice, for example requiring practitioners to be more reflective and analytic about processes of identity construction and their part in these processes.

The future direction of practice for family day care – again as for other children's services – will also need to work on the tensions between diversity and normalization. We read in several chapters of family day care becoming increasingly subject to regulation in various forms – standards, inspection, predetermined outcomes, curriculum and so on – as well as to what has been termed the 'discourse of quality', an approach to evaluation based on establishing conformity to a predetermined norm (Dahlberg *et al.* 1999). The foundations which underpin this superstructure of regulation have been provided by one discipline, child development – a discipline which Burman (1994) describes as 'paradigmatically modern...arising at a time of commitment to narratives of truth, objectivity, science and reason' (Burman 1994, p.18).

It is not my intention here to be critical of regulation. There are conditions in which regulation may be in the interests of family day carers and children. We can see these forms of regulation as produced within a particular historical context (the search for more effective technologies for shaping children and their futures in an increasingly competitive world), and inscribed with the assumptions and values of modernity. Child development has offered a narrative of progress to predetermined ends, and the possibility of devising technologies which serve as means to these ends.

But this movement to greater regulation stirs a number of questions in my mind. How do these processes of normalization and regulation in practice square with concerns for diversity? Can we envisage greater diversity in the theory and practice of early years work emerging, at first in islands of dissensus or local cultural projects? Can family day carers – or networks of family day carers who share values and understandings – become part of such projects?

The centre-based early childhood services in Reggio Emilia provide one example of the possibility of being different, of conducting a local cultural project of childhood, which has now become global through the association of many other centres around the world inspired by this particular pedagogical approach (cf. Dahlberg *et al.* 1999 for discussion of the pedagogical approach in Reggio). Can we imagine groups of family day carers participating in constructing new thinking and practice, working with many disciplines and knowledges, possibly even with widening global networks of other early years practitioners? And, last but not least, can family day care diversify to experiment with other forms of evaluation – for example, meaning making and contextualized judgements of value – not instead of, but as an alternative to, quality and its norm-based methods?

References

Burman, E. (1994) *Deconstructing Developmental Psychology.* London: Routledge.

Cameron, C., Moss, P. and Owen, C. (1999) *Men in the Nursery: Gender and Caring.* London: Paul Chapman Publishing.

Connell, R.W. (1987) *Gender and Power: Society, Power and Sexual Politics.* Cambridge: Polity Press.

Coomans, G. (2002) 'Labour supply issues in a European context', paper given at the European conference on *Employment Issues in the Care of Children and Older People.* Sheffield Hallam University, 21–22 June 2002.

Dahlberg, G., Moss, P. And Pence, A. (1999) *Beyond Quality in Early Childhood Education and Care; Postmodern Perspectives.* London: Falmer Books.

Esping-Andersen, G. (1990) *The Three Worlds of Welfare Capitalism.* Cambridge: Polity Press.

Esping-Andersen, G. (1999) *Social Foundations of Postindustrial Economies.* Oxford: Oxford University Press.

Hochschild, A. (1995) 'The culture of politics: traditional, post-modern, cold-modern and warm-modern ideals of care.' *Social Politics 2*, 3, 331–345.

Jensen, J.J. and Hansen, H.K. (2002) *Care Work in Europe: Danish National Report for Workpackage Three.* http://144.82.35.228/carework/uk/ index.htm

Lewis, J. (2001) 'Legitimizing care work and the issue of gender equality.' In M. Daly (ed) *Care Work: The Quest for Security.* Geneva: International Labour Organisation.

Moss, P. and Petrie, P. (2002) *From Children's Services to Children's Spaces: Public Policy, Children and Childhood.* London: Falmer Routledge.

Singer, E. (1993) 'Shared care for children.' *Theory and Psychology 3*, 4, 429–449.

Social Services Inspectorate (2000) *The 9th Annual Report of the Chief Inspector of Social Services.* London: Department of Health.

Notes

1   The question of the current or future role of family day care in the Majority World is important, but lies beyond the remit of this volume and the knowledge of this author.

2   I use 'pedagogical approach' to refer to a tradition, strong in Continental Europe, of working with children and young people (and in some cases, as in Denmark, with adults). It is a tradition that adopts a holistic approach, addressing the whole child, the child with body, mind, emotions, creativity, history and social identity. Learning, care and, more generally, upbringing are closely-related (indeed inseparable) activities at the level of daily work. They are not separate fields

needing to be joined up, but inter-connected parts of the child's life (for a fuller discussion of pedagogy and the profession of pedagogue, see Moss and Petrie 2002). However, within a broad pedagogical approach, considerable differences are possible, in theory and practice, for example concerning processes of learning or the meaning of care.

3 In the last 15 years, in addition to New Zealand, administrative responsibility for childcare services has been brought into education in Spain, Sweden and parts of the UK (England and Scotland). The extent of integration, over and beyond administration, varies, hence my use of the qualifier 'fully'.

4 Danish family day carers earn, on average 2650a month compared to 3000–3300 for non-school occupations with professional training – pedagogues, nurses, social workers and occupational therapist – and 3500for school teachers (Jensen and Hansen 2002).

The Contributors

Carmen Dalli PhD is a senior lecturer in education and Director of the Institute for Early Childhood Studies at Victoria University of Wellington in New Zealand. Her research and publications are in the areas of development in the early childhood years, early childhood education policy and professionalism and ethical practice in early childhood services.

Elizabeth Everiss is Manager of the Centre for Early Childhood Education at the Open Polytechnic of New Zealand, a major provider of tertiary distance education in New Zealand. She previously worked as a senior adviser for the Ministry of Education and has extensive experience in policy work for the early childhood sector. She has a particular interest in family day care and has researched and published in this area.

Ulrike Gelder PhD is a research associate in the School of Geography, Politics and Sociology at the University of Newcastle upon Tyne, UK. She holds a German childcare and youth work qualification and has worked in several day care settings caring for very young children up to teenagers. In 2002 she completed her doctoral thesis comparing the social and economic experience of family day care providers in England and the new Germany.

Malene Karlsson FL is a doctor who researches for the National School Authorities in Sweden. She has a long and broad experience of family day care, having worked as a co-ordinator, editor and researcher. She worked as an expert for the EEC Childcare Network, writing a report on family day care in Europe, and for the National School Authorities, producing National Advice for family day care in Sweden.

Marta Korintus is Director of Research at the National Institute for Family and Social Policy in Budapest, Hungary. She has over twenty years of experience of regulating and monitoring childcare services for children under the age of three. She is one of the members of the working group who developed the model and the criteria for family day care in Hungary.

Irene J. Kyle PhD is an independent researcher and consultant whose work focuses on childcare, family resource programs, community development and related social policy. Before becoming a researcher, she worked for 20 years in a supervisory and administrative capacity in a number of child and family services, and was a senior policy analyst for childcare with the Ontario Ministry of Community and Social Services. Irene was principal author of the *Ontario Report* of the National Child Care Study (1992) and has many recent publications in the field of child care and family support services.

Kathy Modigliani Ed.D. is Director of the Family Child Care Project in Arlington, Massachusetts, United States. She conducts research and advises on practice in the field of family childcare quality improvement, provider education and organization, and policy development. At Wheelock College she recently led the development of the new accreditation of the National Association for Family Child Care. Previously she was on the faculty and in the research division at the Bank Street College of Education, taught in two- and four-year colleges, and served as founder-teacher-director of a multi-cultural child care centre at the University of Michigan. Kathy is significantly involved in the lives of her two grandchildren.

Ann Mooney is a research officer at the Thomas Coram Research Unit, Institute of Education, University of London, UK. She has many years of experience in the field of childcare, working on projects concerned with the effects of non-parental childcare and enhancing quality in early childhood services. Before joining Thomas Coram, Ann spent two years at the University of California, Irvine, United States, working on the NICHD study of early childcare. The focus of her work, which is very much policy-orientated, has recently broadened to include studies of informal care.

Peter Moss is Professor of Early Childhood Studies at the Thomas Coram Research Unit, Institute of Education, University of London, UK. He has researched a wide range of issues related to services for children, including the workforce, and has also done a lot of cross-national work. Recent books include *Beyond Quality in Early Childhood Education and Care: Postmodern Perspectives* (with Gunilla Dahlberg and Alan Pence) and *From Children's Services to Children's Spaces* (with Pat Petrie).

Liane Mozère is Professor in Sociology at the University of Metz, France. She has carried out a number of research projects on day care in France during the last 30 years as well as research on women's labour more generally, including a research project concerned with Filipino women-servants.

Sue Owen is Director of the Early Childhood Unit at the National Children's Bureau in the UK, and was previously Deputy Director at the Early Years National Training Organization. She has worked in the early years field for 30 years, during which time she has maintained a continuing interest and involvement in childminding. She has worked for the National Childminding Association in the UK and is currently researching the development of locally defined quality indicators for childminding networks.

Miriam K. Rosenthal is a developmental psychologist and a Professor of Child Development at the Hebrew University in Jerusalem, where she established 25 years ago, and is presently directing, a Graduate Program in Early Childhood Studies, under the joint auspices of the School of Social Work and the School of Education. During these years she has been investigating, together with her graduate and doctoral students, various aspects of early child care and education. Her work has been published in academic journals, as chapters in edited books and in a book *An Ecological Approach to the Study of Child Care: Family Day Care in Israel* published by Erlbaum Associates in 1994.

Ann Sanson is the Deputy Director of the Australian Institute of Family Studies. She is a developmental psychologist with considerable experience in children's development in a family and community context. She is the leading investigator on two Australian longitudinal studies – the Australian Temperament Project and the Longitudinal Study of Australian Children.

June Statham PhD is a senior research officer at the Thomas Coram Research Unit, Institute of Education, University of London, UK. She has over twenty years experience of policy-related research on children's services and has published widely in the field of early years services, family support and special educational needs. She has directed a number of major research projects for the Department of Health, the Department for Education and Skills and the National Assembly for Wales, and currently co-ordinates the research unit's programme of responsive work for the Department of Health.

Sarah Wise is a principal research fellow at the Australian Institute of Family Studies leading the Children and Parenting Program. She has a background in policy relevant research in the field of child care. She is currently managing the Institute's Child Care in Cultural Context study, and is an investigator on another collaborative quantitative child care study on the impacts of multiple and changeable child care on children's development.

Subject Index

accreditation (Australia), 200, 203, 210
accreditation (UK), 85–86
accreditation (USA), and cultural sensitivity
   child-rearing values, 222–25
   choice, need for, 229
   consensus, reaching, 217, 226–27
   cultures, learning from each other's, 230
   decision, on accreditation, 228
   flexibility, 226–27
   goals of, 218
   home-childcare linguistic continuity, 229
   information gathering, 218–19
   inter-state variations, 215–16
   materials, making available in other languages,
      229–30
   Observer Workbook, 228
   observer's visit, 227–28
   participants, 219
   provider, choice of term, 232n1
   public funding, limited, 216
   quality, consensus for definition of, 216–17,
      218
   Quality Standards Self-Study Workbook, 227
   regulation, minimal, 216
   relationships, 220, 220t, 231
   self-observation, 227–28
   self-study programme, 227
   success, of system, 231
   term, of accreditation, 228–29
agencies, use of
   Australia, 16
   Canada, 130–31
   Israel, 16
   New Zealand, 16
attachment theory, 15, 236
Australia, family day care in
   costs, 199
   funding, 198–99
   provision, 197–98
   see also accreditation (Australia); cultural
      context, of family day care (Australia);
      quality assurance (Australia)

baby-farming, 14
Bronfenbrenner's ecological model, 13, 94, 97,
   196, 201
business, family day care as, 15, 16

childminding (UK), 123–24, 125, 239
market place conditions, managing (France),
   172–73
self-employment (Hungary), 37, 38
Tagesmütter (Germany), 51–53

Canada *see* quality assurance (Canada)
care, functions of, 17
care work, socially devalued, 175
career progression, 53, 55–56, 236
centre-based care
   Israel, 14
centre-based care, and home-based care, 12, 15
Child Care Act (1972) (Australia), 81
child development theory, as underpinning
   regulation process, 241
Childcare in Cultural Context (Australian Institute of
   Family Studies), 197, 204
childhood services, need for integrated, 19
childminding networks (UK), 125
   accreditation, 85–86
   approved networks (NCMA), 85–86
   cell structure schemes (NCMA), 82, 83
   childminders, recruitment and retention of, 86,
      87, 88
   Childminding in Business, 83, 85
   Children Come First, 85
   Community Childminding model, 83, 85
   community development model, 82
   disadvantaged areas, success in, 86–88
   employer-supported schemes, 83–84
   funding, 87
   illegal (unregistered) childminding, 81, 82
   local authority sponsored schemes, 83
   network, definition of, 83
   registration and inspection, 78, 80, 84, 85
   salaried childminders scheme, 81–82
   support groups, need for, 80–83, 90–91, 99
   traditional flexibility of, 86
   voucher scheme, for nursery education, 84–85
   see also quality assurance (UK); sponsored
      family day care (UK)
Childminding Research Unit (UK), formation of,
   81
Children Act (1989) (UK), 78, 180, 181–82
Children and Youth Service Act (KJHG)
   (Germany), 42, 43
Children and Youth Services Act (Germany),
   44–45, 54
children in need *see* sponsored family day care
   (UK)
competencies, childminder

Author Index

Abrahamsen, G., 159
Andersson, B-E., 149
Annerblom, M-L., 159
Ashton, Baronness, 111–12
Attia, I., 95
Aviezer, O., 99

Bachman, F., 49
Ball, S.J., 123
Bandura, A., 143
Barefoot, B., 203
Beu, W., 49
Birchinal, M., 208
Blair, M., 202
Blüml, H., 43
Boisvert, 66
Boulton, M.G., 43, 49
Bowlby, J., 15
Brabeck, M., 137, 143
Brannen, J., 112
Brennan, D., 81
Bromer, J., 218, 227, 228
Bronfenbrenner, U., 15, 196
Bryant, B., 43, 82, 204
Burman, E., 241

Cameron, C., 16, 115, 120, 121, 122, 240
Cameron, J., 61, 68
Causse, L., 174
Challis, L., 82
Chang, H.N., 229
Chaudry, N., 139, 160
Clark, A., 13
Clarke-Stewart, A., 149
Clifford, R., 181, 207
Cochran, M., 14, 143
Cohen, N.E., 141
Collie-Holmes, M., 61, 63
Coney, S., 61
Connell, R.W., 240
Cook, H.M., 60
Coomans, G., 235–36
Corsaro, W., 202
Creps, C., 220

Dahl, G., 157
Dahlberg, G., 19, 20, 90, 130, 160, 201, 202, 240, 241
Dalli, C., 59–75, 244
De Bord, K., 70, 71
Deci, E.L., 143
Dillon, J., 83, 125, 180, 181
Doherty, 66
Dunster, L., 66, 71
Duurloo, L., 61

Early, D., 208
Edgerton, M., 206
Eheart, B., 70, 160
Eheart, B.K., 143
Emlen, A., 90
Esping-Anderson, G., 237, 238
Everiss, E., 59–75, 62, 63, 67, 69, 70, 244

Faÿ-Sallois, F., 164
Feagans, L., 204
Felstead, A., 116, 121
Ferri, E., 129, 187
Fischer, J.L., 143, 160
Foucault, M., 165
Fournier, C., 174
Frölich, W., 43
Fuller, B., 201, 202

Galinsky, E., 71, 88, 216
Gallimore, R., 93
Garden, M., 164
Gatt, L., 101
Geenen, E.M., 43
Gelder, U., 41–56, 48, 244
Giddens, A., 137
Goelman, H., 72, 141
Gonzalez-Mena J., 201
Grant, J., 112
Gunnarsson, L., 20

Habermas, J., 173
Halldén, G., 157
Hansen, H.K., 243n4
Harkness, S., 93, 196
Harms, T., 181, 207
Harris, M., 43, 82, 204
Harrison, L., 202
Hauser, R., 42
Himmelweit, S., 43
Hochschild, A., 235

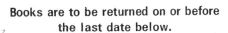